THE BIRTH OF DOUBT

Program in Judaic Studies
Brown University
Box 1826
Providence, RI 02912

Number 366
THE BIRTH OF DOUBT

by
Moshe Halbertal

THE BIRTH OF DOUBT

CONFRONTING UNCERTAINTY IN EARLY RABBINIC LITERATURE

Moshe Halbertal

Translated from the Hebrew by
Elli Fischer

Brown Judaic Studies
Providence, Rhode Island

Library of Congress Cataloging-in-Publication Data

Names: Halbertal, Moshe, author. | Fischer, Elli, Rabbi, translator.
Title: The birth of doubt : confronting uncertainty in early rabbinic literature / Moshe Halbertal ; translated from the Hebrew by Elli Fischer.
Description: Providence, RI : Brown Judaic Studies, [2020] | Series: Brown Judaic Studies; 366 | Includes bibliographical references and index. | Summary: "In the rabbinic laws in the Mishnah, the Sages constructed an entire field of instructions concerning how to behave in situations of uncertainty ranging from matters of ritual purity, to lineage and marriage, to monetary law, and to the laws of forbidden foods. Reflecting on the weight assigned to different possible errors that could be made and examining the norms of uncertainty opens a window for understanding the early rabbinic that reflected rules aimed not at avoidance but rather at dwelling in the midst of uncertainty, thus rejecting sectarian isolationism meant to minimize a community's friction with uncertainty"-- Provided by publisher.
Identifiers: LCCN 2020011985 (print) | LCCN 2020011986 (ebook) | ISBN 9781951498757 (paperback) | ISBN 9781951498764 (hardback) | ISBN 9781951498771 (ebook)
Subjects: LCSH: Rabbinical literature--History and criticism. | Uncertainty. | Uncertainty--Religious aspects. | Jewish law--Interpretation and construction. | Judaism--History--Talmudic period, 10-425.
Classification: LCC BM496.6 .H35 2020 (print) | LCC BM496.6 (ebook) | DDC 296.1/8--dc23
LC record available at https://lccn.loc.gov/2020011985
LC ebook record available at https://lccn.loc.gov/2020011986

Printed on acid-free paper.

In Memory of
Aharon Shemesh

Contents

Acknowledgments

I am grateful to colleagues and friends who offered me their wisdom and support. The comments and insights of Shraga Baron, Hillel Ben-Sasson, Yuval Blankovsky, Avital Davidovich, Tamar Eisenberg-Morsel, Dov Elbaum, Yair Furstenberg, Hillel Mali, Rafael Kroizer, David Kurzweil, Ishay Rozen-Zvi, Joseph Weiler, and the two anonymous readers of the manuscript for Brown Judaic Studies were most helpful. The chapter on "Lineage, Uncertainty and the Boundaries of the Community" received wonderful comments from Yedida Koren, who has worked extensively on this issue. My deepest gratitude to Toby Freilich for her encouragement and advice.

Special thanks I owe to Michael Satlow for inviting me to deliver the series of lectures at Brown University that formed the basis of the book; I have greatly benefited from my conversations with him and from his comments on the manuscript. Elli Fischer produced a remarkable translation of the book from Hebrew and I thank him for the exquisite care he invested in the project. Many thanks to Maurya Horgan, the copyeditor of the book, for her patient reading and valuable comments. I am grateful to the New York University Filomen D'Agostino Foundation for the grants that supported the writing of the book.

In the early stages of thinking about the question of uncertainty in early rabbinic law I was privileged to share my thoughts with my beloved friend Aharon Shemesh may his memory be blessed. I dedicate the book to Aharon in memory of many years of conversation and in longing to a dear scholar and friend.

Translator's Note

In most cases, I translated the word *safek* as "uncertainty" or some variation thereof, generally in the passive sense—"it is uncertain"—to reinforce that *safek* applies to an object, not a subject. "The state of this object is uncertain," rather than "They are uncertain about the state of this object."

In chapter 6, on "Doubt and Vagueness," I use the gender-neutral pronouns "ze" and "hir" to refer to the *androginos* and *tumtum*, the categories of individuals that fall outside the male/female binary. Though rabbinic literature itself defaults to male pronouns, I felt that gender neutrality, in this case, draws attention precisely to the rabbis' construction of the nonbinary status of the *androginos* and the *tumtum*.

For passages from rabbinic literature, I used the translation of the Mishnah, Bavli, and Tannaitic Midrashim available on Sefaria.org as base texts, but I altered them considerably, as dictated by the language and style of the book and by Prof. Halbertal's readings of the texts. Translations of the Tosefta, Yerushalmi, and later Midrashim are largely my own.

I used the 1985 JPS translation of Hebrew Scripture for biblical verses. However, most citations of Scripture in this book are embedded within rabbinic texts that interpret those verses, and so I have tried to alter the translations to comport with how the citing texts interpret them. In some cases, this results in significant deviation from standard translations of Scripture.

When referring to the formative rabbinic work or its anonymous speaker, I refer to "the Mishnah," but when referring to a specific paragraph within that work, I refer to "the *mishnah.*"

Technical rabbinic legal terms—*mamzer, ḥalal, agunah, terumah,* and many more—are defined, or their meanings are otherwise made clear, when the terms are first introduced.

Introduction

One of the most striking features of early rabbinic law is the emergence of vast and diverse legal instructions concerning uncertainty. The Mishnah, the canonical compilation of the sages, addresses cases of uncertainty—*safek*—in all areas of halakhah from matters of ritual purity, to lineage and marriage, to monetary law, and to the laws of forbidden foods. In these disparate realms, the sages constructed an entire field of instructions concerning how to behave in situations of uncertainty. The extensive engagement with uncertainty first appeared, in the history of halakhah, in the Mishnah and the Tosefta, which were both redacted at the end of the second century. These legal compilations preserve traditions and debates dating as far back as the first century BCE, though most of their materials were the product of the rabbinic academies of the first and second centuries CE. If one surveys all the extant nonrabbinic legal material from that era and earlier—the Apocrypha, the Dead Sea Scrolls, Philo, and Josephus—one will not find any directives or discussions of uncertain states. The burst of intense engagement with uncertainty is thus a unique feature of early rabbinic law.

Biblical law itself does not supply much basis for these vast later legal developments. Instances of ad hoc attempts to cope with uncertainty do abound in biblical literature, and at times doubts are settled through a direct appeal to God or with the aid of other occult or divinatory means. However, legislated rules and norms that guide human conduct in the face of uncertainty are very rare in the Bible; they appear in a few passages, such as the wife suspected of being unfaithful (Num 5:11–31), the guilt offering for unknown sins (Lev 6:1–7), and the corpse found in an uninhabited area (Deut 21:1–9). These passages deal with very specific cases and do not provide general guidance for cases of uncertainty.[1] In

1. It is important to note that the case of the possibly unfaithful wife does not issue clear rules of conduct in the case of uncertainty but rather places the decision in God's hands. It seems that, in Scripture, divine justice or "ordeal" is an acknowledged procedure for deciding uncertainties. This emerges from the following verses: "If the thief is not caught, the owner of the house shall depose before God that he has not laid hands on the other's property. In all

contrast to the sparse treatment of uncertainty in biblical law, the highly developed treatment of uncertainty in rabbinic literature, which emerges from the sages' intense preoccupation with such questions, is akin to the proverbial "mountains suspended by a hair." The emergence of the sages' particular interest in uncertainty demands explanation. What can we learn from the very fact of their wide-ranging interest in such questions? What principles guide the instructions they issue about how to behave in cases of uncertainty? Can we draw conclusions from these developments about different ways of viewing halakhah as a whole?

"Uncertainty" has two different meanings. The first is an uncertainty concerning reality. For example, an uncertainty arises when a stone wall collapses on the Sabbath and it is not known whether there were any people under the wall when it collapsed, and, if there were people buried under the rubble, whether they are alive or dead. This sort of uncertainty becomes a halakhic question because it is forbidden to clear rubble on the Sabbath, but the saving of lives overrides the Sabbath. How, then, is one to behave when facing this uncertainty? May one, out of uncertainty, clear the rubble or not? If, as halakhah asserts, the possible saving of lives even in cases of doubt overrides the Sabbath (*m. Yoma* 8:5), how is one to act in

---

charges of misappropriation—pertaining to an ox, an ass, a sheep, a garment, or any other loss, whereof one party alleges, 'This is it'—the case of both parties shall come before God: he whom God declares guilty shall pay double to the other" (Exod 22:7–8). Likewise, the breastplate of the high priest, which is an oracle for revealing the unknown, is called the "breastplate of justice" in Scripture. The sages interpret the word *elohim* in the above verses to refer not to God but to judges: "'The owner of the house shall depose before the *elohim*'—I might think, to inquire of the Urim and Thummim. It is therefore written: 'He whom the *elohim* declare guilty.' The intent is to *elohim* who incriminate (that is, judges)" (*Mekhilta, Mesekhta DeNezikin* 15). Later in that same section, *Mekhilta* derives the requirement to have three judges from the fact that the verses mention *elohim* three times. This same position is taken by those who translate *elohim* as *dayana* ("judges"). In her book *Law and Truth in Biblical and Rabbinic Literature* (Bloomington: Indiana University Press, 2010), Chaya Halberstam develops the claim that the gap between biblical certainty and rabbinic uncertainty is due to the shift from divinely present judgment available in the Bible to human responsibility for administering judgment in the absence of such divine approachability, which is typical of the rabbinic world.

In Tannaitic and later literature, there is a clear tendency to avoid using ordeals, including various magical ways of resolving legal uncertainties. Ishay Rosen-Zvi has shown that in the Mishnah, the ordeal of the suspected wife is shaped in a way that annuls its investigative properties and reformulates it as a ritual of punishment. See Ishay Rosen-Zvi, *The Rite That Was Not: Temple, Midrash, and Gender in Tractate Sotah* [Hebrew] (Jerusalem: Magnes, 2008), 119–23, 165–68.

This prevailing tendency in rabbinic literature, which negates the turn to divine justice and ordeals as a default in cases of uncertainty between litigants and legal uncertainty, is one element that can explain why rules for states of uncertainty blossom in rabbinic literature. Regarding the question of the various forms of ordeals in legal and other contexts in rabbinic literature, see Shraga Bar-On, *Lot-Casting, God and Man in Jewish Literature, from the Second Temple Period to the Renaissance* [Hebrew](Ramat Gan: Bar-Ilan University Press, 2020).

cases where the likelihood of survivors is slim to infinitesimal? The state of affairs of the world is often unknown, yet not every uncertainty poses legal or halakhic questions. The intersection of Sabbath prohibitions, on one hand, and the duty to save lives, on the other, with the abiding uncertainty about whether anyone was buried under the rubble and whether those under the rubble are alive or dead is what transforms a factual uncertainty into a halakhic question that demands an answer.

The second sense of uncertainty does not address an assessment of reality but relates to the rule that should be applied to it. In such cases of normative doubt, the reality is more or less known, and the uncertainty is about how to act when confronting this reality. Such uncertainties are legion in the Mishnah, Tosefta, and halakhic Midrashim, stemming as they do from the emergence of controversy in this literature. The very first *mishnah* presents a debate among the sages concerning the time for reciting the Shema at night. In this case, it is known that one must recite the Shema, and the precise time at night is known as well. The difference of opinion that generates normative uncertainty pertains to the question of whether, at that specific moment, the time for reciting the Shema in the evening has already expired, or not. (It is easy to imagine a case in which the time is unknown—for example, whether it is already past midnight.)

This work will focus on uncertainty of the first type, which concerns factual uncertainty. Such uncertainty might relate to the present state of affairs of the world or to what actually happened in the past or to what might happen in the future.[2] It is worth noting, however, that, since

2. Confrontation with uncertainty has received extensive attention in Decision Theory and Behavioral Psychology and Economics. In these realms of investigation the focus is on what the optimal rational choice in conditions of uncertainty and risk should be, how people behave in such conditions, and how they assess probalities and risks. Lara Buchak provides a careful assessment of the different positions with a compelling defense of the ways in which ordinary people tend to assess risks and make decisions in such conditions of uncertainty (*Risk and Rationality* [Oxford: Oxford University Press, 2013]). While decision theories tend to search for rules for rational choice, my discussion focuses on a different issue, which is normative in its essence and deals with the question what is the proper and moral way of dealing with uncertainty. This question focuses not only on utility analysis of costs and benefits but also on the normative dimensions. The normative question has been the focus in ethics and philosophy in connection with two different realms. The first question is how people should behave when they are uncertain about moral principles and norms. In such a dilemma the facts are known and the uncertainty concerns the proper moral principles. A good starting point for this discussion is Ted Lockhart's book *Moral Uncertainty and Its Consequences* (Oxford: Oxford University Press, 2000). The second question concerns the dilemma of how people should behave when they are uncertain about the facts. This issue was extensively discussed in Michael J. Zimmerman's books, *Living with Uncertainty: The Moral Significance of Ignorance* (Cambridge: Cambridge University Press, 2000) and *Ignorance and Moral Obligation* (Oxford: Oxford University Press, 2014). A central question in the ethical and philosophical literature is the degree to which models borrowed from Decision Theory can be illuminating to the moral questions regarding uncertainty. The approach to this question

rabbinic literature is filled with controversies, we will encounter a good deal of disagreement about how to behave in cases of uncertainty and how to deal with uncertainty. The intensive engagement with uncertainty concerning the state of affairs of the world is thus accompanied by a secondary layer of uncertainty: differences of opinion, occasionally substantial differences, about how to behave in cases of uncertainty. Of course, much of this work will revolve around the elucidation of such disputes, but only in contexts where these disputes address uncertainties in assessing reality.

In coping with factual uncertainties two very different modes must be distinguished in order to fully elucidate the aims of my exploration. The first mode in coping with uncertainty concerns the attempt at getting a better grasp of reality and devising procedures that will enable one, at least partially, to dispel some of the fog and to approach the facts of the matter as closely as possible. A vast field of law is dedicated to this effort in establishing rules of evidence and in constituting procedures of interrogation that aim at truth finding, while dealing with such questions as the degree to which self-incrimination is reliable and what the most trustworthy procedures for examining evidence are. Such rules are abundant in early rabbinic literature, which established norms for identifying reliable witnesses and presented detailed court procedures for interrogating them.

The second mode in coping with uncertainty is dedicated not to extracting more and better information to minimize the uncertainty, but rather to accept the partial state of information as a closed matter and to concentrate on what should be done given such uncertainty. For example, war, given its chaotic nature, serves as a painful arena for these sorts of dilemmas. Can soldiers aim at a specific target even if they are not certain that it is indeed a military target? And what ought to be the acceptable threshold of probability in such matters? Must the threshold of probability pass at least 50 percent in order to legitimize aiming fire at the target? Or should the probability be set higher or lower than that threshold? The stakes of war are such that these dilemmas deal with matters of life and death, and the pervasive fog of war makes such questions present in almost every military operation.[3] In the legal realm, this second mode of

---

depends on the larger moral theory. Consequentialist moral theories can take into account the possible weight of the predictable consequences while deontological theories have difficulty with such considerations. On this debate, see Frank Jackson and Michael Smith, "Absolutist Moral Theories and Uncertainty," *Journal of Philosophy* 103 (2006): 267–83; and the response of Ron Abodi, Adi Borer, and David Enoch, "Deontology Individualism and Uncertainty," *Journal of Philosophy* 105 (2008): 252–79.

3. For an extensive exploration of this question and its moral and legal dimensions in an attempt to establish a threshold of probability while dealing with uncertainty in war, see Adil Ahmad Haque, "Killing in the Fog of War," *Southern California Law Review* 86 (2012):

coping with uncertainty is expressed in questions such as the following: What is the level of certainty needed to incriminate a defendant? or Who among the plaintiffs carries the burden of proof in cases of factual uncertainties concerning property claims? In their intense interest in creating rules that guide the confrontation with uncertainties, the rabbinic academies of the first and second centuries raised such questions as: Can someone eat meat that was bought in the market based on a probability of 51 percent that the meat is kosher? What is the status of an abandoned baby whose lineage is not known? Is killing in self-defense justified when it is uncertain whether a threat exists? My exploration will focus mainly on this second mode of coping with uncertainties, and therefore I will not analyze the halakhic rules that aim at truth finding, such as laws of witnesses. Rather, I will address the vast realm of instructions that guide conduct in conditions of uncertainty.[4]

As will become apparent, the laws of *sfekot* are one of the most intricate, technical and difficult fields of early rabbinic literature, and yet the maze of debates and rules is guided by larger religious, moral, and social concerns. It is worthwhile to mention two of these larger concerns at this introductory stage. In establishing the proper threshold of certainty for action, the problem central to guiding such a decision is the assumed price of error. For example, when a legal system legislates that in order to incriminate someone the evidence ought to present a case that is beyond reasonable doubt, what drives the establishment of such a relatively high threshold of evidence is the dread of erring and punishing an innocent person. A thorough examination of the range of rules established in early rabbinic literature in dealing with uncertainty enables us to grasp the deepest layers of its evaluations by reflecting on the weight assigned to different possible errors. This will become apparent through the analysis of a whole spectrum of diverse thresholds of certainty established in the Mishnah. Examining norms of uncertainty opens another, broader window for understanding the social stance and religious sensibility of the early rabbinic world, especially in relation to the sectarian default. Sectarianism is a way of communal being in which a whole-encompassing environment is created that minimizes the friction with uncertainty, but at the cost of imposed isolation. By examining the rules that were introduced in early rabbinic literature, I hope it will become clear that the

---

63–116. For another discussion that questions the establishment of a fixed threshold of probability while preferring a balancing approach that takes into account the importance of the targets, see Seth Lazar, "In Dubious Battle: Uncertainty and the Ethics of Killing," *Philosophical Studies* 175 (2018): 858–83.

4. Halberstam's book *Law and Truth in Biblical and Rabbinic Literature* analyzes and explores the different modes of truth finding in rabbinic literature and their internal and historical logic.

rules of uncertainty are aimed not at avoiding uncertainty but at dwelling in its midst, thus rejecting the sectarian default.

The very emergence of uncertainty as a significant phenomenon in rabbinic literature, a phenomenon that includes, inter alia, the imaginative invention of states of uncertainty that life does not frequently bring about, invites a broader inquiry: Is there something unique about the halakhic discourse of the Mishnah that warrants the emergence of uncertainty? And how do states of uncertainty and engagement with them serve the overall conception of halakhah?

Yet, beyond the broader perspective on uncertainty as such, the internal logic of the various realms of doubt and the sorts of questions that uncertainty raises in their contexts are unique to each specific realm. Uncertainties regarding forbidden foods, which the first and the second chapters of this work will address, pose unique and distinct questions that include elements of guilt and fear of sin. Rules governing states of uncertainty about prohibitions of foods are also connected to the status of the uncertainly forbidden object as a poisonous and dangerous element or, alternatively, as an element whose forbidden or permitted status is constituted by and defined by halakhah as lacking any inherent "dangerous" quality.

Uncertainty about purity and impurity, the subject of the third chapter, involves questions of the possibility of contact, movement, and placement within space. The mobility of impurity from person to person and object to object gives it a unique dimension, and in many cultural and ritual settings strict obedience to purity laws results in enforcing large-scale social separation between the pure and the impure. Uncertainties concerning matters of purity might therefore relate to the possibility of creating shared spaces in an unknown world.

Uncertainties relating to lineage, which will be addressed in the fourth chapter, trigger questions that penetrate the fabric of the most basic and shared aspects of life. Doubts that emerge concerning lineage can undercut the possibility of marital ties between communities that may find themselves unable to agree about the correct procedure for marriage and divorce, and, consequently, the possibility of intermarriage between these groups is the subject of acute halakhic examination.

Despite the unique character of each of these topics—forbidden foods, purity, and lineage—which are addressed in the first four chapters of this book, they are characterized by a common sensitivity pertaining to the status of the prohibited, the impure, and the unfit and to the degree of danger entailed by making an error with respect to one of them. Likewise, the commonalities in the way uncertainty is addressed in these realms are rooted in how the various rules for uncertainty in the realms of prohibited foods, impurity, and lineage are formed and articulated in opposition to the sectarian alternative that strives to seal off self-contained social and communal spaces that minimize life's uncertainties to the degree possible. The first four chapters, which form the core of the book, can thus be read as a unit in itself.

The fifth chapter of this work, which addresses monetary uncertainty, moves into a completely different realm that stands independently and focuses on ownership rights and the burden of proof. At the heart of this chapter is the tension in early rabbinic literature between the tendency to preserve the status quo when facing uncertainty and the aspiration to offer the fairest alternative with the lowest cost of error. The sixth and final chapter of this work deals not with a specific halakhic realm but with the unique phenomenon of vagueness, in which the most basic distinctions drawn by law confront a complicated reality that resists the binary character of legal and halakhic concepts. These phenomena, like "twilight" (*bein ha-shemashot*), which are addressed in the chapter on vagueness and uncertainty, are fertile ground for the areas of uncertainty that early rabbinic halakhah developed and broadened.

The attempt to understand and clarify the genesis of uncertainty in early rabbinic literature, which is the broader topic of this work as a whole, should, therefore, incorporate two perspectives: one deals with the question of the emergence of uncertainty in general, and the other investigates the unique characteristics pertaining to each realm of halakhah in which uncertainty arises and develops. Uncertainty poses a complex existential and communal challenge in human life, which is fraught with the unknown; and, in order to understand the ways in which a legal world confronts uncertainty, multiple approaches must be adopted. In different chapters of the book I therefore adopt a variety of angles to analyze the sources, and these approaches include a doctrinal analysis of legal rules, an assessment of errors and risk touching on the field of law and economics, and social and communal implications. At the same time, I take into consideration the particular historical background in which these rules emerge.

In the history of halakhah, the treatment of uncertainty became one of the most complex fields of intense study. From the eighteenth century on, the analysis of laws of doubts developed as the main medium in which the intellectual and conceptual achievements of Talmudic learning were articulated in all their magnificence.[5] The present work is concerned with

5. See Yehuda Brandes, "Living and Learning in a World of Doubt: Thoughts on Shev Shmateta," *Akdamut* 19 (2007): 143–64; Michal Tikochinsky, "'Kuntres HaSfekot' (Studies in Uncertainty): Methodology, Objectives, and Meaning" [Hebrew], *Shenaton ha-Mishpat ha-Ivri* 25 (2008): 1–44. See also Noam Samet, "'Ketsot Ha-choshen': The Beginning of 'Lamdanut'—Features and Tendencies" [Hebrew] (PhD diss., Ben-Gurion University, 2016), 71–108. And see the discussion in Shai Wozner, *Legal Thinking in the Lithuanian Yeshivoth: The Heritage and Works of Rabbi Shimon Shkop* (Jerusalem: Magnes, 2016), 208–18; and, more generally, Pinchas

examining the astonishing point of origin of the study of uncertainty in early rabbinic literature. I will address later impressive developments in the treatment of uncertainty only to the extent that they are directly related to the earlier sources I will examine. The focus of this book will be the Mishnah, Tosefta, and halakhic Midrashim that constitute the first phase of development of these subjects, in which the singular language of this discipline was shaped, and in which the basic concepts that would guide future development were posited.

Shiffman, "On the Concept of Doubt ('Safek') in Halakha and Law," *Shenaton ha-Mishpat ha-Ivri* 1 (1974): 328–52.

1

Prohibitions, Uncertainty, and the Price of Error

I

One of the most important chapters in the Mishnah on the subject of uncertainty is the second chapter of tractate *Makhshirin,* within the Order of *Taharot.* This chapter, devoted almost entirely to cases of uncertainty, attests to the sages' systematic and independent interest in the study of uncertainties and assembles, in one place, cases of uncertainty pertaining to a broad variety of halakhic realms: the laws of impurity, lineage, the Sabbath, forbidden foods, and property law. The organizing principle of all these various realms of uncertainty is rules of behavior that share a similar structure, and these rules and the chapter in which they are embedded, will serve as an important starting point for understanding uncertainties about prohibitions in Tannaitic literature and the religious and legal meaning of how they frame and decide these issues:

> 3. Two pools, one that is pure and one that is impure—[if a wall that exudes] moisture is close to the impure one [the moisture] is impure; [if the wall that exudes moisture] is close to the pure one [its moisture] is pure. Half-and-half, it is impure. One mixed impure iron with pure iron [in fashioning a utensil]—<if the majority is from impure [iron], [the utensil] is impure>[1] if the majority is from pure [iron], it is pure. Half-and-half, it is impure.... Rain water fell into waste water—<if most [of the mixture] is from the impure [waste water], it is impure> and if most is from the pure [rain water], it is pure; half-and-half, it is impure. When

1. This version of the text is based on MS Kaufmann with additions and amendments (in angle brackets) based on MS Parma when I deem it necessary. The version of the Mishnah cited throughout this work is based on MS Kaufmann, and the version of the Tosefta is based on MS Vienna. Halakhic Midrashim are quoted in accordance with the reliable textual witness selected by the Historical Dictionary Project of the Hebrew Language Academy, or in accordance with a trustworthy critical edition of that Midrash. Throughout the work, I note textual variants where the changes are important for understanding the content of the halakhah under discussion.

[does this apply]? When the waste water came first [and the rain fell into it]. However, if rain water, even a trace amount, preceded the waste water, [the mixture] is impure.

4. [If] one is plastering his roof or laundering his clothing and rain fell into [the waste water used for those activities]—if most [of the mixture] is from the impure [waste water], it is impure; and if most it is from the pure [rain water], it is pure; half-and-half, it is impure. Rabbi Yehudah says: If it increased [the volume of] the dripping.

5. If a city where Jews and gentiles live has a bathhouse that is used on the Sabbath—if the majority is gentiles, one may bathe there immediately [after the Sabbath], and if the majority is Jews, one must wait until the water could have been heated [after the Sabbath]; half-and-half, one must wait until the water could have been heated [after the Sabbath]. Rabbi Yehudah says: One may bathe in a small bath immediately if there are officials [who use it].

6. If he found vegetables being sold therein—if the majority is gentiles, one may buy [them] immediately [after the Sabbath], and if the majority is Jews, one must wait until they could have been brought from nearby [after the Sabbath]; half-and-half, one must wait until they could have been brought from nearby [after the Sabbath]. If there are officials there, one may buy immediately.

7. If he found a baby cast away therein—if the majority is gentiles, it is a gentile; if the majority is Jews, it is a Jew; half-and-half, it is a Jew. Rabbi Yehudah says: We go by the majority of those who cast away [babies].

8. If one found a lost object there—if the majority is gentiles, one need not proclaim [that he has found something]; <if the majority is Jews, one must proclaim> half-and-half, he must proclaim. If one found bread there, we follow the majority of bakers, and if it was bread of pure flour, we follow the majority of those who eat pure flour. Rabbi Yehudah says: If it was bread of coarse flour, we follow the majority of those who eat coarse flour.

9. [If] one found meat there, we follow the majority of the butchers. If it was cooked, we follow the majority of those who eat meat.

10. If one found fruit on the road—if most [farmers normally] gather it in for home use, it is exempt [from tithes and *terumah*], and [if most farmers gather it in] for sale in the marketplace, it is liable [for tithes and *terumah*]; half-and-half, it is *demai* [produce from which it is uncertain whether tithes were already taken]. A granary in which Jews and gentiles deposit [their produce]—if the majority is from the gentiles, [the produce] is certain [*tevel*, from which tithes and *terumah* have not been apportioned], and if the majority is from the Jews, it is *demai*; half-and-half it is certain [*tevel*], according to Rabbi Meir. But the sages say: Even if they are all gentiles, but one Jew deposited [produce] in it, [it is] *demai*.

> 11. [If] fruit of the second [year of the sabbatical cycle became mixed with and] exceeded that of the third [year fruit], or that of the third exceeded that of the fourth, <or that of the fourth exceeded that of the fifth> or that of the fifth exceeded that of the sixth, or that of the sixth exceeded that of the seventh, or that of the seventh exceeded that of the [year] following the seventh, we follow the majority. Half-and-half, [we act] stringently. (*m. Makhshirin* 2:3–11)

A close look at the general structure of this chapter shows that the redactor of the Mishnah wove into tractate *Makhshirin* an independent literary unit that is not related solely to matters of purity and impurity, and it includes a series of uncertainties from different realms of halakhah. Beyond these diverse realms of halakhah, the chapter presents as well three different rules for dealing with uncertainties. The first *mishnah* (2:3) in the unit, which serves as a bridge between this unit and the tractate in general, deals with the purity and impurity of liquids and fluids. It presents the first rule in dealing with uncertainty, that of following proximity:

> Two pools, one that is pure and one that is impure—[if a wall that exudes] moisture is close to the impure one [the moisture] is impure; [if the wall that exudes moisture] is close to the pure one [its moisture] is pure. Half-and-half, it is impure.

The same *mishnah* continues with another rule of dealing with uncertainty, that of "annulment by majority":

> One mixed impure iron with pure iron [in fashioning a utensil]—<if the majority is from impure [iron], [the utensil] is impure> if the majority is from pure [iron], it is pure. Half-and-half, it is impure.

This *mishnah* teaches us that a vessel that has been composed from impure and pure iron is defined by the majority of the iron. The impure iron is annulled even with a slim majority of pure iron.[2]

From these cases, the chapter continues to an independent unit composed of a collection of determinations about uncertainty that are grouped according to another independent organizing principle, namely, uncertainties that arise as a result of Jews and gentiles living together in a mixed city.[3] The resolution of these sets of uncertainties are decided by a third

2. The source of this halakhah is in tractate *Kelim* 11:4, and its states that a utensil that was made of a mixture of impure and pure iron is defined by the majority. The editor of this chapter in the Mishnah did not distinguish between a situation in which a prohibited element is known to be mixed within a majority and the question of the status of a found item with an unknown origin; both of these situations are decided by slim majority. On annulment by majority, see below.

3. The expression "if he found ... therein," which begins *mishnayot* 6–9, fashions direct attention to the city as an organizing issue. By means of the verb "found," the chapter moves

different rule that dictates following the majority. According to this rule, the status of a person or an object whose origin is uncertain is decided by a probabilistic assessment that is based even on a slim majority.

This exceptional chapter in tractate *Makhshirin* presents three rules of behavior in conditions of uncertainty, and the organizing axis bonding them together is the identical pattern of their formulation in the chapter. The pattern consist of the following: majority (or proximity) to one side, half-and-half, and majority (or proximity) to the other side. I will first focus on the third principle of following the majority, the principle that leads most of the cases that are presented in the chapter, cases that are drawn from the reality of life in a mixed city.

This lived reality in the mixed city generates conditions of uncertainty in a broad range of fields, and one of the uncertainties raised by the Mishnah pertains to the question of pedigree:

> If he found a baby cast away therein—if the majority is gentiles, it is a gentile; if the majority is Jews, it is a Jew; half-and-half, it is a Jew. Rabbi Yehudah says: We go by the majority of those who cast away [babies].

Alongside the determination of this uncertainty pertaining to pedigree, there is a similar determination made regarding prohibited foods:

> [If] one found meat there, we follow the majority of the butchers. If it was cooked, we follow the majority of those who eat cooked meat.

The principle of following the majority in cases of food prohibitions is a basic institution of Tannaitic halakhah. As formulated in a different context:

> One who finds a slaughtered hen in the marketplace, and likewise, one who gave a hen to someone in the marketplace to slaughter and does not know his status, we follow the majority. (*t. Ḥullin* 2:2)[4]

---

on, in *mishnah* 10, to deal with a topic that has nothing to do with a mixed city, but it is related to deciding based on a majority. At the end of *mishnah* 10, the chapter returns to the city and the mixed reality of the granary. The end of *mishnah* 10 is missing the context of a found object and deals, rather, with an object that was taken, though the subject is a mixed city. *Mishnah* 11, which deals with neither a found object nor a mixed city, is connected to *mishnah* 10 through their mutual attention to the question of a majority of fruits.

4. The majoritarian principle is reiterated in *t. Taharot* 6:1: "The carcasses and [properly] slaughtered [animals] in a city follow the majority. Rabban Shimon ben Gamliel says, even if but one carcass is sold in the city, all meat found in that city is [considered] a carcass, because there are carcasses present." Does Rabban Shimon ben Gamliel dispute the majoritarian principle where there is a "present minority" (*mi'ut matzui*) because, in his words, "there are carcasses present"? Or does he maintain that, even though most stores sell properly slaughtered meat, the meat of carcasses is still more commonly found, and this is what determines the majority. See below, pp. 26–27.

This principle has no substantive biblical precedent, and through its establishment by the sages in these passages, it became a major principle of how uncertainty has been approached in the history of halakhah.[5]

The rendering of decisions about uncertain statuses on the basis of a majority, even a bare majority, in cases pertaining to various areas of halakhah—such as meat whose kosher status is uncertain or an abandoned child—offers us an initial important insight into the conceptual and social ramifications of early rabbinic regulations concerning uncertainty. This insight is sharpened when we recognize that the Mishnah's majoritarian principle is in fact an alternative to another possible attitude toward uncertainty, one that reflects an unambiguous and paralyzing dread of uncertainty. Such fear of uncertainty would have produced a completely different rule than the one found in the Mishnah. It would have been formulated roughly as follows: "As long as the source of the meat is unknown, it is forbidden to eat it." According to such a position, meat cannot be rendered permissible based on a greater-than-50-percent likelihood of its having been prepared kosher. A much stronger basis is needed to permit this meat. According to this hypothetical position, one who finds meat in the street may, at most, sell it to a non-Jew. It would be forbidden for a Jew to eat it, though. The same applies to an abandoned child; as long as it is not known that the child is of Jewish origin, it may not be treated as a Jew.[6]

It is possible that the absence of any discussion of uncertainty in the literature of the Dead Sea sect is rooted in a basic general attitude similar to the one described, according to which there are no "laws of uncertainty" because eating meat requires knowing with certainty that the meat can be sourced to a worthy slaughterer and from someone known to cook kosher. The sect's practice of communal eating may indicate that, in practice, it was forbidden for members of the sect to eat anything prepared outside

---

5. The expression "incline after the majority," which is quoted as the biblical prooftext for the majoritarian principle, has a completely different, even negative, meaning when read straightforwardly in context: "Do not follow the crowd in doing wrong. Do not give perverse testimony in a dispute in order to incline after the majority" (Exod 23:2). That is, do not follow the majority to pervert justice. This admonition does not apply to questions of likelihood of prohibition but is directed at judges and witnesses, that they not pervert justice to please the majority.

6. The rule that seems to be unambiguous in the Mishnah was narrowed in the first generation of Babylonian Amoraim: "Rav said: 'They taught this only with respect to providing for him, but not with respect to pedigree.' Shmuel said: 'To clear rubble from on top of him [in Shabbat].' Did Shmuel really say that? Didn't Rabbi Yosef say in Rabbi Yehuda's name in Shmuel's name: 'We do not follow the majority when it comes to saving lives'? Rather, Shmuel's statement applies to the first clause: 'If the majority is gentiles—it is a gentile.' Shmuel said: 'But this is not so when it comes to clearing rubble from on top of him'" (*b. Ketubot* 15b). Rav thus qualifies the Mishnah's rule, and Shmuel, according to the way his statement is interpreted in the passage, likewise qualifies, but in the opposite direction.

the sect.[7] One of the social definitions of sectarian existence is the construction of a demarcated and all-encompassing social reality that reduces friction with the environment and, consequently, conflict with the reality of uncertainty. Such a sweeping prohibition removes, with a wave of the hand, all primary interest in the sorts of uncertainty of which the Mishnah speaks.

This is, of course, only conjecture about the reason for the absence of laws governing uncertainty from Second Temple literature. It is not unreasonable, however, to assume that, if such rules were to be formulated by today's halakhists, a bare majority would be rejected as grounds for permitting the consumption of meat whose origin is unknown. A contemporary halakhist would tell a questioner who found meat in the street: "If you don't know where it's from, it's forbidden." Presumably, in such cases, to use a general legal analogy, it would be permissible to eat the meat only if it is kosher beyond a reasonable doubt (as in the rules of evidence in contemporary criminal law) or, at a lower level of certainty, when there are strong grounds to believe that the meat is kosher (as in the rules permitting self-defense). Rendering a decision based only on a statistical majority is astonishing and has far-reaching implications for questions of this type.

II

The way that the principle of following the majority is formulated in *Makhshirin* leaves no room for doubt that a likelihood of just over 50 percent is sufficient to permit the prohibited. The Mishnah requires no obvious or special majority, as the Mishnah explicitly distinguishes between a case where there is a majority and a case where there is a probability of "half-and-half," and only in the half-and-half case is the situation treated as an uncertainty that mandates stringency. A closer look at the Mishnah in toto shows that in other halakhic contexts there are cases of uncertainty that require a greater probability than a bare majority to decide the uncertainty in favor of permissibility. Such a requirement for a higher degree of likelihood appears in context of determining the death of a husband whose fate is unknown, in order to permit his wife to remarry:

7. The sect's laws of separation, which, inter alia, forbid eating and drinking with anyone who was not a member in good standing, were formulated in the Community Rule: "nor to eat or drink what is theirs, nor yet to take anything from them, unless purchased" (1QS V, 16–17) (translated in *The Dead Sea Scrolls Reader*, ed. Donald W. Parry and Emanuel Tov, 2nd ed., 2 vols. [Leiden: Brill, 2013], 1:14–15).

> We do not testify [that he is dead] except based on the face, with the nose, even if there are marks on his body or his clothes. We do not testify [that he is dead] unless his soul has departed; even if they saw him disemboweled, crucified, or being eaten by a wild beast, we do not testify [that he is dead] unless his soul has departed.
>
> ... if he fell into water, whether delimited waters or endless waters, his wife is forbidden [to remarry]. Rabbi Meir said: It happened that someone fell into a large pit and emerged three days later. Rabbi Yose said: It happened that a blind man descended into a cave to immerse himself, and his attendant followed him down; they waited long enough for their souls to have departed and permitted their wives to remarry. Another incident happened in Asia: Someone was lowered into the sea, and nothing was raised back up but his leg. The sages said: If it was above the knee, [his wife] may remarry; if it was below the knee, she may not remarry. (*m. Yevamot* 16:3–4)

A different version of these rules is taught in the Tosefta:

> If one fell into waters, whether delimited or endless, his wife is forbidden [to remarry]—these are the words of Rabbi Meir. But the sages say: into delimited waters, she may [remarry]; into endless waters, his wife is forbidden [to remarry], for perhaps a wave will toss him and eject him onto dry land.... Rabbi said: It happened during the years that they were dredging the bed of the Jordan, and one person entered a fish stream. His friend waited long enough for his soul to depart, and then went and told his household. In the morning, the sun shone and [the missing man] discerned the opening of the cave. He returned to find a funeral notice posted in his house. Rabbi Meir said: It happened that someone fell into a large pit and emerged three days later. They said to him: miraculous occurrences are not invoked. (*t. Yevamot* 14:5–6)

In contrast to the *mishnah* in *Makhshirin*, the threshold for determining the death of the husband according to the *mishnah* in *Yevamot* is much higher than a simple majority; according to the sages, deciding that the husband is dead, and thus permitting his wife to remarry, requires a much greater probability. They thus maintain that, even if a man is known to have fallen into the sea, his wife is not permitted to remarry unless it was possible to observe in all directions that the husband did not emerge from the water. According to Rabbi Meir, even this very high probability is insufficient; the uncertainty about the husband's death is not determined unless his body has been found and identified.[8] The Mishnah thus recognizes a

8. One who studies the chapters of the Mishnah that deal with *agunah* (a "chained woman" whose husband has disappeared and who cannot remarry without a writ of divorce from him or confirmation of his death) will discover a stringent approach to questions of determining death on the basis of circumstantial evidence, and, in contrast, much broader leniency (subject to dispute) in the rules of testimony for an *agunah* than in other areas of

higher level of probability than a regular majority, and it mandates this level in the very specific halakhic context of determining a husband's death.

The Mishnah presents a diametrically opposed approach to uncertainty in cases of saving lives. In such cases, even a low probability, far less than a statistical likelihood, warrants action that is otherwise forbidden on the Sabbath. As the Mishnah states, "If a wall collapsed on someone, and it is uncertain whether or not he is there [in the rubble], and it is uncertain whether or not he is alive, and it is uncertain whether or not he is a Jew, we remove the rubble from on top of him" (*m. Yoma* 8:7). The Mishnah permits abrogation of the laws of the Sabbath not only when the odds are even but even when there is a much lower probability. It describes a case in which there are several uncertainties that, cumulatively, decrease the likelihood of rescue to below the threshold of a bare majority, or even of fifty-fifty odds.

The Bavli abstracts a principle from the law stated in this *mishnah*: "Rabbi Yosef said that Rabbi Yehudah said that Shmuel said: 'They did not follow the majority with respect to saving lives'" (*b. Yoma* 84b). We could have imagined another ruling concerning saving life on the Sabbath in which the possible price of the mistake of desecrating the Sabbath would have been given a different weight. In the Karaite halakhah, for example, saving life overrides the Sabbath, but in case of uncertainty whether life would be saved, a person is not allowed to perfom work during the Sabbath. Rabbi Yehuda Hadasi, the Karaite sage of the twelfth century, formulated the Mishnaic rule in completely different terms: "An old person or a child or a baby that fell to the pit or to a river or to the sea or the lake, or a pile of stones fell on them … and in this occasion the sages will know that they are still alive and can be cured from their situation, they will desecrate the sacred day to save them" (*Eshkol ha-Kofer*, 148). It is clear that desecrating the Sabbath was permitted in the Karaite tradition when there was clear knowledge that it would actually save life and not in conditions of uncertainty.[9] The ruling of the Mishnah that is taken for granted within

---

halakhah. In *agunah* cases, a woman's testimony about herself, the testimony of a lone witness, hearsay evidence, and the indirect testimony of a gentile are all accepted, even as they are not accepted in other halakhic contexts. On the tension between these two components within the Mishnah, see Yehuda Brandes, "Agunot: Chained Women and Meta-Halakhic Principles" [Hebrew], *Akdamut* 18 (2007): 55–72; see n. 57 there for later attempts to unify these two realms under one lenient rubric.

9. See the formulation of Eliyahu Bashyazi, the Karaite sage of the fifteenth century: "And the sage Rabbi Joseph the seer said that when the danger [of loss of life] is uncertain it is prohibited to desecrate the Sabbath. Rather the probability of danger should be higher than the probability of health.... In conclusion the [Karaite] sages rule that saving of life overrides the Sabbath when the probability of danger is higher than the probability of health" (*Aderet Eliyahu* [Odessa, 1870], 112). In contrast to rabbinic law, in cases of uncer-

the rabbinic tradition is not trivial altogether, and it teaches that the price of a mistake in which there is a possibility that life will be lost has greater weight in facing uncertainty of this kind. Likewise, for the same reason, namely, the importance of life, even a probabilistic determination with a high likelihood is rejected as grounds for incrimination in capital cases. The threshold established in the Tannaitic tradition is far more stringent than the common threshold in cases of criminal law—"beyond a reasonable doubt." The Tosefta exemplifies the inadmissibility of circumstantial evidence, even when it establishes facts beyond reasonable doubt:

> What is "[based only on] conjecture"? [The judges say:] Perhaps you will say, "We saw him running after his fellow with a knife in his hand; [the victim] entered into a store, [the pursuer] followed him into the store, and then we entered and found [the victim] killed, with the knife in the murderer's hand, dripping blood." Perhaps you will say, "With all of this, who killed him?" (*t. Sanhedrin* 8:2)

The Tannaitic sources thus assert different levels of probability with respect to different realms of decision making. The complicated range of different probabilistic requirements is related to the fact that the height of the threshold of probability necessary to decide situations of uncertainty expresses the gravity of the potential cost of error. The higher the cost of error in the eyes of those who set the rules for these cases of uncertainty, the greater the degree of likelihood necessary. Even though *Makhshirin* brings together different halakhic realms, such as purity, forbidden foods, and pedigree, under a single majoritarian rule, the case of marriage, according to the halakhah of the Mishnah, is fundamentally different, as it creates a binding relationship that is permitted only when there is a high degree of likelihood. The cost of error in a case where a woman is released from marriage is high, inter alia, because the mistake can be exposed by the return of the husband who had been presumed dead.[10] In cases of saving lives, a low level of probability is sufficient, because the importance of saving lives is such that it permits what is normally forbidden on the Sabbath even when the chances of an actual rescue are low. Similarly,

---

tainty one is not allowed to desecrate the Sabbath unless there is higher probablitiy that life would be saved. See Daniel Lasker, "Karaism and the Study of Judaism," *Mehkarei ha-Katedra Al Shem Yosef ve-Sil Maiser* [Hebrew], (2000): 26–27.

10. In *agunah* cases, there is, of course, a high price for setting a strict threshold to release her, because such a threshold keeps her in her chained state. The high price of error is therefore symmetrical. This symmetry is reflected in the various conflicting trends toward stringency and leniency that can already be found in the Tannaitic literature regarding the rules of evidence (see n. 8 above). Additionally, the risk of the husband's possible (and tragic) return is a reason to be more permissive about admitting evidence, because this very risk ensures that the witness will testify cautiously and precisely. See *Mishneh Torah*, Laws of Divorce 13:29.

imposition of the death penalty requires an effectively unattainable level of certainty.[11]

It is no accident that the most profound statement on the value of life in all of Tannaitic literature appears in the context of the high threshold of certainty required to convict in capital cases and emphasizes the cost of executing a man erroneously and without warrant.

> How do we press the witnesses in a capital case? We bring them in [to the court's chambers] and press them: "Perhaps what you say [isn't eyewitness testimony] is but your own assessment, or from rumors, or hearsay from a trustworthy individual. Or perhaps you were unaware that by the end we'd interrogate you, with examination and inquiry. Know that capital cases are not like monetary ones. In monetary cases, [a false witness] can return the money and achieve atonement. But in capital cases, the blood of [the victim] and all his future offspring hang upon you until the end of time.... It was for this reason that man was first created as one person [Adam], to teach you that anyone who destroys a life is considered by Scripture to have destroyed an entire world; and anyone who saves a life is as if he saved an entire world." (*m. Sanhedrin* 4:11–12)

The diverse spectrum of instructions concerning the proper threshold of certainty that is needed for permitting, acting, or punishing depends on the assessment of the price of error in each of these realms. Exposing these diverse legal responses in the Tannaitic literature teaches us that a closer look at the way in which legal systems deal with uncertainty might serve as a key to understanding the underlying evaluations of the system. It is in confronting the uncertain that the evaluations become clear.

---

11. Commenting on the *mishnah* in which Rabbi Tarfon and Rabbi Akiva say, "Had we been on the Sanhedrin, no one would have ever been executed," the Bavli states: "How would they have acted? Rabbi Yohanan and Rabbi Elazar both say: [They would have asked witnesses to murder:] Did you see whether he killed a terminally ill person or someone who is hale? Rabbi Ashi said: Even if it can be determined [by postmortem examination] that [the murder victim] was hale, perhaps there was already a laceration where the sword entered" (*b. Makkot* 7a). The same *mishnah* in *Makkot* records a dissenting view from that of Rabbis Akiva and Tarfon, which opposes a high threshold for evidence in capital cases and points out the corresponding price of excessive stringency: "Rabban Shimon ben Gamliel says: They would increase the number of murderers in Israel." Perhaps the rationale of Rabban Shimon ben Gamliel is valid only with regard to evidence in murder cases and not in other capital cases, where the cost he indicates does not exist. See *Tosafot Yom Tov* on this *mishnah*. For an incisive analysis of the tension expressed in the Mishnah between dread of mistake and uncertainty and the aim of implementing the law, see Halberstam, *Law and Truth*, 102–5.

III

A more penetrating understanding of rules governing uncertainty and the price of error emerges from an acute Tannaitic dispute about uncertainty and self-defense. The discussion of this question develops out of the sages' understanding of the unique law of the "tunneler": "If the thief is found while tunneling, and he is beaten and dies, there is no bloodguilt in his case. If the sun has risen on him, there is bloodguilt in that case. He must make restitution; if he lacks the means, he shall be sold for his theft" (Exod 22:1–2). The verse asserts that one who kills a burglar who is tunneling is exempt, whereas if he kills him while the sun shines on him, he is liable. In the latter case, the thief is only liable to pay for what he stole; his blood has not been permitted.

The sages understood these verses as pertaining to a distinction between defense of one's life from a threat, in which case killing the threat is justified, and defense of one's property, in which case killing the thief is unjustified and is considered murder.[12] The Tosefta formulates this distinction and, typical of Tannaitic literature, offers instruction for cases of uncertainty as well.

> One who is coming through a tunnel: If he is coming to kill, we rescue him [from sin] at the cost of his life; if he is coming to take money, we do not rescue him [from sin] at the cost of his life [i.e., we do not take his life to prevent him from sinning]. If it is uncertain whether he is coming to kill or take money, we do not rescue him [from sin] at the cost of his life [i.e., we do not take his life to prevent him from sinning] as it says, "If the sun has risen on him, there is bloodguilt." Does the sun rise only on him? Doesn't the sun rise over the whole world? Rather, just as the rising sun means peace for the world, so too this person; as long as you know that there is peaceful intent within him, we do not rescue him [from sin] at the cost of his life [i.e., we do not take his life to prevent him from sinning], whether by day or by night. (*t. Sanhedrin* 11:5)

The first part of this Tosefta passage asserts that one may kill, in self-defense, someone who certainly poses a threat to his life, but protection of property does not justify killing the thief. If there is uncertainty about whether the tunneler has murderous intent or only wishes to rob the homeowner, the homeowner may not kill someone who poses an uncertain threat.[13]

---

12. On the turn within Tannaitic literature toward understanding this passage as a threat to life, see Haggai Schlesinger, "Din Ha-ba Ba-maḥteret Be-mishnatam shel Tanna'im: Bein Haganah Atzmit Le-anishah" (The Law of the Tunneler in Tannaitic Teachings: Between Self-defense and Punishment), *Shnaton Ha-mishpat Ha-Ivri* 29 (2017–2018): 181–234.

13. The explication of the verse that appears later in this Tosefta passage in support of

A close study of the explication of the same verses in *Mekhilta De-Rabbi Yishmael* demonstrates that there is a Tannaitic dispute regarding self-defense in situations of uncertain threats:

> "If the thief is found while tunneling ...": What is this? One about whom there is uncertainty as to whether he is breaking in to steal or to kill. You say that it is uncertain as to whether he is coming to steal [or kill, but perhaps it is merely uncertain whether he is coming to steal][14] or not? If when it is certain that he is coming to steal, one who kills him is liable, then a fortiori [he is liable if he kills someone] when it is uncertain whether or not he is coming to kill [emend to: steal]. (*Mekhilta De-Rabbi Yishmael, Nezikin* 13, MS Oxford)

---

this law seems to contravene the rule of conduct for cases of uncertainty that appears in the first part of the passage. This explication, which originates in *Mekhilta De-Rabbi Yishmael,* is predicated on a metaphorical reading of the expression "if the sun has risen on him" and is based on the fact that the verse specifies that the sun rises for the thief by using the words "on him." According to the explication, the rising of the sun indicates not the distinction between day and night but the clarity of the nonthreatening nature of the thief's intentions. If it is known that the thief does not threaten the life of the homeowner, only his property—"there is peaceful intent within him"—the homeowner may not kill the thief. One can infer from this explication that, if the thief's intentions are unclear, and there is some likelihood that he intends to kill the homeowner, the homeowner may, on the basis of this uncertainty, kill the thief.

The contradiction between the first part's explicit rule of conduct for cases of uncertainty and the latter part's implied rule of conduct for the same case stems from the fact that the explication cited in support of the law recorded in the first part is rooted in an entirely different conception of rules of conduct for cases of uncertainty. The explication indeed supports the distinction between a threat to life and a threat to property, as asserted by the first part of the Tosefta passage, but it does not support the very same paragraph's rule for cases of uncertainty. MS Vienna of the Tosefta contains an addendum to the explication as it appears in MS Erfurt: "as it says, 'If the sun has risen on him, there is bloodguilt.' Does the sun rise only on him? Doesn't the sun rise over the whole world? Rather, just as the rising sun means peace for the world, so to this person; as long as you know that there is peaceful intent within him, we do not rescue him [from sin] at the cost of his life [i.e., we do not take his life to prevent him from sinning], whether by day or by night. And whenever you do not know that there is no peaceful intent within him, whether by day or by night, we do not rescue him [from sin] at the cost of his life [i.e., we do not take his life to prevent him from sinning]." The last, additional line that appears in MS Vienna purports to resolve the contradiction between the first part of the Tosefta passage's rule for uncertain cases and the explication, in that it asserts that the thief is not killed in cases of uncertainty. Nevertheless, it is clear that this line was added in order to resolve the contradiction between the first and second parts of the passage. Moreover, it is obviously forced, because the additional line is structured in a way that would draw contrast between two situations, but in fact it establishes the same ruling for both situations. In *b. Sanhedrin* there is a *baraita* that explicitly contravenes the *Mekhilta* passage, though its internal logic is problematic vis-à-vis the verse to which it relates. See *b. Sanhedrin* 72a. On the Tosefta text and its significance, see Schlesinger, "Din Ha-ba Ba maḥteret," 207–9 and n. 69.

14. This addition is warranted on the basis of MS Munich of the *Mekhilta,* as likewise accepted by the editor of the *Mekhilta* text that appears in the "Ma'agarim" database of the Historical Dictionary Project of the Hebrew Language Academy.

The *Mekhilta* asserts, in contradistinction to the Tosefta, that this biblical passage allows a homeowner to kill a thief in a case where it is uncertain whether the thief threatens the homeowner's life. However, if the uncertainty is only whether the tunneler intends to steal, the homeowner may not kill him. This is derived a fortiori, for it is forbidden to kill in order to protect property even if it is clear to the homeowner that his property is threatened; certainly, then, if his need to defend his property is uncertain, killing is not warranted.

In contrast, when it comes to defending life, the homeowner may kill someone even if it is uncertain whether he poses a threat.[15] Based on this conception of uncertainty, the explication continues on to a significant expansion of the laws of saving lives on the Sabbath:

> From here one can infer to saving a life [on the Sabbath]. For bloodshed defiles the land and causes the Divine Presence to depart, yet it overrides uncertainty, then a fortiori saving a life [on the Sabbath] overrides uncertainty."[16]

This passage makes the important determination that murder is more severe than desecration of the Sabbath, which sets the stage for the a fortiori inference: if the more severe transgression of murder is set aside for the mere possibility of saving the homeowner's life, then certainly the Sabbath prohibitions are set aside for the possibility of saving a life. This explication teaches not only that saving a life overrides the Sabbath, but

---

15. The Tannaitic sources, both Tosefta and *Mekhilta*, therefore distinguish between a thief who threatens property, who may not be killed in self-defense, and an intruder who intends to threaten lives, whom it is permitted to kill. As noted, the two sources disagree about cases of uncertainty. The distinction between defense of property and defense of life is blurred by the Bavli's explanation of the license to kill the tunneler: "Rava says: What is the rationale for [the law of] the tunneler? There is a presumption that a person does not stand by idly when it comes to his money. [The tunneler] therefore said to himself: 'If I go in, he will rise against me and not leave me; so if he rises against me, I will kill him.' And the Torah stated that if someone comes to kill you, rise and kill him first" (*b. Sanhedrin* 72a). According to this understanding, any break-in whose purpose is burglary will escalate into a threat to life because the homeowner will rise up to defend his property, in which case the burglar will try to kill him in order to take the property. The homeowner, being justified in standing up to defend his property, is therefore defending his own life.

The Yerushalmi cites a Tannaitic dispute that includes a view that prima facie permits killing in order to protect property: "Rabbi Ḥiyyah taught: In the tunnel there is no bloodguilt; outside the tunnel there is bloodguilt. Rabbi Shimon ben Yoḥai taught: Even outside the tunnel, there is no bloodguilt, because a person's money is as dear to him as his life. He will see him, he will want to take his money from him, and he will rise up against him and kill him" (*y. Sanhedrin* 8:6; col. 1310, lines 1–4). The debate is about whether one may kill a burglar who is not tunneling—for example, he broke into a storehouse or is stealing from a field, in which case it is clear that he has no intention of threatening the homeowner's life.

16. The line "We must thus perforce accept not the second supposition, but the first: It is uncertain as to whether he is coming to steal or kill" belongs at the end of the previous discussion in the *Mekhilta*.

that even the mere possibility of saving a life overrides the Sabbath due to the importance of saving lives.[17] This derivation of a law governing uncertainty about saving a life on the Sabbath rests on the premise, which is prior to the *Mekhilta*'s explication, that self-defense overrides the prohibition of murder even in cases of uncertainty.

Later in the *Mekhilta* passage, there is an explication attributed to Rabbi Ishmael that corresponds to the position earlier in that passage, namely, that one may kill even if the need for self-defense is uncertain: "'If the sun shone upon him, there is bloodguilt': Now does the sun shine upon him alone? Rather, just as the sun means peace for the world, so too this person, if it is known that he is at peace with him, and he killed him nonetheless, he is liable." This explication presumes that it is forbidden to kill the thief if it is certain that he does not threaten the life of the homeowner, and that his sole interest is stealing property. However, when there is no such certainty, and it is possible that he will kill the homeowner, it is permitted to kill him.[18]

The Tannaitic sources are thus in disagreement about whether one may, in self-defense, take the life of someone who might or might not be threatening him. The Tosefta tradition maintains that it is forbidden to kill someone when there is uncertainty about whether self-defense is war-

---

17. On this, see the parallel passage in *Mekhilta, Shabbat* 1, where an abbreviated version of the passage appears with attribution to Rabbi Ishmael. In the Tosefta, this exposition is attributed to Rabbi Akiva: "Rabbi Aḥa said in the name of Rabbi Akiva: It is said: 'If the thief is found while tunneling….' Is the homeowner certain or uncertain? I would say uncertain. If it is permitted to kill someone out of uncertainty in order to live, then certainly Shabbat is overridden to save a life at risk" (*t. Shabbat* 15:17). For a different reading of Rabbi Ishmael's position in the *Mekhilta* and its relation to the source of the Tosefta in Shabbat, see Tzvi Novick, *What Is Good and What God Demands: Normative Structures in Tanaitic Literature,* Journal for the Study of Judaism Supplements 144 (Leiden: Brill, 2010), 65–67. It is possible that the expression "saving lives" (*piku'aḥ nefesh*) already implies a case of uncertainty regarding the saving of lives, as the expression is borrowed from a *mishnah* in Yoma: "We clear [*mefakḥin*] the rubble from on top of him." In such a case, where a person is buried under rubble, it is impossible to know whether he is alive or dead. See Aharon Shemesh, "The History of the Halakhic Concept '*Piku'aḥ Nefesh Doḥe Shabbat*'" [Hebrew], *Tarbiz* 80 (2012): 481–506, here 482.

18. See also *Mekhilta De-Rabbi Shimon Bar Yoḥai,* which likewise states that in a case of uncertainty one may kill the tunneler: "Later it says: 'For this case is like that of a man attacking another and murdering him' (Deut 22:26). That case is thus like this case. Just as in that case, it is uncertain that there are lives [at stake], so too in this case, it is uncertain whether there are lives [at stake]; just as in that case, if he gestured at killing, rise up and kill him first, so too in this case, if he gestured at killing, rise up and kill him first" (*Mekhilta De-Rabbi Shimon Bar Yoḥai* 22:2; based on the edition of Liora Elias Bar-Levav, *Mekhilta de-Rabbi Shimeon Ben Yohai on the Nezikin Portion: Text, Terms, Sources and Editing* [Jerusalem: Magnes, 2014], 355, lines 10–13). *Mekhilta De-Rabbi Shimon Bar Yoḥai* compares the case of the rape of a young woman to the case of the tunneler on the presumption that in both cases it is permissible to kill the trespasser/rapist, who also potentially threatens the life of the young woman/homeowner.

ranted, whereas the *Mekhilta* tradition permits killing even when there is uncertainty about whether self-defense is warranted.

It is understandable that there would be disagreement about this question. Uncertainty when it comes to self-defense poses a particularly acute problem due to the symmetry of the cost of error. If the homeowner kills the intruder and it turns out that his sole intent was stealing property, the homeowner's mistake caused the death of an innocent man. However, if the homeowner errs in not acting because of his uncertainty, and it turns out that the intruder indeed came to commit murder, then his error cost him his life.[19] Any rule of conduct for this uncertain situation will bear a high cost of error.

In contrast to the disagreement about self-defense in cases of uncertainty, when it comes to saving lives, there is no view in all of Tannaitic halakhah that challenges the ruling that even the uncertain possibility of saving a life overrides the Sabbath. Furthermore, as formulated by the Mishnah—"If a wall collapsed on someone, and it is uncertain whether or not he is there [in the rubble], and it is uncertain whether or not he is alive, and it is uncertain whether or not he is a Jew, we remove the rubble from on top of him" (*m. Yoma* 8:7)—the threshold of certainty that permits the desecration of the Sabbath is much lower than a fifty-fifty chance. The cost

19. Another disagreement about a case of uncertainty relating to capital crimes appears in *m. Sanhedrin* 10:7: "If a murderer became mixed among others, they are all exempt. Rabbi Yehudah says: They are brought into confinement." The anonymous first Tanna's view is clear and easily understood: When there is uncertainty, innocents cannot be punished along with an unidentifiable murderer among them. Rabbi Yehudah's view, that all of them are confined to jail, where they die, is hard to understand. It triggered a reinterpretation of the *mishnah* and sparked a dispute among Babylonian and Palestinian Amoraim: "Rabbi Yoḥanan said: The *mishnah* is about a murderer who became mixed among innocents. Resh Lakish said: The *mishnah* is about a murderer who had not yet been condemned, who got mixed up with a murderer who had already been condemned. Shmuel said: The *mishnah* is about one ox among [other] oxen. If the *mishnah* is about an ox among oxen, about this it is taught, 'they are brought into confinement!?'" (*y. Sanhedrin* 9:3; col. 1313, lines 17–22). The harshness of Rabbi Yehudah's statement led Resh Lakish and Shmuel to suggest far-fetched alternative interpretations in order to deny the possibility that Rabbi Yehudah maintained that innocents can be sacrificed as long as the murderer is punished along with them. Resh Lakish limits the *mishnah* to a case where all parties in the mixture are guilty of murder, except that one's court proceedings had already concluded and the other's had not. Shmuel applies the *mishnah* only to an ox that killed a person and then was mixed up among other oxen. In the Bavli (*Sanhedrin* 79b), the possibility that the case refers to a murderer mixed among innocents is rejected, and the view of Rabbi Yoḥanan as cited in the Yerushalmi is not mentioned. Additionally, the disagreement over the meaning of the *mishnah* is cited with some differences: According to the anonymous editor of the Bavli, Shmuel maintains that the *mishnah* refers to an ox whose verdict was concluded that was mixed among oxen that gored people to death but whose verdicts had not yet been concluded. This further limitation on the scope of the case is not impelled by Shmuel's statement as quoted in the Yerushalmi, because killing oxen that had not gored was not nearly as problematic as killing human beings. Shmuel could have limited the *mishnah* to oxen without combining his view with that of Resh Lakish.

of error in this case is much higher, as refraining from Sabbath desecration means that the possibility of saving a Jewish life goes unfulfilled.[20]

The disagreement about the proper rule of conduct for self-defense in cases of uncertainty, and the way that the permissibility of saving lives on the Sabbath is inferred from the permissibility of killing in self-defense, teach us an important principle about rules of conduct for cases of uncertainty: the threshold of certainty needed to act in cases of uncertainty is a function of the cost of error. Thus, the correct rule for self-defense in cases of uncertainty, where the cost of error is high, is the subject of disagreement among Tannaim, and the disagreement stems from the fact that the cost of error is symmetrical no matter which rule is used to decide the uncertainty. In contrast, when it comes to saving lives on the Sabbath, which is inferred, according to one view, from the permissibility of saving one's life through self-defense, there is no dispute; violating the Sabbath to save a life, even when it is uncertain that the attempt will succeed, is permitted according to all opinions. Moreover, the level of certainty necessary to enable life-saving action and to justify violating the Sabbath is low. The cost of the error of Sabbath desecration, severe as it is, cannot be compared to the cost of failure to save a life that could have been saved.

The rules of conduct governing uncertainty in various contexts are thus key to understanding the worldview of a halakhic legal system, in that they reflect the relative and absolute weight that it assigns to error. It is this weight that often determines the rules of conduct for cases of uncertainty and the degree of certainty needed to act or to refrain from acting. The fact that the Mishnah, in its sensitivity to the cost of error, acknowledges that there are situations that demand a high level of probability to decide an uncertainty, reinforces the importance of the Mishnah's ruling that a simple majority is followed in cases of prohibitions of foods.[21]

---

20. It is apparent from the *mishnah* in *Yoma*'s formulation of this rule of conduct in a case of uncertainty that saving the life of a gentile does not override the Sabbath. Menaḥem Meiri (*Bet Ha-beḥirah on Yoma* 84a, s.v. "*piku'aḥ nefesh ein holkhin bo*") characteristically limits this ruling to gentiles who are not disciplined by religion and thus asserts that it does not pertain to nations and religions that set boundaries and impose laws. In contrast to the *mishnah* in *Yoma* that gives preference to Jewish lives, the *mishnah* in *Sanhedrin* predicates the value of human life on the fact that the first human was created individually. There it is clear that the subject is a human being *qua* human being, despite various versions that later added the word "Israel" to limit the dictum to Jewish lives. See E. E. Urbach, "'Whoever Preserves a Single Life …': The Evolution of a Textual Variant, the Vagaries of Censorship, and the Printing Business," *Tarbiz* 40 (1971): 268–84.

21. Calculating the cost of error as the benchmark for the degree of certainty required for rules of conduct in cases of uncertainty is reflected in the rulings of Maimonides, who asserts that even though a woman is not permitted to remarry on the basis of circumstantial evidence of her husband's death, when it comes to inheritance and other fiscal matters, that same evidence is admitted, and the husband is deemed to be dead:

> If a man drowned in endless waters and witnesses came and testified that he had drowned in their presence—and all trace of him was lost—the heirs may take the

Rules governing cases of uncertainty are, as noted, a yardstick by which a legal system assesses the cost of error. Likewise, such rules serve as a means of ranking the severity of a transgression and of characterizing the source and nature of a prohibition. An example of such characterization can be found in tractate *Orlah*, which establishes one of halakhic history's main rules for governing uncertainty: "If there is uncertainty about [whether a certain fruit is] *orlah*, in Eretz Yisrael it is forbidden, and in Syria it is permitted.... New [wheat] is forbidden everywhere by the Torah, *orlah* by 'halakhah,' and *kilayim* by rabbinic law" (*m. Orlah* 3:9). The level of severity of the prohibition is ascertained by means of the rule governing an uncertain case thereof. Since *orlah* is forbidden in Eretz Yisrael by the Torah and elsewhere only by halakhah, produce whose *orlah* status is uncertain is forbidden in Eretz Yisrael but permitted in Syria. The same applies to uncertainty concerning *kilayim*: it is permitted outside of Eretz Yisrael because its prohibition is a rabbinic enactment and not from the Torah.[22] We learned from the rules of conduct for cases of uncertainty in

---

> inheritance in reliance upon the testimony of the witnesses, although ab initio we do not permit his wife to remarry in reliance thereon. Similarly, if witnesses came and testified that they had seen a man fall into a den of lions or leopards, or that they had seen him hanging and the birds eating his flesh ... in all of these cases and the like, if thereafter all trace of him was lost, the heirs take the inheritance in reliance upon the testimony, even though his wife may not be permitted to remarry in reliance thereon. For we say that the strictness of the rule making such testimony ineffective in so far as the capacity of the man's wife to remarry is concerned is due to the fact that a prohibition entailing the penalty of extirpation is involved therein, but with respect to matters pecuniary, if the witnesses testified to things which raise a presumption of death, asserting that they had seen all those things—and all trace of the man was lost and it was rumored that he had died—the heirs may take the inheritance in reliance upon such testimony. Such is the daily practice of all the courts and we have heard of no dissent in this matter. (*Mishneh Torah*, Laws of Inheritance 7:3; translation from *The Code of Maimonides, Book Thirteen: The Book of Civil Laws*, trans. J. J. Rabinowitz [New Haven: Yale University Press, 1949], 280–81])

22. There is an Amoraic dispute about the meaning of the assertion that *orlah* outside of Eretz Yisrael is forbidden by dint of "halakhah" as opposed to being forbidden by the Torah (like new grain) and by rabbinic enactment (like *kilayim*): "Shmuel said: Like local practice. Rabbi Yoḥanan said: Halakhah given to Moshe at Sinai. Rabbi Yassa asked before Rabbi Yoḥanan: It is halakhah given to Moshe at Sinai, yet you say thus? He said: When the halakhah was given, it was given thus. He said: If you left the land of Israel only to hear this dictum, it is sufficient" (*y. Orlah* 3:9; col. 347, lines 18–21; see the parallel in *b. Kiddushin* 38b). Whereas Shmuel understands the prohibition of *orlah* outside Eretz Yisrael as an ancient enactment, Rabbi Yoḥanan gives it the stricter status of halakhah given to Moshe at Sinai. Rabbi Yassa then asks Rabbi Yoḥanan why we do not rule stringently on uncertainties that arise with respect to halakhah given to Moses at Sinai. Rabbi Yoḥanan answers that this halakhah was established ab initio so that its uncertainty would be permitted, as opposed to uncertainty about a Torah prohibition or obligation.

The principle of ruling stringently in cases of uncertainty concerning a prohibition or obligation from the Torah is repeated in tractate *Mikva'ot*:

tractate *Makhshirin* that stringency in cases of uncertainty with respect to Torah law, as asserted by the *mishnah* in *Orlah,* applies only if the uncertainty is balanced. If there is a majority, however, even barely, it is permitted to eat even something whose prohibition is from the Torah.

IV

For those who have studied the intricacies of halakhah in depth, the principle of following the majority with respect to forbidden foods has become very familiar, almost self-evident. Returning to the first attestation of the formulation of this principle, in that tightly organized chapter of *Makhshirin,* allows us to see it not merely as a tradition handed down as a fait accompli, but as the product of decisions that occasionally went against earlier practices. Symptomatic of the boldness that such halakhic decision making entails is how even those who are loyal to halakhah sometimes have difficulty accepting such rulings in practice. Likewise, there are voices from within the tradition that oppose these rulings.[23] The primary

---

> *Mikva'ot* are [considered] mixed [when they are connected by an opening] the size of the tubular part of a flask, in its thickness and in its opening, such that two fingers can be rotated all the way around. If there is an uncertainty as to whether or not [the opening] was the size of the tubular part of a flask, it is invalid, because this is from the Torah. Likewise, [we rule stringently in a situation of uncertainty] regarding an olive's bulk of a corpse, an olive's bulk of a carcass, and a lentil's bulk of a vermin. (*m. Mikva'ot* 6:3)

The Tosefta formulates the ruling of this *mishnah* as follows: "An olive's bulk of a carcass, and a lentil's bulk of a vermin, about which it is uncertain whether or not there is the requisite quantity, this uncertainty is deemed impure; uncertainty about anything that is based in the Torah but whose quantities are given by the sages is deemed impure" (*t. Mikva'ot* 5:3). Since the obligation to immerse is from the Torah, the Mishnah rules stringently when there is uncertainty about the suitability of the connection that is supposed to link, and thus render fit, two otherwise deficient *mikva'ot*. The same applies to uncertainty whether the minimum quantity for corpse impurity or vermin impurity is met. Even though these quantities were determined by the sages, since these forms of impurity are rooted in the Torah, their uncertainties are treated stringently. The rule, "uncertainty with respect to Torah law is rendered stringently; uncertainty with respect to rabbinic law is rendered leniently," which appears in the Talmudim in various contexts, thus originates in Tannaitic literature, which ranks the source and severity of a prohibition by ruling on the status of its uncertainty. Another source that ranks a prohibition by ruling on the status of its uncertainty appears in *t. Shabbat* 2:6. See also below, chapter 6, p. 173.

In the medieval era, the greatest halakhists debated whether the rule to act stringently in cases of uncertainty about a biblical prohibition is a rabbinic decree or is itself a biblical rule. Maimonides maintained that uncertainty about a Torah precept is treated with stringency by dint of a rabbinic enactment. See *Mishneh Torah,* Laws of Impurity of Corpses 9:12. Rashba (Rabbi Shlomo ibn Adret), on the other hand, held that the Torah itself mandates stringency in a case of uncertainty regarding a Torah precept. See *Torah Ha-bayit Ha-arokh* 4:1.

23. The Bavli maintains that there is a minority opinion of Rabbi Meir that is concerned

opposition was to the idea that a majority, even a bare majority, is sufficient to permit something forbidden. In cases where there is a significant minority (*mi'ut matzui*), the medieval rabbis shy away from following a majority without examination.[24] Inter alia, the principle requiring a high degree of likelihood is extended from the realm of marriages and missing husbands to the general realm of prohibited foods, in direct opposition to what emerges from the plain meaning of the Tannaitic sources. The discussion of uncertainty in Tannaitic sources, as it pertains to forbidden foods, seems to be a safeguard against the dread of uncertainty and prohibition that may have been characteristic of other traditions. Indeed, this may explain the absence of any discussion of uncertainty in ancient traditions other than those of the sages.

V

Considering the importance of the majoritarian rule in cases of uncertainty and of the contextual question of the price of error leads to another major insight, pertaining to the relationship between halakhic realism and nominalism. This issue has been addressed at length in the scholarly literature, and it can be articulated as follows: The realist view maintains that halakhah reflects a connection between legal concepts and real-world forces and substances. In the case of biblical prohibitions, halakhic realism maintains that the prohibited object possesses some negative property that is prior to the prohibition—some sort of invisible poisonous substance that the Torah identifies—which is, in fact, the reason for the prohibition. This dangerous substance is not material and cannot be detected by the senses; it is an ethereal, spiritual substance whose existence and danger are revealed by the Torah.

The nominalist view, in contrast to the realist view, maintains that biblical prohibitions do not express or reveal any intrinsically negative aspect of the prohibited object. According to the nominalist approach, the

about the minority case and does not follow the majority. The Bavli infers that this is Rabbi Meir's view from a statement of his in the Tosefta: "Rabbi Meir would say: A man should not consummate with his deceased brother's wife until she first menstruates. Likewise, co-wives and relatives [of the deceased husband] should not be married or betrothed until they first menstruate, lest these turn out to be infertile [*ayloniot*] and the others therefore disqualified. But the sages say: They retain their presumption [*ḥazakah*] and are deemed fit" (*t. Yevamot* 9:6). Another Tannaitic opinion that might be concerned about a minority is that of Rabban Shimon ben Gamliel in *t. Taharot* 6:1. See n. 4 in this chapter.

24. See *Tosafot* on *Yevamot* 36b, s.v. *"ha"*; Naḥmanides writes, "It is a tradition that we happily receive that we do not rely on a fragile majority with a significant minority unless there is no alternative" (*Ḥiddushei Ha-Ramban* on Ḥullin 3b, s.v. *"bodek"*); see also *Responsa Rashba* 1:274.

reason for a prohibition can be, inter alia, God's will, the object's moral value, or its social or educational objectives. Thus, for instance, the nominalist approach might hold that the purpose of food prohibitions is to restrain and impose discipline on physical appetites, or that the purpose of the prohibition against consuming milk with meat is rooted in opposition to a pagan custom of seething a kid in its mother's milk, or that seething a kid in its mother's milk is cruel, at least symbolically. The common denominator of all of the rationales within the nominalist view is that there is no negative property, substance, or power intrinsic to the prohibited object that explains its prohibition.[25] The prohibited object is not "poisonous," as the realist view posits.

In recent years, realist readings have proliferated from various directions within the critical study of halakhah. However, none of this extensive treatment deals with the question of what can be learned about the sages' approach to this issue from their rules of conduct in cases of uncertainty.[26] The study of such cases, such as those found in *Makhshirin*, demonstrates a clearly nominalist view. Had prohibited meat, for example, been spiritually poisonous and detrimental to the soul, the sages would not have permitted it on the basis of a bare statistical majority. Where there is uncertainty about poisonous substances, where there is real concern that the substance in question is toxic and hazardous, people do not allow for solutions based simply on which outcome is most likely. The cost of error is too high if one views prohibitions as poison, and, accordingly, the threshold it would demand in order to permit would be higher. As we explore in the coming chapters other areas of regulations of uncertainty, such as impurities and lineage, the question of realism versus

---

25. The distinction between nominalism and realism was developed in Yochanan Silman, "Halakhic Determinations of a Nominalistic and Realistic Nature: Legal and Philosophical Considerations" [Hebrew], *Dine Israel* 12 (1984): 249–66. A newer and sharper formulation of this distinction has been proposed in Yair Lorberbaum, "Halakhic Realism," *Dine Israel* 30 (2015): 9–77. On how the nominalist approach does not undermine the attribution of rationales to the commandments, see ibid., 22–43. Lorberbaum raises the possibility that there is an intra-halakhic realism according to which the prohibited object has no harmful property or poisonous essence outside the halakhic system itself (ibid., 49–54). My usage of the concept of "halakhic realism" does not include such a possibility, which is itself quite complicated.

26. Among the various studies, see Daniel Schwartz, "Law and Truth: On Qumran, Sadducean, and Rabbinic Views of Law," in *Dead Sea Scrolls: Forty Years of Research*, ed. Devorah Dimant and Uri Rappaport, Studies on the Texts of the Desert of Judah 10 (Leiden: Brill, 1992), 229–40; Vered Noam, "Is It True That 'A Corpse Does Not Defile'? On Ritual Contamination in Tannaitic Literature" [Hebrew], *Tarbiz* 78 (2009): 157–88; see also Noam, "Essentialism, Freedom of Choice and the Calendar: Contradictory Trends in Rabbinic Halakhah," *Dine Israel* 30 (2015): 121–37; Christine Hayes, "Legal Realism and the Fashioning of Sectarians in Jewish Antiquity," in *Sects and Sectarianism in Jewish History*, ed. Sacha Stern, IJS Studies in Judaica 12 (Leiden: Brill, 2011), 119–46. See also Jeffrey Rubenstein, "Nominalism and Realism Again," *Dine Israel* 30 (2015): 79–120.

nominalism will surface with greater clarity. It is important to note that in conditions of uncertainty people are willing to assume risks, and the assumption that a prohibition is poisonous does not necessarily imply a complete avoidance of any shred of doubt. What is unique in the rule of the Mishnah is the decision to rely on a mere majority of 51 percent, which leads to the rejection of the equation of prohibited foods with spiritual danger.

A Mishnaic unit that, like the one in *Makhshirin*, is devoted in its entirety to rules of conduct in cases of uncertainty and attests to the emergence of uncertainty as an independent halakhic subject in Tannaitic literature, appears in tractate *Shekalim*. The starting point for the unit is an uncertainty about what specific shekel coins were earmarked for, but, as in *Makhshirin*, the *Shekalim* unit progresses to other realms of uncertainty that are organized under the same rule of conduct:

> Money found between [the chests for] shekels and free-will offerings, if it is closer to the [chest for] shekels, it falls to the shekels; if closer to the [chest for] free-will offerings, it falls to the free-will offerings; if it is in the middle, it falls to the free-will offerings.... [If it is found] between unconsecrated money and the second tithe, if it is closer to the unconsecrated money, it falls to the unconsecrated money; if it is closer to the second tithe, it falls to the second tithe; if it is in the middle it falls to the second tithe. This is the general rule: The money goes to what is closer even to be more lenient. When it is in the middle, it goes to the more stringent. (*m. Shekalim* 7:1)

The principle of following whatever is closer establishes a probabilistic consideration whose intent is to decide the status of an object whose origin is unknown.[27]

Later in the chapter, rules of conduct are presented for situations of uncertainty on the basis of various probabilistic assessments, beyond the principle of following the most proximate:

> Flesh found in the Temple courtyard: If it was [cut into] limbs, [it is assumed to be of] burnt offerings; if it was [cut into] pieces, [it is assumed to be of] sin offerings; if [found] in Jerusalem, [it is assumed to be of] peace offerings.... If it was found in outlying areas: If it was [cut into] limbs, [it is assumed to be] improperly slaughtered; if it was [cut into] pieces, it is permitted. But at the time of the [three pilgrimage] festivals,

27. See also *m. Bava Batra* 2:6: "A fallen [bird] found within fifty cubits [of a dovecote] belongs to the owner of the dovecote. Outside of fifty cubits, it belongs to the finder. If it is found between two dovecotes, if it is closer to this one, it is his, and if it is closer to that one, it is his. If it is halfway between, they split it." The ensuing discussion in the Bavli addresses the relationship between two decision principles of these Mishnaic units: majority and proximity. See *b. Bava Batra* 23b–24b.

when meat is abundant, even if it was [cut into] limbs it is permitted. (*m. Shekalim* 7:3)

When meat has already been cut into pieces, there are grounds to presume that someone took pains to prepare it for eating and that it is from a properly slaughtered animal. In contrast, when a limb is found intact, it indicates that the source of the meat is an improperly slaughtered animal, which is why no one bothered cutting it into smaller pieces.[28] During pilgrimage festivals in Jerusalem, when meat is in abundance, they would not bother cutting it into small pieces, so even if a whole limb is found, it is deemed kosher.

The rules contained in the unit on uncertainty in *Shekalim,* like the unit in *Makhshirin,* allow for the eating of "found" meat using additional considerations to tip the balance of uncertainty. What these two units have in common, which attests to the sages' independent and highly developed interest in uncertainty as a separate domain of inquiry,[29] is the permission they grant to eat meat of unknown provenance, based solely on probabilistic considerations—considerations that indicate that the sages were far from realist understandings of prohibitions and from paralyzing fear of uncertainty.

---

28. The Tosefta offers another mark by which unconsecrated meat can be differentiated from consecrated meat: "Meat found in the Temple courtyard: if it is strung together, it is permitted, because consecrated meat is not strung together. [If it was found] atop a trash pile anywhere, it is permitted" (*t. Shekalim* 3:10).

29. Aside from the numerous cases of uncertainty discussed in the Mishnah in various contexts, there are other groups of such cases in Tannaitic literature that further indicate independent interest in uncertainty. See *m. Zevaḥim* ch. 8; *Kinnin* chs. 1–3; *Yevamot* ch. 11; *Terumah* chs. 4–5; *Orlah* ch. 2; *Taharot* from midway through ch. 3 until the end of ch. 6; *t. Taharot* chs. 3–8.

2

Uncertainty and the Marketplace: Majority, Sectarianism, and Guilt

I

A marketplace is a physical space to which various local agricultural and manufactured products are funneled by means of wholesalers and brokers. Therefore, one who buys merchandise in the marketplace cannot trace its provenance.[1] One who purchases a product from a farmer's fieldside stall or a craftsman's workshop can identify the source of the merchandise with certainty. In contrast, one who makes purchases in the marketplace enters an area that is rife with uncertainty; entering the market-based cycle of exchange requires a complex confrontation with uncertainty.

The Torah commands that, from agricultural produce that has grown in the Land of Israel, diverse allocations have to be made before the owner is allowed to consume the produce. The first allocation is *terumah,* which is concentrated for priestly consumption and pertains to roughly 2 percent of the produce; the second and third allocations are tithes of the produce to be allocated to the Levite and the poor; and the fourth is tithe of the produce that has to be brought by the owner of the produce to be consumed by him in a pilgrimage to Jerusalem. As was apparent in the collection of uncertainties described in the first chapter of tractate *Makhshirin,* it is uncertain whether produce from Jewish farmers or sellers had tithes and *terumah* taken, so one who purchases produce in the market cannot be sure of their status (*m. Makhshirin* 2:10; *t. Demai* 1:12). Since the buyer of the fruits in the marketplace has no way of identifying their source (this is the very definition of a marketplace), he enters a field of uncertainty

1. On the flow of merchandise to market and its character as the site of exchange, see Joseph Menirav, *Prakmatia: The Marketing System on the Jewish Community in Palestine during the Mishna and Talmud Era* [Hebrew] (Ramat Gan: Bar-Ilan University Press, 2009), 23–123. On the Shuk as a complex gendered space and its nature, see Cynthia Baker, *Rebuilding the House of Israel: Architectures of Gender in Jewish Antiquity,* Divinations (Stanford, CA: Stanford University Press, 2002), ch. 3.

concerning about how "kosher" such fruits are. Proper apportionment of *terumot* and tithes levies a significant tax of some 20 percent of crops, which does not even account for the hefty tax burden that the government imposes for its own needs. The considerable scope of the mandatory gifts naturally caused farmers to refrain from fully apportioning tithes and *terumot*. Farmers such as these could permit themselves to pass the burden of these duties down the supply chain that mediates between them and the consumer, perhaps all the way to the consumers themselves. They could even use a quasi-halakhic justification by asserting that these duties are supposed to devolve upon the consumer of the produce, not its grower, not the wholesalers, and not the brokers.[2] The significant cost of fulfilling the obligation of *terumah* and the tithes, combined with complex legal and halakhic options for performing these obligations, produced a broad and varying range of commitment among Jewish farmers, merchants, and consumers. Indeed, extant literary evidence attests to different and varied levels of care in observing these obligations.[3] Additionally, the markets of the mixed cities of Palestine sold the produce of gentile farmers, which was also obligated in *terumot* and tithes, but from which its growers did not normally apportion those *terumot* and tithes. As indicated in tractate *Makhshirin*, this only intensifies the market's status as a place rife with uncertainty.[4]

---

2. See *Sifre Devarim* §105 (p. 165): "They said: The stores of the sons of Ḥanan were destroyed three years before the land of Israel, for they would exclude their produce from the tithes. They would expound: 'You shall set aside a tenth part ... and you shall eat' (Deut 14:22–23)—excluding the seller; 'the yield of your sowing'—excluding the buyer."

3. Ruth Alster points out that the word *demai* and its context of produce of uncertain status do not indicate the produce of an *am ha-aretz* specifically, in contrast to the produce of *ḥaverim*, who were trusted to apportion *terumot*. Undifferentiated produce of Jews, sold at market, were *demai*. On the relationship between the broad term *demai* and the distinction between an *am ha-aretz* and a *ḥaver* in the editing of the Mishnah, see Ruth Alster, "Mashma'ut Ha-munaḥ 'Demai' Be-sifrut Ha-Tanna'it" (The Meaning of the Term "Demai" in Tannaitic Literature), *Sidra* 29 (2014): 5–38.

4. The produce of gentiles is obligated in the apportionment of *terumot* and tithes, as indicated by the following *mishnah*: "A granary in which Jews and gentiles deposit [their produce]—if the majority is from the gentiles, [the produce] is certain [*tevel*, from which tithes and *terumah* have not been apportioned]" (*m. Makhshirin* 2:10). In the Talmudim, there developed the opinion that the status of a gentile's produce is the subject of a Tannaitic dispute, though it emerges from a close study of the Tannaitic sources that the view exempting gentiles from *terumot* and tithes seems to be nonexistent among Tannaim. Ze'ev Safrai wrote, "The view that gentile produce is exempt from tithes does not appear in the Tannaitic literature, and in general only the opinion that a gentile is obligated in land-dependent commandments finds expression" (*Mishnat Eretz Yisrael, Demai* [Ramat Gan: Bar-Ilan University Press, 2012), 149 [*Demai* 5:9]). Hanan Mazeh deals with the question of the place of gentiles in the halakhah of *demai* in Tannaitic sources and the Yerushalmi; I thank him for allowing me to read a draft of the chapter he is writing on this subject.

Aside from the concerns that arise from exchanges in the market, these uncertainties are likely to permeate the most basic fabric of coexistence. The possibility of eating in the home of a neighbor or relative depends on the presumption, which is far from obvious, that the hosts are meticulous about *terumot* and tithes, and that the refreshments served are permitted. In Tannaitic literature, the Mishnah and Tosefta of tractate *Demai* are devoted to the attempt to create rules of conduct for such states of uncertainty. Close study of this complex of rules provides a complicated portrait that interfaces with commerce, the market, neighborliness, and prohibition.

A full picture regarding these questions would require a rigorous discussion of tractate *Demai* in its entirety. However, we can still raise several important principles that are revealed in the rules relating to *demai*. The Mishnah does not require one who purchases produce in the market to apportion *terumot* and tithes in full, out of uncertainty. Fixing *demai* produce demands the apportionment to the priests of just 1 percent of the produce, as the *terumah* of the tithe. The Tannaitic literature that establishes the small portion that must be allocated from *demai* produce presumes that every Jew is careful to apportion *terumot*; therefore, one who buys produce is exempt from apportioning *terumah*. Likewise, the first tithe and the pauper's tithe, about which it is uncertain whether they were allocated, cannot be taken from the buyer in accordance with the rule that the burden of proof devolves upon the party that seeks to take something away from the other party. This rule would require the pauper or Levite to prove that no tithes had been apportioned from the produce; since there is no way to prove this claim, the owner of the produce is exempt from giving these tithes. Thus, the obligation imposed on *demai* produce includes only the duty to give the tithe of the first tithe—the *terumah* of the tithe—to a priest and to apportion the second tithe, which is consumed by its owner in Jerusalem or redeemed for money that the owner then spends on produce in Jerusalem (see *t. Sotah* 13:10). After the destruction of the Temple, produce was exempt from the second tithe; the produce would be redeemed for a *perutah* (a "penny"; a coin of the least value), and so the only obligation remaining with respect to the uncertain produce of *demai* was 1 percent of the yield.[5]

This limited form of obligation applying to *demai* produce makes feasible the existence of a marketplace where Jews can exchange produce and merchandise, as the cost of buying *demai* produce is relatively small. If the buyer had been required to apportion the full burden of tithes, he would have avoided buying produce in the marketplace and would do business only with a defined and demarcated group of trustworthy people, with

5. On the second tithe after the destruction of the Temple, see *t. Sanhedrin* 3:6.

whom he would share the burden of tithing. The Mishnah's construction of obligations vis-à-vis *demai*, which amount to 1 percent of purchased produce, thus enables entry into the marketplace, rife with uncertainty, with a low price of admission.

In addition, the Mishnah establishes other leniencies with respect to *demai* produce, exempting wholesalers even from the limited duties that apply to *demai* (*m. Demai* 2:4–5). Furthermore, the sages' halakhah created a mechanism for apportioning the *terumah* of the tithe and the second tithe during the meal itself; this halakhic mechanism makes it feasible to participate in a meal of produce whose status is uncertain (*m. Demai* 7:12).[6] A full discussion of all these processes would, as noted, require further inquiry into tractate *Demai*; however, it is worthwhile to focus on one central ruling that pertains to the marketplace as a locus of uncertainty.[7]

The unique space of the market, along with Tannaitic literature's enabling of entry therein, forms the background for one of the most central developments of the doctrine of uncertainty within the Bavli, becoming a basic principle of the halakhah governing uncertain cases of prohibited foods and constituting an inexhaustible source of attempts at conceptual elucidation. Carefully tracing the growth of this development will show that it originates in the Tannaitic enabling of exchange at market.

The Bavli states an important qualification to the majoritarian principle in Rabbi Zeira's name: "Anything fixed in place [*kavu'a*] is likened to being fifty-fifty, whether the result is leniency or stringency" (*b. Ketubot* 15a). This qualification asserts that we indeed follow the majority when there is uncertainty about an object that has left its place. However, if the uncertainty arises in the place of the object, or with regard to the place of the object, the uncertainty is treated as being completely balanced, with a likelihood of 50 percent, irrespective of the question of the majority.

The Talmud offers the following example: "It was taught [in a *baraita*]: Nine stores all sell properly slaughtered meat, and one sells the meat of a

---

6. On leniencies with regard to *demai* and their broader implications, see Ruth Alster, "Religious and Social Aspects of the Laws of Demai in Talmudic Literature" [Hebrew], PhD diss., Bar-Ilan University, 2010), 87–166. The Bavli explains the various leniencies in the laws of *demai* by claiming that most *amei ha-aretz* tithe. According to this view, *demai* is a rabbinic enactment requiring stringency in cases of uncertainty. As Alster shows, this position has no sources in Tannaitic literature or in the Yerushalmi, where, as stated, it is uncertain whether tithes were apportioned from undifferentiated produce of Jews. On the Bavli's discussion, see ibid., 185–217.

7. The attempt to lessen the cost of participation in the market, which stems from the special rules governing uncertainty that are fashioned in Mishnah *Demai*, does not absolve one who is meticulous about tithes and *terumot* from trying to minimize the obstacles posed by the market; such a person is deemed responsible for other people, other buyers, and consumers of produce that was in his control. See *m. Demai* 3:1–6.

carcass; if he bought from one of them but does not know from which he bought, his uncertainty is deemed prohibited. If [the meat] was found, follow the majority." If meat was purchased from a store, and the buyer does not know whether it is a store that sells kosher meat or not, or if he forgot which store he bought the meat from, then even though most stores in town are kosher, this case is treated as a fifty-fifty uncertainty; in this case, the meat is forbidden out of uncertainty. Since the uncertainty arose when the meat was in its place, it is considered "fixed in place" (*kavu'a*). In contrast, if the meat was found in the streets of that same city, its source is determined on the basis of the majority, and since most stores sell kosher meat, the meat may be eaten. This meat is called "separated" (*parish*), meat that had been separated from its place, which is subject to the principle: "Anything that separated, separated from the majority."

At first glance, there is no probabilistic difference between one who bought meat in a store and is uncertain as to whether the store was kosher and one who found the meat in the street and is uncertain as to whether it is from a kosher store. Nevertheless, according to the Talmudic rule, these two questions have completely different solutions. The question as to whether the meat was bought in a kosher store is treated as a perfectly balanced uncertainty, irrespective of considerations of majority and minority. On the other hand, the question as to whether the found meat is from a kosher store is decided in favor of the majority. In other Talmudic passages, the broad distinction between the "fixed in place" (*kavu'a*) and "separated" (*parish*) is applied in various contexts pertaining to uncertainty. In medieval and modern halakhic and Talmudic literature, there have been several attempts to illuminate the difference between "fixed in place" and "separated" in an obvious effort to understand why, despite the apparent absence of any probabilistic difference, there is an essential difference in how the uncertainty is decided.

The discussion in the Talmud cites two possible Tannaitic sources for Rabbi Zeira's dictum. One of them is the aforementioned *baraita*: "Nine stores all sell properly slaughtered meat, and one sells the meat of a carcass; if he bought from one of them but does not know from which he bought, his uncertainty is deemed prohibited. If [the meat] was found, follow the majority."[8] This *baraita*, as it appears in the Talmudim, does not

8. A formation similar to this *baraita* is cited by the Yerushalmi as well: "Nine stores all sell carcass ([properly slaughtered]) meat, and one sells the properly slaughtered ([carcass]) meat; if he mixed them up, he suspects. With regard to found [meat], we follow the majority" (*y. Shekalim* 7:4, col. 629, rows 17–21). The scribe who emended MS Leiden of the Yerushalmi from "carcass meat" to "properly slaughtered meat" at the beginning of the statement, and from "properly slaughtered meat" to "carcass meat" further on, compared its formulation with that of the *baraita* in the Bavli, which deals with a case where most stores sell kosher (slaughtered) meat and only one sells non-kosher (carcass) meat. The formulation of the *baraita* in the Bavli seems more reasonable, as does the scribal emendation, because without

appear in the Mishnah or Tosefta. A parallel Tannaitic source with a similar structure and number of features as the *baraita* of the Bavli and Yerushalmi appears in Tosefta *Demai* with respect to the laws of the market. A close study of the parallel source shows a different and much broader context than the distinction developed in the Bavli:

> If the entire city is selling *vadai* (produce that is certainly untithed), and one is selling *demai*, and he bought, and he does not know which one he bought from, it is prohibited. He apportions *terumah* and tithes, gives them to a priest, and the rest is his.... If the entire city is selling fixed [= tithed produce] and one is selling unfixed, and he bought, and he does not know which one he bought from, it is prohibited. If the entire city is selling properly slaughtered meat and one is selling carcass meat, and he bought, and he does not know which one he bought from, it is forbidden. When does this apply? When he bought but does not know from whom he bought. However, if he bought from the market, we follow the majority. (*t. Demai* 4:6–10)

Commentators on the Tosefta have noted the similarity between this passage and the *baraita* about the nine stores, but it is worth considering the significant difference between them.[9] The Tosefta qualifies the majoritarian principle. If kosher meat is sold in each city, but one local merchant sells non-kosher meat, and an uncertainty arises as to whom the meat was bought from, the overwhelming majority is not taken into consideration, and the meat is forbidden. In contrast, if the meat was bought in the market, the majority is followed, and the meat is permitted. Whereas the Bavli's *baraita* distinguishes between meat bought in a store and "found" meat, the Tosefta's distinction is between meat purchased from a particular seller, whether from his store or his home, and meat bought in the market. It would seem that the rationale for the Tosefta's differential ruling is not based on the Bavli's distinction between *kavu'a* and *parish*. (Prima facie, it would seem that meat bought from a market stall should be

---

the scribal emendation there is nothing novel in saying that if one forgot where he made his purchase, he must show concern that the meat in his possession is not kosher, because most of the stores sell non-kosher meat. Moreover, the difference between the case of bought meat and the case of found meat would not be clear, because in both cases the majority would be followed. Apparently, the Bavli's formulation of the *baraita* is a reworking of an earlier version, which appears in the Yerushalmi. The expression "he mixed them up" (*nitḥalfu lo*) in the Yerushalmi's version of the *baraita* was made more explicit in the Bavli version: "if he bought from one of them but does not know from which he bought." Likewise, the expression "he suspects" (*ḥoshesh*) is replaced by the more abstract and decisive formulation, "his uncertainty is deemed prohibited."

9. See Saul Lieberman, *Tosefta Kifshutah, Zera'im*, vol. 2: *Berakhot–Terumot* (Jerusalem: Jewish Theological Seminary, 1993), 237. The source he cites is from Rabbi Nissim of Kairouan, *Sefer Ha-mafte'aḥ: Ketubot*, in *Teshuvot Ha-Ge'onim*, S. Assaf edition (Jerusalem, 1927), 195.

considered *kavu'a*.)[10] According to the Tosefta, the difference between the cases is linked to the special, distinct status of the marketplace. If the meat was purchased from a specific person, before reaching the marketplace through the medium of wholesalers and brokers, then it would have been possible to ascertain the provenance of the meat and whether this person sells kosher or non-kosher meat. The purchaser's confusion and failure to remember where the meat was bought do not negate his prior ability, and duty, to ascertain the source. In contrast, when purchasing at the marketplace, it is fundamentally impossible to ascertain the source of the meat, because products arrive at the marketplace from different suppliers and in various contexts. The Tosefta therefore determines that, when one buys from the marketplace as opposed to buying from a specific person at his home or shop, the uncertainty of the meat's provenance is decided in accordance with the majority by means of a statistical decision. Majoritarian decision making is, in fact, the principle that enables marketplace purchases. The series of rulings that appears in the Tosefta of tractate *Demai*, which demarcates the marketplace as a defined and demarcated space vis-à-vis various prohibitions, is inextricably linked to the general question of *demai*, as *demai* produce is, first and foremost, produce purchased in the marketplace.[11]

In the version of the *baraita* that appears in the Bavli and Yerushalmi, the Tosefta's phrase, "if he bought from the market," is replaced with "if

---

10. The formulation of Maimonides softens the differences between the Tosefta's formulation and the formulation of the Bavli's *baraita*: "

> If there are ten shops, nine of which sell properly slaughtered meat while one sells carcass meat, and if a person has purchased meat in one of them and does not know which shop it was, the meat is forbidden, since in the case of a fixed object [*kavu'a*] the possibility one way or the other is assumed to be equal. If, however, the meat is found abandoned in the marketplace, the rule follows the majority of the shops, according to the principle that whatever emerges (*parish*) is regarded as having emerged from the majority." (*Mishneh Torah*, Laws of Forbidden Foods 8:11; [translation adapted from *The Code of Maimonides, Book Five: The Book of Holiness*, trans. L. Rabinowitz and P. Grossman [New Haven: Yale University Press, 1965], 193)

It seems that Maimonides was familiar with the Tosefta version and therefore added that the found meat was "abandoned in the marketplace." Nevertheless, as noted, our version of the Tosefta speaks of meat purchased, not found, in the market: "If he bought from the market."

11. An important presumption with regard to the marketplaces in question is that most of the produce available there is from Jews, so when one buys from a merchant, even if the merchant is not Jewish, the produce is considered *demai* and not *vadai*: "The presumption of a merchant everywhere is [that his produce is] *demai*, whether he is a gentile, Jew, or Samaritan. When does this apply? When he is brought [produce] of Jews, but if he is brought [produce] from a gentile or from a Samaritan, the presumption is that it is *vadai*" (*t. Demai* 4:20). See Saul Lieberman's comments on this text, based on the Yerushalmi cited in *Tosefta Kifshutah: Zera'im* (Jerusalem: Jewish Theological Seminary of America, 1992), 81 n. 45 on *t. Demai* 4:20).

[the meat] was found." As a result, the unique context of the question concerning the marketplace, as presented in its source in the Tosefta, is erased. Instead of the distinction between purchasing from a private seller in his home, where the provenance of the produce can be determined with certainty, and purchasing in the marketplace, a distinction developed between a stationary shop and meat found on the street, a distinction that was interpreted as a fundamental difference between *kavu'a* and *parish,* whose underlying logic is difficult and convoluted. In addition, the Bavli and Yerushalmi version of the *baraita* could have been understood without resorting to the principle of *kavu'a* and *parish* that the Bavli develops; in keeping with the similar explanation offered for the Tosefta version, the *baraita* can be understood to distinguish not between *kavu'a* and *parish,* but between a buyer and a finder. A buyer, whose purchase is the result of his own initiative, has the means to investigate the kosher status of the meat, unlike a finder, for whom it is impossible to ascertain the meat's provenance *ab initio.* The *baraita* of the Bavli and Yerushalmi thus expands the license granted by the Tosefta, which emphasizes the distinction between a buyer in a marketplace and a buyer from a private vendor, into a distinction between buyers and finders. Thus, the distinction between *kavu'a* and *parish* is not evident from Tannaitic literature; rather, it developed as a result of the differences between the text of the Tosefta and that of the *baraita* in the Talmudim.[12]

The majoritarian principle enables participation in marketplace exchanges, because the marketplace, as a space that funnels merchandise from a variety of unsupervised sources to itself, will always contain forbidden merchandise. Whereas Tannaitic literature devotes an entire tractate—*Demai*—to such states of uncertainty and provides rules of conduct in spaces, whether homes or marketplaces, that contain elements whose prohibited status is uncertain, there is no mention of questions and rulings like these in the Second Temple literature, which predates the Mishnah. The absence of rules for dealing with uncertain circumstances does not indicate a lack of obsession over the possible, uncertain, indeterminate presence of something prohibited on the part of the Dead Sea sect and other groups. Rather, in a sense the opposite is true: The absence from Second Temple literature of any attempt to formulate rulings for cases of

12. The fact that the Mishnah, in contrast to the Talmud, does not acknowledge the distinction between *kavu'a* and *parish* in majority-based rulings produces some interesting exegetical tensions wherein the Talmud tries to inject the novel criteria of *kavu'a* and *parish* into Mishnaic rulings that are based on a majority or a lack thereof, e.g., *b. Kiddushin* 73a, regarding those of unknown paternity; as well as *b. Ketubot* 15a and *y. Ketubot* 1:10, col. 960; *b. Zevaḥim* 73a–b; and *b. Yoma* 84b. The discussion in Bavli *Ketubot* quotes another Tannaitic source from which the distinction between *kavu'a* and *parish* seems, at first glance, to emerge. On the meaning of this source and its relationship to the question of *kavu'a* and *parish,* see the next chapter, on uncertainty with respect to impurity, n. 6.

uncertainty seems to stem from the fact that a Jew, who was supposed to be meticulous about these things, would, by default, apportion the tithes and *terumot* in full from any produce he bought in the marketplace, since he could not presume that they had been apportioned already. It was possible to avoid apportioning the full gamut of tithes and *terumot* only if the produce came from a known, reliable source—that is, from a very small marketplace and an extremely limited system of exchange.

In the Tannaitic literature, the emergence of discussion about uncertainty and the proliferation of rules of conduct for such circumstances is rooted not in the appearance of stringency-inducing dread of transgression but in an attempt to mitigate such impulses and allow a certain degree of contact with a complex reality that generates doubts and misgivings. The Mishnah's rulings were the product of opposition to the default attitude, which was likely to produce a ruling that one may not eat produce of unknown provenance unless one apportions the *terumot* and tithes in full. Moreover, according to this default attitude, in order to avoid uncertainty, one must limit, to the extent possible, any contact with a world that does not observe prohibitions and obligations in full. Such an approach might suit the sectarian policy that aims at establishing a self-contained all-encompassing reality that will diminish friction with such uncertainties to the minimum.

II

Aside from following the majority, one of the main ways to decide cases of uncertainty in Tannaitic literature is *ḥazakah,* that is, maintaining the status quo of the object of uncertainty, whether to prohibit or to permit. The term *ḥazakah* has three different meanings in the Mishnah. The first meaning, which does not pertain to uncertainty, is "possession" as a form of acquisition. Ownership of real estate is transferred to the buyer at the moment that he demonstrates possession of it by cultivating it, even if only symbolically.[13]

The second meaning of *ḥazakah* in the Mishnah is "presumption"; that is, uncertainty is clarified by means of a *ḥazakah,* which provides probabilistic information about a case. Thus, for example, the Mishnah states:

---

13. On *ḥazakah* as a form of acquisition, see *m. Kiddushin* 1:5 and *t. Kiddushin* 1:3. Sometimes a person's demonstration of possession serves not as a form of acquisition by symbolic cultivation of the land—"he locked, fenced in, or breached in any quantity" (*t. Kiddushin* 1:3)—but as evidence of prior acquisition. On this, see *m. Bava Batra* 3:3. Additionally, there are acts of *ḥazakah* that generate ownership on the strength of the very fact of usage. See *m. Bava Batra* 3:5–6.

> If the wall of a courtyard falls, we obligate him to build up to four cubits. There is a presumption [*ḥazakah*] that he has given until one brings proof that he has not given. From four cubits and up, we do not obligate him. If he built an adjacent wall, we make it all incumbent upon him. There is a presumption [*ḥazakah*] that he has not given until he brings proof of having given. (*m. Bava Batra* 1:4)

Joint owners of a yard can compel one another to rebuild a partition between them that has collapsed. Since halakhah requires the partners to share in the building expenses, there is a *ḥazakah*, a presumption, that gives credibility to one partner's claim that he paid his share; it would have been possible to compel him, and we cannot assume that the second partner built the wall without charging the first partner for his share in the building expenses. In contrast, if one of the partners wants to raise the partition wall above four cubits, he cannot require the partner to share in the cost of raising the wall, unless the partner built a wall on his side of the partition adjacent to the newly raised wall, indicating that he plans to build a roof over the walls and to make use of the wall under construction by his neighbor. In such a case, since it was not possible to charge the partner at the outset, we assume that he has not yet paid his share, unless he proves that he has.

This sense of *ḥazakah* appears frequently in the Mishnah, and it is essentially similar to a decision based on a majority in that it decides uncertainty by identifying the higher-probability outcome.[14] The distinction between this sort of *ḥazakah* and a decision based on a regular majority in the Mishnah stems from the fact that the *ḥazakah* principle is articulated as a broad rule that does not relate to any known statistical information about a specific state of affairs. In a regular majority-based ruling, as in the *mishnah* in *Makhshirin*, there is definite information about who constitutes the majority of residents. This type of *ḥazakah* principle, in contrast, provides broad probabilistic information in situations where we cannot ascertain the facts of the specific case in front of us. The uncertainty is decided by an agglomeration of *ḥazakot* that provide broad probabilistic assumptions and serve as a default for deciding cases of uncertainty.[15]

The third meaning of *ḥazakah* in Tannaitic literature is "status quo"; when uncertainty is introduced to a case, the past or present status is maintained unless there is additional evidence that the status has changed.

---

14. Additional examples from the Mishnah and Tosefta that use *ḥazakah* to decide uncertainty on the basis of probabilistic assumptions include *m. Kilayim* 9:7; *Bekhorot* 8:6; *Niddah* 2:5; *t. Yevamot* 6:9; *Horayot* 2:11; *Ohalot* 17:13; *Taharot* 4:5.

15. Such probabilistic assumptions are called "majorities that are not before us" (*b. Ḥullin* 11a–b), as distinguished from "majorities that are before us" wherein the claim of a majority is based on discrete knowledge about a given state of affairs—like the decisions based on the majority of a city's population in tractate *Makhshirin*.

This form of decision adds no probabilistic information that would clarify the uncertainty. Rather, it asserts that, when there is uncertainty, the prevailing order should be left alone, whether to permit or prohibit, until there is substantive evidence in favor of change. This third type of *ḥazakah*, whose later development added multiple layers of complexity, originates in Tannaitic literature; in the Mishnah and Tosefta, it is applied to decide uncertainties in various halakhic realms.

Thus, regarding an uncertainty about whether a nazirite became defiled, "The *ḥazakah* of one who is impure is [to remain] impure, and the *ḥazakah* of one who is pure is [to remain] pure, for there is support for this matter" (*m. Nazir* 9:2).[16] The status of the nazirite in a case of uncertainty about defilement is determined by the status quo ante.[17] In another *mishnah*, which addresses the permissibility of eating the meat of a slaughtered animal, *ḥazakah* serves to render the meat fit for consumption:

> If one slaughters a gravely ill animal, Rabban Shimon ben Gamliel says, "[It is fit for consumption] as long as its fore and hind leg convulse." Rabbi Eliezer says, "It is sufficient if it squirts [blood]." ... The sages say, "Unless its fore or hind leg convulses or it shakes its tail, whether for cattle or caprines."... About what is this said? When it had a *ḥazakah* of being gravely ill. However, if it had a *ḥazakah* of healthiness, even if did not exhibit one of these signs, it is fit [for consumption]. (*m. Ḥullin* 2:6)

Slaughtering a dying animal renders it fit for consumption only if there are signs that the animal dies because it was slaughtered and did not die beforehand. The convulsion of certain limbs of the animal at the time of the slaughter constitutes evidence that it was alive at the time. In the absence of these symptoms, there arises uncertainty about whether the animal indeed died prior to being slaughtered and is therefore forbidden to eat. Nevertheless, if the animal had a *ḥazakah* of being healthy prior to being slaughtered, the uncertainty stemming from the lack of convulsions at the time of the slaughter is decided by maintaining the animal's prior *ḥazakah* of health, and the animal may be eaten. The known state of affairs prior to the introduction of uncertainty is what determines the halakhic ruling that applies after the uncertainty is introduced.

In accordance with this type of *ḥazakah*, the Mishnah also asserts that, if an object or person underwent a physical change that effects a change in halakhic status, the moment of status change is deemed to be the moment

---

16. Later in that chapter are *mishnayot* that discuss other uncertainties that are decided using the principle that "there is support for this matter." Not all of these cases are predicated on the principle of *ḥazakah*, and, in some of them, one gets the impression that the statement "there is support for this matter" is a probabilistic claim.

17. See J. N. Epstein, *Introduction to the Mishnaic Text* [Hebrew], 2 vols. (Jerusalem: Magnes, 2001), 2:1037–38, which links this *mishnah* to the issues of uncertainty that are discussed in *m. Nazir* ch. 8.

that the physical change became known for certain, or immediately prior, and, until that moment, the person or object retains the status quo ante. Thus, for example:

> If a *niddah* (a woman rendered impure by menstruation) examined herself on the morning of the seventh day [after menstruation] and found she was pure (i.e., no blood was found upon examination), and at twilight she did not [examine herself again before immersing in order to] separate [her impure period from her period of purity], and after some days she examined herself and found she was impure, she has a *ḥazakah* of having been pure [in the interim]. If she examined herself on the morning of the seventh day and found she was impure, and at twilight she did not [examine herself again before immersing in order to] separate, and after some time she examined herself and found she was pure, she has a *ḥazakah* of having been impure [in the interim], and she renders things impure [retroactively] for twenty-four hours back and from [the previous] examination to [the latest] examination. (*m. Niddah* 10:2)[18]

The assumption that in cases of uncertainty the status quo is retained until the emergence of additional evidence is also articulated in Mishnah *Gittin*. This interesting and complex formulation begins with the assertion that a husband who traveled far away is presumed to be alive in every respect.[19] The Mishnah then addresses a case in which an uncertainty arises about whether the husband is alive:

> Rabbi Elazar ben Parta said three things before the sages, and they upheld his words: That [a husband in] a city that was besieged by soldiers, [on] a ship foundering at sea, or who was being led to trial [for a capital crime] is presumed alive. However, [a husband in] a city sacked by soldiers, [on] a ship that was lost at sea, or who was being led to his execution is treated with the stringencies of those who are alive and the stringencies of those who are dead; [neither the] a daughter of an Israelite who married a priest nor the daughter of a priest who married an Israelite may eat *terumah*. (*m. Gittin* 3:4)

---

18. See also *m. Niddah* 1:1, where there is a dispute between the House of Hillel, the House of Shammai, and the sages. Charlotte Elisheva Fonrobert analyzed extensively the ways in which the different rules of presumption of an uncertainty applied to menstruation serve among other means as objectifiying women's bodies (*Menstural Purity: Rabbinic and Christian Reconstructions of Bibilical Gender*, Contraversions [Stanford, CA: Stanford University Press, 2000], 85–102).

19. "[If] one brings a *get* and left [the husband] elderly or ill, he gives it to [the wife] with the presumption [*ḥazakah*] that he is alive. [If] the daughter of an Israelite was married to a priest, and her husband went overseas, she eats terumah on the presumption [*ḥazakah*] that he is alive" (*m. Gittin* 3:3). It is clear from the Yerushalmi that this *ḥazakah* does not constitute evidence but is a rule of conduct for uncertain circumstances that establishes the preference for the status quo: "Bar Kappara taught: Even if he left [the husband] one hundred years old, and his journey took another hundred years, he gives [the *get*] to [the wife] under the presumption that [the husband] is alive" (*y. Gittin* 3:3, col. 1063, lines 45–47).

If a man is known to be standing trial for a capital crime, residing in a besieged city, or aboard a foundering ship, there are doubts about whether he is alive. Nevertheless, by means of a *ḥazakah* that reflects his status quo ante of being alive, we decide the uncertainty and presume him to be alive. In contrast, when this man's condition changed, and it became more likely that he was dead—he had been condemned to death, his ship was lost at sea, or the city was conquered—then the *ḥazakah* is nullified and his status is decided on the side of stringency of both living and dead. This *mishnah* teaches that, as long as there is no likelihood that warrants stringency, the uncertainty is decided by means of *ḥazakah*.[20]

One of the Mishnah's more interesting uses of *ḥazakah*, whether of the second or third type, is when it does not serve to decide uncertainty but has a prior function of preventing the emergence of uncertainty. For instance, we learn, "A conduit of water that comes from afar is fit, as long as it is guarded so that no person interrupts it. Rabbi Yehudah says: It retains its *ḥazakah* and is permitted" (*m. Parah* 8:11). The purifying water of the red heifer requires water that was never used or drawn. Against the *mishnah*'s anonymous first opinion that the entire length of a conduit must be guarded to ensure that its waters are not disqualified by human interference, Rabbi Yehudah applies a *ḥazakah* that, in this case, does not decide an emergent uncertainty but removes the concern for uncertainty, thereby rendering superfluous the need for vigilant guarding of the conduit and the fitness of its waters.

The function of *ḥazakah* as something that limits the emergence of uncertainty and delimiting its boundaries appears once again in context of the red heifer: "Rabbi Yehudah says: We guard it so that it is not used for any work. They said to him: If so, there is no end to this. Rather, it retains its *ḥazakah* and is deemed fit" (*t. Parah* 2:1).[21] The Tosefta's phrase "there is no end to this" constitutes an assertion that purports not to decide an uncertain status but to delimit the boundaries of the uncertainty's emergence. The claim that "there is no end to this" also appears in another important and very common context as a barrier against the dread of

---

20. See also *t. Gittin* 2:13. The Mishnah states:

> [If] a woman and her husband went overseas and her son was with them, and she returned and said, "My husband died and then my son died," she is credible. [If she said], "My son died and then my husband died," she is not credible. Nevertheless, we are concerned about her claim [i.e., that it is true], so she performs levirate divorce and may not perform levirate marriage. (*m. Yevamot* 15:8)

It is apparent that the Mishnah's decision regarding this uncertainty and the credibility of the woman's testimony hinges on the woman's prior status, before going overseas.

21. In this Tosefta passage, Rabbi Yehudah's opinion is reversed with respect to the *mishnah* quoted above. This is apparently his opinion. See also *m. Yoma* 1:1 and below, n. 23.

uncertainty. The Mishnah defines the duty to search and destroy *ḥametz* (leavened grain products) in advance of the festival of Pesaḥ:

> On the evening of the fourteenth [of Nissan] we search for *ḥametz* by candlelight. Any place into which *ḥametz* is not brought need not be searched. So why did [the sages] say [to search the first] two rows in a wine cellar? When it is a place into which *ḥametz* is brought. The House of Shammai say: Two rows across the entire façade of the wine-cellar. The House of Hillel say: The two outer rows, which are the uppermost. We need not be concerned lest a weasel dragged [*ḥametz*] from house to house and from place to place, for then [we would also need to be concerned that it dragged *ḥametz* from courtyard to courtyard, and from city to city—there is no end to this. (*m. Pesaḥim* 1:1–2)

The search for *ḥametz* is limited only to those places into which people are likely to bring *ḥametz*.[22] With the contention that "there is no end to this,"[23] the Mishnah blocks concern that a rodent may have dragged *ḥametz* from an as-yet-unsearched place to someplace that had already been searched, or from a place into which *ḥametz* is brought to a place where it is not brought. If we would be concerned for the transfer of *ḥametz* from one place to another within the same house, or from one house to another within the same courtyard, we would need to worry about the transfer of *ḥametz* from one courtyard to another and from one city to another. There would be no end to our consternation in the face of uncertainty. This rule, a kindred spirit of the *ḥazakah* rule from Tosefta *Parah*, likewise (and uniquely) delimits the boundaries of uncertainty and not the method of deciding it. In this realm *ḥazakah* serves as an anchor to stop the spiraling and delibitating power of doubt when it encounters religious obligation and commitment. Interestingly, this rule, which appears in a *mishnah* whose purpose is to delimit and contain uncertainty vis-à-vis the elimination of *ḥametz*, did not allay the anxieties that underlie frenzied pre-Pesaḥ cleaning and disinfecting, which remain widespread to this day.

As mentioned, the Tannaitic sources present two distinct notions of *ḥazakah* for deciding uncertainties: *ḥazakah* based on probability, and *ḥazakah* based on retaining the status quo ante when faced with uncertainty. In one of the more interesting Tannaitic sources on treating cases of uncertainty, there is a dispute about which of these two notions of *ḥazakah* should be applied when they lead to opposite results. This dispute emerged with respect to the obligation to separate tithes and *terumah*, which applies to produce from the Land of Israel. In the border regions of the Land of Israel, there is no small amount of uncertainty about which

22. See *t. Pesaḥim* 1:2–3 for a list of places where there is need to be concerned for the presence of *ḥametz* since it is not brought there.

23. On the function of the phrase "there is no end to this" as a barrier to uncertainties and concerns, see *m. Yoma* 1:1 and *Sifra, Aḥarei Mot* 5:3. See also *t. Sotah* 1:1.

halakhic jurisdiction the produce belongs to. To decide these cases, the sages applied *ḥazakah*:

> One who purchases [produce] from a donkey caravan in Tyre or from the warehouses of Sidon is exempt [from separating *terumah*]; from the warehouses of Tyre or from the donkey trains of Sidon is obligated. Rabbi Yosah ben Rabbi Yehudah says: One who purchases from the warehouses of Tyre is exempt, and the donkey caravans go without saying. From one donkey driver in Tyre—he is obligated. Rabbi Yehudah says: A donkey train that descends to Keziv is obligated, because there is a *ḥazakah* that it comes from the Galilee. But the sages say: It retains its *ḥazakah* of being exempt unless you know where it is from." (*t. Demai* 2:17)

Tyre is adjacent to the northern border of the Land of Israel, and Sidon is to the north of Tyre, farther from the border of the Land of Israel. It is therefore presumed, due to proximity, that the produce in a Tyrian storehouse was imported from the Land of Israel and is therefore subject to tithing, unlike the produce in the distant storehouses of Sidon. In contrast, produce brought to Tyre by donkey caravan did not originate in Land of Israel, as the relatively short distance from Tyre to the Land of Israel would not require organized, group transportation. However, it can be surmised that a donkey caravan that reached distant Sidon originated in the northern Land of Israel. These are all probabilistic considerations. Rabbi Yosah ben Rabbi Yehudah's position is likewise based on a probabilistic presumption that a donkey train that descends to Keziv came from Galilee.

In contrast to these probabilistic *ḥazakot*, the sages put forward a completely different position, based on a *ḥazakah* that is predicated not on probability but on the situation as it emerges before us. If this produce is outside of Eretz Yisrael, it is exempt from tithing, because its present location determines its status by default, absent certain knowledge.[24] It seems that the sages deemed probabilistic considerations negligible next to the given halakhic reality, which should not be altered without more significant evidence.[25]

---

24. See Saul Lieberman's comments: "The sages, apparently, dispute all of this and maintain that even along the border of Eretz Yisrael, if its present location is exempt [from tithes], [the produce] is exempt, and we follow its status" (*Tosefta Kifshutah, Zera'im*, vol. 1: *Berakhot–Terumot*, 198).

25. Occasionally, *ḥazakah* as a probabilistic determination is combined with *ḥazakah* as status quo. For instance, "Rabbi Meir would say: A man should not consummate with his deceased brother's wife until she first menstruates … lest these turn out to be infertile [*aylo-niot*] and the others therefore disqualified. But the sages say: They retain their *ḥazakah* and are deemed fit" (*t. Yevamot* 9:6). According to Rabbi Meir, a man may not consummate levirate marriage with a minor, lest she turn out to be infertile, in which case it is forbidden to perform levirate marriage with this girl, as she is his brother's wife. The sages disagree, claiming: "They retain their *ḥazakah* and are deemed fit." They assert that a minor has a

A complex thicket of cases pertains to disputes about which facts define the status quo ante that determines the halakhah that is not changed by the introduction of uncertainty. A dispute of this sort appears in the Mishnah *Mikva'ot* and the corresponding Tosefta: "If a *mikveh* was measured and found deficient, all purifications which were made on its bases, whether in a private domain or in a public domain, are retroactively impure" (*m. Mikva'ot* 2:1).

The *mishnah*'s case deals with a *mikveh* that was known to be fit but, when measured, was found to be lacking the requisite forty measures of water. The uncertainty in this case is when the *mikveh* became unfit. The *mishnah* asserts that all vessels and human beings who immersed in that *mikveh*, going back to when the *mikveh* was known to be fit, are retroactively deemed impure. Later the *mishnah* asserts that this rule applies only to severe forms of impurity; less restrictive forms of impurity are deemed pure in such cases, due to the uncertainty.

Rabbi Yosah disagrees. According to him, in such cases of uncertainty, everything that had been immersed in that *mikveh* to remove any impurity, whether severe or mild, is deemed impure:

> Rabbi Yosah deems it impure, for Rabbi Yosah would say: "Anything that has a *ḥazakah* of impurity will always remain in its state of impurity until it is known to have become pure." Nevertheless, [if the] uncertainty [is about its fitness] to become impure and to render other things impure, [it] is deemed pure. (*m. Mikva'ot* 2:1)

Since the person or vessel immersed in the *mikveh* that was discovered to be deficient was impure, it remains subject to its preexisting *ḥazakah* of impurity. Therefore, according to the principles of *ḥazakah*, if the problem was reversed—the uncertainty was whether pure vessels became impure—they stand on their *ḥazakah* of purity.

The Tosefta that deals with the same case of a *mikveh* that was found deficient reports a dispute about *ḥazakah*:

> Rabbi Shimon said: There was an incident with a pool of Diskos in Yavneh, which was measured and found deficient. Rabbi Tarfon rendered pure, and Rabbi Akiva rendered impure. Since this *mikveh* had a *ḥazakah* of purity, it remains pure until it becomes known that it has become impure. Rabbi Akiva said: Since this *mikveh* has a *ḥazakah* of impurity, it is always deemed impure, until it is known to have been pure. (*t. Mikva'ot* 1:8)

The bone of contention between Rabbi Tarfon and Rabbi Akiva is which status to consider the status quo that should not be altered in the face of

ḥazakah of fitness for levirate marriage on the basis of her present status. This *ḥazakah* may also rely on the notion that most women are fertile and not *ayloniot*.

uncertainty. Does the *ḥazakah* relate to what is known about this *mikveh*'s past, in which case its disqualification is delayed until the moment its deficiency is discovered, or, as Rabbi Akiva maintains, is the present, deficient status of the *mikveh* the determinative status quo, in which case the *mikveh* is retroactively disqualified all the way back to the last time it was known to be full and fit?[26] This question was later reformulated in terms of a conflict between *ḥazakah de-me'ikara* (presumption based on prior status) and *ḥazakah de-hashta* (presumption based on present status).[27]

The term *ḥazakah* has a fourth meaning in the Mishnah, which is not a mode of acquisition, a probabilistic rule, or a means of deciding cases of uncertainty by preserving the status quo. The fourth meaning of *ḥazakah* also pertains to states of uncertainty, but the *ḥazakah* serves not as a claim or a consideration used to decide uncertainty but as a tentative and provisional way that defines the mode and method in which the uncertainty is decided. A *mishnah* in *Ketubot* exemplifies this unique usage of the concept of *ḥazakah*:

> If she was pregnant, [and they asked her:] "What is the nature of this fetus?" [And she replied:] "It is by Mr. So-and-so, and he is a priest." Rabban Gamliel and Rabbi Eliezer say: She is believed. Rabbi Yehoshua says: We do not live by [the words of] her mouth. Rather, she is presumed (lit. "has a *ḥazakah*") to be pregnant by a Gibeonite or a *mamzer* until she brings evidence for her words. (*m. Ketubot* 1:9)

Rabban Gamliel and Rabbi Eliezer believe the pregnant woman's testimony regarding the fitness of the fetus's father. In his dissent, Rabbi Yehoshua's invocation of *ḥazakah* is not a claim to resolve the uncertainty. He does not contend that there is a higher probability of the father, and

---

26. A similar question about determining the time that a halakhically significant change occurred to an object appears in the Mishnah: "One who put produce aside to apportion *terumah* and tithes from them, or money on which to redeem the second tithe, may apportion on the presumption that it still exists. If they were lost, he must be concerned about twenty-four hours. These are the words of Rabbi Elazar" (*m. Gittin* 3:8). In the Yerushalmi and Bavli on this *mishnah*, there is an Amoraic dispute concerning the twenty-four hours in question. Does it refer to twenty-four hours forward from the placement of the money or produce, or twenty-four hours backward from when it was discovered that the money or produce was gone or ruined? The straightforward meaning of the *mishnah* seems to be that the continued existence of the money or produce can be presumed until the last twenty-four hours before their loss was discovered, even though they had not been seen for many days prior to the discovery of their loss. The Talmud comments that Rabbi Elazar disputes the *mishnah* in *Mikva'ot* that retrojects the present, deficient status of the *mikveh*. Perhaps he would agree with Rabbi Tarfon's view in the Tosefta. For a similar dispute on this question of *ḥazakah*, between Rabbi Meir and the sages, see *m. Taharot* 5:7 and *t. Taharot* 6:6.

27. Rabbi Yosah's words in the *mishnah* in *Mikva'ot* seem to indicate that the rationale for retroactively rendering the immersed vessels impure stems not from the present status of the *mikveh* but from the present, impure status of the vessels. See the discussion in *b. Niddah* 2b.

therefore the fetus, being a Gibeonite or *mamzer*, because there is no such likelihood. He likewise does not refer to any prior status that can serve as a default for deciding the uncertainty. The sentence that reflects Rabbi Yehoshua's position—"she is presumed to be pregnant by a Gibeonite or a *mamzer*"—is not a rationale for resolving the uncertainty but the means by which it is decided. That is, according to Rabbi Yehoshua, we regard this woman as having had sexual relations with someone of unfit lineage until she brings evidence to the contrary.

The usage of the term "she is presumed" (*harei hi be-ḥezkat*) distinguishes the decision of this case from other, more absolute and conclusive ways of resolving uncertainties. In this case, the decision is not absolute. It is tentative in character, valid only until she brings additional evidence. Deciding the uncertainty by assuming that this woman had sexual relations with someone of unfit lineage is not supported by probability or by any prior status, but by undermining the woman's credibility and control and policing her sexuality. The term *ḥazakah*, as used by Rabbi Yehoshua, describes how uncertainty is tentatively and singularly decided as a tentative default position, not as an absolute determination.[28]

The assessment of the relative weight of the various, and sometimes conflicting, types of *ḥazakah* and their relationship with other options for deciding uncertainties is the subject of some of the most impressive and detailed elaborations in the history of halakhah. Even at the earliest, Tannaitic stages of development of the notion of *ḥazakah*, however, it is

---

28. It is sometimes difficult to ascertain from the Mishnah's formulation whether *ḥazakah* is being used as a rationale for deciding an uncertainty or as an expression that describes the tentativeness of the decision. It is apparent that the earlier *mishnayot* in the first chapter of *Ketubot*, which present a series of disputes between Rabban Gamliel, Rabbi Eliezer, and Rabbi Yehoshua, do not relate to *ḥazakah* as a claim:

> One marries a woman, and does not find [physical signs of] her virginity. She says, "After you betrothed me I was raped and your field has been flooded [i.e., it is your loss]." And the other one says, "Not so, rather, before I betrothed you [you lost your virginity], and [consequently] my purchase was made under false pretenses." Rabban Gamliel and Rabbi Eliezer say, "She is believed." Rabbi Yehoshua says, "We do not live by [the words of] her mouth. Rather, she is presumed to be [*be-ḥezkat*] a non-virgin from before she became betrothed and that she deceived him, until she brings proof for her words." (*m. Ketubot* 1:6)

This *mishnah*, and the following *mishnayot*, are an important and complex site of discussion in the Talmud and among the medieval sages about *ḥazakah*. However, Rabbi Yehoshua's usage of *ḥazakah* in our *mishnah* (1:9) seems similar to the usage he makes of it in all of the *mishnayot* in this series of disputes with Rabban Gamliel and Rabbi Eliezer; it therefore would not relate to the weight of *ḥazakah* as a rationale for deciding uncertainty.

Another example of using *ḥazakah* as a sort of hybrid between *ḥazakah* as a rationale and *ḥazakah* as a unique way of deciding uncertainty appears in the Tosefta: "The daughter of a *ḥaver* who married an *am ha-aretz*, the wife of a *ḥaver* who married an *am ha-aretz*, or the slave of a *ḥaver* who was sold to an *am ha-aretz* retain their *ḥazakah* until they are subject to suspicion. Rabbi Shimon ben Elazar says: They must accept [the practices of a *ḥaver*] upon themselves from the beginning" (*t. Demai* 10:18).

possible to identify an idea that lies at its core and from which we can learn about how the sages viewed prohibitions.[29] The assumption that, in cases of uncertainty, decisive weight is granted to the status quo ante, whether this results in prohibition or permission, follows basic human and legal logic, but it softens the hazardous aspect of forbidden foods. This sort of *ḥazakah* offers no probabilistic information that pertains to the uncertainty; there is no reason to assume a greater probability that the prior status of a person or an object will persist. In the language of Talmudists of the modern era, a *ḥazakah* does not clarify uncertainty but serves as a rule of conduct that determines behavior while facing the uncertainty.[30] The principle of *ḥazakah* determines, for instance, that in the case of a piece of kosher meat about which there arose a doubt that perhaps it is not kosher, we retain its *ḥazakah* of being kosher in the absence of alternative information that would decide the uncertainty in favor of stringency.

If prohibited foods had a poisonous quality to them, we would never decide uncertainties with outcomes of equal likelihood by means of a *ḥazakah* principle that adds no real information about reality. This insight, which distinguishes prohibitions from poisons, finds expression in the Talmud itself in one of the most important passages about *ḥazakah*. The passage, in *Ḥullin*, distinguishes between a potentially dangerous situation, in which the rules for deciding uncertainties by means of a majority or a *ḥazakah* do not apply, and a prohibition, whose status is indeed decided by means of a majority or a *ḥazakah*. Regarding this gap between prohibitions and hazards, the Talmud formulates an important rule: "Danger is more severe than a prohibition" (*b. Ḥullin* 10a).[31] Likewise, and more importantly, *ḥazakah* grants preferred status to the present or prior state of affairs, thereby choking off the wide world of spiraling anxiety that the awareness of uncertainty can awaken. The concept of *ḥazakah* thus creates a stable halakhic anchor in a world filled with uncertainty. It limits the capacity of uncertainty to generate an unending and ever-intensifying obsessive form of investigation and examination.[32]

---

29. For other examples of the usage of *ḥazakah de-me'ikara*, see *t. Bekhorot* 2:14; *t. Terumah* 10:8.

30. See Rabbi Shimon Shkop, *Sha'arei Yosher* (Warsaw: Pospiech, 1925), *sha'ar* 2, chapter 2, s.v. "*nireh li,*" and chapter 5, s.v. "u-veha."

31. Ḥatam Sofer formulated the distinction between danger and prohibition as follows: "The distinction is easy to understand. With respect to prohibitions, even if he happens to consume something of the non-kosher minority, he has committed no sin, for he followed the Torah by relying on the majority. He Who admonished us not to eat non-kosher meat also permitted us to rely on the majority. This does not apply in cases of danger to human life. If he happens to consume the dangerous minority, it is impossible to restore his life. This is simple" (*Ḥiddushei Ḥatam Sofer* on *Ḥullin* 9b). See as well his responsa Orach Chaim, 83.

32. See the classic formulation of Maimonides in his commentary on *m. Nazir* 9:2:

The idea of "there is support for this matter" is that the issue would be unending

In the Mishnah and Tosefta, two directives took shape in relation to uncertainties about prohibitions. These directives had far-reaching implications on the development of halakhah. The first directive asserts that, under conditions of uncertainty, the majority is determinative, even a bare statistical majority. The second directive asserts that uncertainty is decided by the principle of *ḥazakah,* which preserves the prior halakhic status of the object of uncertainty, whether the prior state prohibited or permitted the object, if there is no other information that can bring clarity. These two directives indicate a nominalist, antirealist attitude toward the broader concept of prohibition.[33] In a world of poisons and hazards, these two rules for dealing with situations of uncertainty would be untenable. Likewise, and more importantly, the basic directives governing uncertainties teach us that confronting uncertainty does not mean taking precautions and demarcating the *terra incognita* that must be avoided or trod carefully. The intense preoccupation with legislating norms or confronting uncertainty does not flow from fear of falling, from concern that sin lies crouching in wait for us, or from concern that transgression can lurk around any corner. On the contrary! One who deals with uncertainty demarcates the boundaries of prohibition and does not permit its indefinite expansion.

III

Alongside the principle of following the majority in cases of uncertainty, the first layer of halakhah in the Mishnah and Tosefta posited another principle with far-reaching implications for situations of uncertainty: nullification by a majority (*bittul be-rov*). This principle determines that a slab of prohibited meat that got mixed up with two slabs of kosher meat is nullified by the majority, making it permissible to eat each of the three slabs of meat in the resulting mixture. The idea of nullification can be viewed as a derivative of the principle of following the majority, since

---

if we follow every possibility. Rather, the principle is that if a certain state of affairs has been established, we leave it under that presumption until something definite removes that presumption. But anything that has uncertainty of merely another possibility does not remove the presumption.

33. Another case in the Mishnah where uncertainty is decided in a way that indicates a clearly nominalist tendency is as follows: "One says to a woman, 'I betrothed you,' and she says, 'You did not betroth me'; he is forbidden to [marry] her relatives, and she is permitted to [marry] his relatives. She says, 'You betrothed me,' and he says, 'I did not betroth you'; he is permitted to [marry] her relatives, and she is forbidden to [marry] his relatives" (*m. Kiddushin* 3:10). This decision regarding this uncertainty attests that the woman is both betrothed and not betrothed simultaneously. Halakhic realism cannot tolerate such a position. A similar example of an uncertainty being decided in a way that would be self-contradictory if it were premised on realist assumptions can be found in *m. Yevamot* 16:5, 7–8.

each individual slab has more than a 50 percent chance of being one of the permitted slabs. According to this logic, which predicates the law of nullification on the majoritarian principle and views it as a specific application of the laws relating to uncertainties, it would be forbidden for one person to eat all three slabs, one after the other, as it is nevertheless clear that one of the three slabs is prohibited. This is indeed the conclusion reached by several halakhists, medieval and modern.

In contrast, the more mainstream approach is that it is permissible to eat all three slabs of meat together; nullification originates not with the laws relating to uncertainties but in the idea that a mixture, as a single unit, is defined and characterized by the majority of its ingredients; therefore, in this case, it is permitted in its entirety.[34] We will see that this distinction between the two understandings of nullification is rooted in Tannaitic sources themselves. Here, too, we can imagine an entirely different approach, one that maintains that any such mixture is forbidden, come what may, unless it is known that the food is completely free of anything prohibited. As with the majoritarian principle, the nullification principle attempts to demarcate, within the expansive realm of fear of transgression, uncertainty, suspicion, and aversion, the exact place of the relevant prohibition; the laws governing mixtures come to contain and delimit the reach of prohibition more than they extend it.

The fact that one slab of meat is nullified by a majority of two seems self-evident to anyone with a rudimentary halakhic education. At the time of its formulation, however, this ruling was an innovation of major consequence that had no clear biblical basis and may even have been in direct opposition to an existing practice that would disqualify any mixture that contained any sort of prohibited matter.[35] Indeed, it seems that among

---

34. For a survey of the different views, see *Beit Yosef* on *Yoreh De'ah* 109.

35. Leib Moscovitz maintains that the principle of nullification by majority is not mentioned at all with respect to mixtures of dry goods with dry goods, and that, according to the Mishnah and Tosefta, a slab of prohibited meat that got mixed up with permitted meat forbids every slab of meat in the mixture, no matter how small the quantity of prohibited meat. Moscovitz limits the majoritarian principle in Tannaitic literature to situations where the presence of something prohibited has not been established (*la itẓḥazek issura*), that is, where we do not know that there is a prohibited slab that fell into a mixture. Rather, the majoritarian principle applies when we do not know whether a particular object is from a permitted or prohibited source. See Leib Moscovitz, "Le-ḥeker Dinei Ta'arovet 'Yavesh Be-yavesh' Be-sifrut Ḥazal" [A Study of the Laws of "Dry with Dry" Mixtures in Rabbinic Literature], *Asufot–Yearbook of Jewish Studies* 11 (1998): 309–58. Prima facie, contra Moscovitz, the *mishnah* in *Makhshirin* that we discussed earlier relates explicitly to the mixture of something known to be forbidden into permitted ingredients: "A granary in which Jews and gentiles deposit [their produce]—if the majority is from the gentiles, [the produce] is certain [*tevel*, from which tithes and *terumah* have not been apportioned], and if the majority is from the Jews, it is *demai*; half-and-half it is certain [*tevel*], according to Rabbi Meir. But the sages say: Even if they are all gentiles, but one Jew deposited [produce] in it, [it is] *demai*." Moscovitz explains

the sages there was a minority opinion that recognized nullification by majority but limited it to a case where a prohibited item that got mixed up with permitted items of the same kind—for example, if a slab of non-kosher meat got mixed up with similar cuts of kosher meat—is not nullified. As Rabbi Yehudah states:

> [If] blood became mixed with water: if it [still] has the appearance of blood, it is valid. If [blood] became mixed with wine, we view [the wine] as if it were water. If [the blood] became mixed with the blood of [another] animal, or with the blood of a [kosher] wild animal, we view it as if it were water. Rabbi Yehudah says: Blood does not nullify blood. (*m. Zevaḥim* 8:6)[36]

It is possible that Rabbi Yehudah's view reflects an earlier halakhah or an alternative to the concept of nullification by majority, at least with respect to mixtures of like items (*min be-mino*).

Since the sages apply nullification by majority as the default rule for all prohibitions, they specify the exceptions in which one must be stringent by excluding the possibility that they, like other prohibited items, can be nullified by majority. Thus, for instance, the Mishnah establishes:

---

that this *mishnah* refers to a granary about which there is no definite knowledge that gentiles deposited produce there; the phrase "gentiles deposit" means that they normally deposit produce there. Consequently, *la itzḥazek issura*—the presence of prohibited produce has not been established in this case ("Le-ḥeker Dinei Ta'arovet 'Yavesh Be-yavesh' Be-sifrut Ḥazal," 316–17). According to Moscovitz, if it were known that a gentile deposited produce in the granary, in any quantity, all the produce in the granary would be deemed forbidden, even if most of the produce in the granary was of Jewish provenance.

It is very difficult to square this interpretation with the *mishnah* itself, especially since the sages' view in the latter part of the *mishnah* seems to indicate that, in this case, one Jew actually deposited produce in the granary, not that it is typical for a Jew to deposit produce in the granary. Moreover, *t. Demai* 1:13 clearly refers to a case where deposits are known to have been made, as it instructs, "He is obligated proportionally." Apparently, Moscovitz was constrained in his interpretation of this *mishnah*.

Yet, even if we could accept this interpretation of the *mishnah* about the granary, the prior *mishnah* in the same chapter deals with a case where the majoritarian principle obtains even when it is known that something prohibited was deposited or mixed in: "One mixed impure iron with pure iron [in fashioning a utensil]—<if the majority is from impure [iron], [the utensil] is impure> if the majority is from pure [iron], it is pure. Half-and-half, it is impure. From the case of the impure iron that was mixed in the utensil it is clear that the *mishnah* that rules that the majority is followed does not distinguish between a case in which it is known that a prohibited object was mixed within the group or it is unknown. In both instances the majority is followed. Additionally, explicit proof that nullification by majority in Tannaitic literature obtains even in cases where the presence of something forbidden has been established appears in *t. Terumot* 6:1. It is clear there that the nullification of one part in a hundred, the ratio necessary to nullify *terumah,* is a rabbinic law; according to Torah law, *terumah* that fell into unsanctified produce is nullified by a regular majority. See also Saul Lieberman's notes to *Tosefta Zera'im*, p. 136, lines 1–2.

36. See also *m. Ḥullin* 6:5; *t. Terumot* 21–22; and Rabbi Yehudah's opposition to the possibility of nullification.

> Libation wine is prohibited, and any amount of it renders other items forbidden. Wine in wine or water in water—in any amount. Wine in water or water in wine—if it imparts flavor. This is the rule: [a mixture] in kind—in any amount; of one kind in another kind—if it imparts flavor. (*m. Avodah Zarah* 5:8)

The severity of idolatry prevents any possibility of nullification by majority when an item used in idolatrous practice gets mixed up with items of the same kind. When it gets mixed up with something of a different kind, it is nullified only if it does not impart any flavor to the mixture. A similar degree of stringency applies to the realm of the sacred:

> Anything that is forbidden [to offer] on the altar renders other things forbidden in any amount: an animal that copulated with a woman, an animal with which a man copulated, an animal set aside, a worshiped animal, a prostitute's fee, a dog's exchange, a hybrid, an animal with a terminal defect, and an animal born by Caesarean section. (*m. Temurah* 6:1)

Something offered on the altar is meant to be completely free of any forbidden admixture, and anything that may not be offered on the altar is never nullified; such things, in any amount, render anything they get mixed up with forbidden to offer on the altar.[37]

In addition, there are prohibitions that are never nullified, not because they are uniquely severe[38] but because there are other ways to permit

---

37. See also *m. Zevaḥim* 8:1. In addition, the *mishnah* in Tractate *Avodah Zarah*, after positing that any amount of libation wine renders other things forbidden, adds another list of prohibited items—libation wine and others—that, in any amount, render other things prohibited:

> The following things are prohibited and prohibit in any quantity: libation wine, objects of idolatry, skins torn at the heart [as part of an idolatrous practice], an ox that is to be stoned, the calf which will have its neck severed, the bird offerings of a leper, the hair of a nazirite, the firstborn donkey [that has not yet been redeemed], meat mixed with milk, the scapegoat, and nonsanctified animals slaughtered in the Temple courtyard—all these are prohibited and prohibit in any quantity. (*m. Avodah Zarah* 5:9)

The rabbis of both Talmudim were bothered by the question of what distinguishes the items on this list that they render other things prohibited even in the smallest of quantities. One common factor seems to be that these prohibitions emerge in an obviously cultic context, as opposed to carcasses and improperly slaughtered animals. Each of the listed prohibitions is related to an object that was used to commit a severe transgression or was dedicated for sacred use. That is, it is not forbidden to eat or otherwise benefit from because of its essential nature alone. Regular hair, a regular donkey, meat, and milk can all be used. According to the reasoning of the Talmudim, these are all objects whose benefit is prohibited in any form (*issurei hana'ah*) as well as significant objects that cannot be nullified. See the discussion in Rashi on *b. Zevaḥim* 74a, s.v. "*u-basar ve-ḥalav*"; and Tosafot on *b. Zevaḥim* 74a, s.v. "*elu asurin*." See also the Talmud's discussion in *b. Zevaḥim* 72a.

38. Objects that have been sanctified also are not nullified by a majority:

them. Thus, with respect to *tevel* (produce from which tithes and *terumot* [priestly gifts] have not yet been apportioned):

> If one takes leaven from wheat dough and places it into rice dough, if [the rice dough] has the taste of grain, it is obligated in *ḥallah*; if not, it is exempt. If so, why did they say, "*Tevel* of any amount renders [food] forbidden"? [That was said in a case of] kind [mixed] with its own kind. When it is mixed with another kind, [it renders the mixture forbidden] when it imparts taste. (*m. Ḥallah* 3:10)[39]

This principle is repeated in the Tosefta:

> Rabbi Shimon says: All things that can become permitted, such as *tevel*, the second tithe, consecrated objects, and new grain, were given no fixed amount by the sages. But all things that cannot become permitted, like *orlah* and *kilayim* of the vineyard, were given a fixed amount by the sages. (*t. Terumot* 5:15)[40]

In addition to specific prohibitions that cannot be nullified, the sages also enumerated specific objects that, due to their significance, are not nullified. The Tannaim disagreed about the scope of this category.[41] As mentioned, the prevention of any possibility of nullification, and the prohibition of an entire mixture due to the presence of any quantity of a forbidden food, serves, in the Mishnah, as a means of ranking unique or severe prohibitions, to which the broader practice of nullification by majority does not apply. At the level of more severe prohibitions than those that are nullified by a regular majority, the sages were stricter about *terumah*, *ḥallah*, tithes, and firstfruits, which are nullified only when they are one part in a hundred, and *orlah* and *kilayim* of a vineyard, which are nullified as one part in two hundred.[42]

Not only does rabbinic halakhah nullify prohibited matter in a majority of permitted matter, but the Mishnah even asserts that, if a quantity of permitted matter falls into a mixture that initially did not have a sufficient

---

> One who weaves a thumb-to-forefinger length of wool from a firstborn into a garment—must burn the garment; from the hair of a nazirite or from a firstborn donkey into a sack—must burn the sack. And with regard to sanctified objects—they sanctify [whatever they are sewn into] in even the smallest quantity. (*m. Orlah* 3:3)

In the Yerushalmi (*y. Orlah* 3:3), Rabbi Yoḥanan limits the ruling about sanctified objects to those sanctified objects that can be permitted.

39. See *t. Terumot* 5:18; see also *m. Shevi'it* 7:7.

40. For another reason why any quantity of *tevel* forbids other items, see *b. Avodah Zarah* 73b. The medieval commentators question this contradiction. See Lieberman's lengthy discussion in *Tosefta Kifshutah: Berakhot–Terumot*, 375–76.

41. See the dispute between Rabbi Meir and the sages in *m. Orlah* 3:6–7. See also *m. Ḥullin* 7:5, which presents cases where entire limbs or significant slabs of meat are not nullified.

42. Regarding the notion that *terumah* is nullified in a regular majority according to the Torah, see *t. Terumot* 6:1 and the notes of Lieberman, *Tosefta Kifshutah: Zera'im*, 136 nn. 1–2.

quantity of permitted matter to nullify the prohibition, the additional permitted matter nullifies the prohibition. The boldness of applying the majoritarian principle even in such cases brought the Mishnah to establish an important rule about uncertainty: "A measure of *terumah* that fell into less than a hundred [measures] and then [additional] non-sacred [produce] fell in, is permitted if it was by accident and forbidden if it was on purpose" (*m. Terumah* 5:9). According to this *mishnah*, one cannot purposefully and predeterminedly mix prohibited matter into a larger quantity of permitted matter and thus take advantage of a decision principle that would permit the uncertainty. The rule of nullification by majority is thus addressed to one who confronts an existing state of uncertainty, not to one who intentionally inserts himself into a state of uncertainty in order to permit it.[43]

We can imagine an alternative view to the principle of nullification by majority in which each and every prohibition has the same status as *tevel* and libation wine, which are never nullified, and which render a mixture forbidden in any quantity. A position that recoils from the halakhah of the Mishnah and from the very idea of nullification by majority appears in the first generation of Amoraim, in the name of Rav and Shmuel: "Rav and Shmuel both say: All biblical prohibitions—[render] their own kind [prohibited] in any quantity, and another kind if it imparts flavor" (*b. Avodah Zarah* 73b). Rav and Shmuel, according to the Talmud's anonymous editorial layer, predicate their position on an expansion of the *mishnah* that formulated its ruling with respect to libation wine and objects used in idolatry by means of a generalization: "This is the general rule: Kind with its own kind—in any quantity; with another kind—if it imparts flavor." It is clear, however, that the Mishnaic tradition treats certain prohibitions as uniquely

43. This Mishnaic principle is formulated in the Talmud as a rule: "Prohibited matter is not nullified ab initio" (*ein mevatlin issur lekhatḥila*). See *b. Beitzah* 3b. See also the Tannaitic dispute in Tosefta *Terumot* (5:6):

> If nuts were cracked, pomegranates cloven, barrels broken open, gourds cut, [or] loaves sliced, they are nullified at one part in two hundred. If they fell [into a mixture] and then were broken open, whether by accident or on purpose, they are not annulled. These are the words of Rabbi Meir. Rabbi Yudah and Rabbi Shimon say: Whether by accident or on purpose, they are annulled. Rabbi Yosah says: By accident, they are annulled. On purpose, they are not annulled.

Nuts, pomegranates, barrels, gourds, and loaves are not annulled in mixtures, due to their significance, unless they were broken or cut up. The sages disagree about the status of these objects if they were cut up or broken after falling into a mixture. It seems that the *mishnah* in *Terumah* accords with the view of Rabbi Yosah among the opinions that appear in the Tosefta passage, as he, too, differentiates an accident from a purposeful act. See also *y. Orlah* 3:6, where the Talmud explains the opinion of Rabbi Yehudah and Rabbi Shimon to accord with our *mishnah*: in the case of these significant objects, the person who cut or broke them "already has his penalty in hand." That is, he caused damage to himself, so there is no reason to penalize him, even if he nullified these significant objects on purpose.

severe, whereas all other biblical prohibitions are nullified by a majority.[44] This view of Rav and Shmuel, which is not accepted in practice, reflects the Babylonian sages' initial recoiling from the Mishnah's far-reaching approach to uncertainties and majorities vis-à-vis prohibitions. It is possible that this reluctance also echoes an earlier halakhah, preserved in a minority position in the Mishnah, and perhaps even the view espoused by Jewish groups that were outside the tradition of the sages.

One of the more interesting examples of the conceptual design of the realm of uncertainties and nullification by majority in the Mishnah appears in the distinction between prohibition and money in cases of admixture. As mentioned, *terumah* that fell into non-sacred produce is nullified if it is one part per hundred, in which case one may eat the entire mixture. However, one must still set aside from the mixture the equivalent of the amount of *terumah* that fell in and give that amount to a priest, since the priest's ownership of the *terumah* is not nullified. Thus, the Mishnah states:

> *Terumah*, the *terumah* of the tithe taken from *demai* (produce from which it is uncertain whether tithes were taken), *ḥallah*, and the firstfruits are nullified in one part per hundred; they combine with one another, and one must apportion [the equivalent of the mixed-in *terumah*]. *Orlah* and *kilayim* of the vineyard are nullified in one part per two hundred; they combine with one another, and there is <no>[45] need to apportion [their equivalent]. (*m. Orlah* 2:1)

The distinction drawn between forbidden foods and money is significant because, while the prohibition is nullified by the majority, the majority does not nullify ownership. For that reason, if a measure of *terumah* falls into a hundred measures of non-sacred produce of the same kind, one must take one measure from the mixture and give it to a priest. In contrast, when it comes to the prohibition of *orlah*, since there is no adverse ownership, the prohibition is nullified without any need to remove the measure of *orlah* produce that fell into the mixture.[46] This teaches us that if, for example, one person's object fell into a pile of similar objects belonging to another, and it is impossible to identify it, it is not nullified by the majority, and the owner of the pile must return the equivalent of the coin that fell into the pile.

---

44. In addition, see *t. Terumot* 8:22, where all other prohibitions are explicitly distinguished from *tevel* and libation wine.

45. This is based on MS Parma. In the first part, instead of "there is no need to apportion," which is the text of MS Kaufmann, the text should read "one must apportion," in accordance with the MS Parma text.

46. See also *t. Terumot* 5:9. And see *y. Orlah*: "Rabbi Abbahu in the name of Rabbi Yoḥanan [said]: Because of the theft from the tribe" (2:1, col. 338, lines 38-40). The Yerushalmi also concluded from this that, with regard to *terumah* that a priest does not care about, there is no need to remove the equivalent of the amount that fell in: "It was taught thus: Any *terumah* that a priest does not care about, like the *terumah* of *kelisim* (a type of legume), carob, and barley in Edom, need be removed" (ibid.).

The Mishnah juxtaposes its treatments of the nullification of *terumah* and the nullification of *orlah* to contrast them and to emphasize that the domain of permissibility that applies to forbidden foods does not apply to monetary uncertainty.[47] This distinction between money and prohibitions reinforces the novelty of the idea of nullification by majority. Although a human being's claim to his own property is not nullified if that property happens to fall into and get lost in the property of another, God, Who commands the observance of these prohibitions, does not act as a claimant who is entitled to defend his interests. Where a prohibition of foods, which is supposed to guide human action, lapses, a monetary claim remains in force.

IV

A study of the whole chapters devoted to uncertainties and majority in the tractates of *Terumah* and *Orlah*, and several other contexts in the Mishnah and Tosefta reveals a duality that accompanies the emergence of halakhah as a whole. A piece of something forbidden falling into something permitted is a common occurrence, and the attempt to impose a network of precise rulings on such cases is a blatant tendency of rabbinic halakhah. The scrupulous distinction between mixtures of one kind and mixtures of two kinds; between the various prohibitions on eating and benefiting from particular items; and between that class of items that cannot be nullified due to their significance and those that cannot be nullified because they can be permitted stems, inter alia, from the rejection of a single, unambiguous answer. Such a position would leave no room for dealing with uncertainty and making subtle distinctions between various contexts, because whenever something prohibited might be present, even in the tiniest amounts, there is no uncertainty; the mixture is forbidden. The sages' complex distinctions in these areas stem from their rejection of such a sweeping potential directive. An analysis of the sages' statements shows that they work, inter alia, to moderate, not expand, the fear of uncertainty. Likewise, since nullification by majority is the starting point for all of these states of uncertainty, impeding the default option of nullification serves to outline a hierarchy of severity of the prohibition or of the nullified item in various and ramified halakhic contexts.

Yet, alongside the clear tendency to develop a set of instructions to guide behavior in various contexts, including states of uncertainty, the Mishnah also presents us with hypothetical borderline cases; the sages' whole interest in such highly developed debates is the creation of purely intellectual, subtle insights that are not at all tied to the attempt to guide

47. See *b. Beitzah* 38b, which discusses how money cannot be nullified.

human action. One of the most interesting and surprising things about the Mishnah's and the Tosefta's considerable engagement with uncertainties and nullification is the vast and, prima facie, baffling spectacle of hypothetical possibilities of nullification by majority. The halakhic acrobatics of the Mishnah reaches a climax in such cases that is higher than in any other subject it addresses. Studying these cases shows that the motivation for producing halakhah that has barely any relevance for actual behavior is the drive toward conceptual clarification, which is a subject of inquiry in its own right.[48]

Let us examine the following example from a *mishnah* that links uncertainty to nullification by majority:

> Two baskets or two stockpiles, into one of which a measure of *terumah* has fallen, and it is not known into which it has fallen, they are summed with one another. Rabbi Shimon says: even if they are in two cities, they are summed with one another. (*m. Terumot* 4:12)

In the Tosefta's treatment of the same question, Rabbi Yehudah's view, which does not appear in the *mishnah*, is added:

> Two baskets in two stockpiles, two stockpiles in two upper chambers, two stockpiles in one upper chamber: all of these are summed. Rabbi Yehudah says: they are not summed. (*t. Terumot* 6:12)

This passage presents a case in which a measure of *terumah* fell into one of two containers of non-sacred produce, each of which contained fifty measures of produce. Since we do not know into which container the *terumah* fell, the sages maintain that the two containers combine to reach the sum of one hundred measures, which is sufficient to nullify one measure of *terumah*. Rabbi Shimon elucidates, and perhaps expands, this principle: this summing of the contents is effective even if the containers are far from one another, in two different cities. Rabbi Yehudah disagrees, maintaining that in such a case the *terumah* is not nullified.

It is hard to imagine that a borderline case like this one would actually occur, or that a response to such an unlikely eventuality must be prepared in advance. Rather, it serves, inter alia, to clarify a concept that can be defined as follows: Is the nullification of *terumah* in one part per hundred a probabilistic concept—that is, one may eat a pile of one hundred measures into which one measure of *terumah* fell because with regard to each individual fruit in the pile, there is less than a 1 percent chance of its being prohibited. Alternatively, perhaps the reason it is permitted is because in

---

48. On this characteristic duality of the Mishnah and how it treats, with equal seriousness, practical matters and hypothetical borderline cases, see I. Rosen Zvi, "Introduction to the Mishnah," in *Rabbinic Literature: Introductions and Studies* [Hebrew], ed. D. Rosenthal et al. (Jerusalem: Yad Ben Zvi, 2018), 60–63.

a one-hundred-to-one majority, the non-sacred produce, as the prevailing unit, nullifies the *terumah* and defines the identity of the entire unit as being permitted. It is possible that the purpose of recording the disagreement between Rabbi Shimon and Rabbi Yehudah in a case like this is to test the conceptual question underlying nullification.[49] Rabbi Shimon maintains that the two containers of fifty measures combine with one another, even if they are physically separate, because the totality of the uncertainties results in a likelihood of less than one in one hundred. According to Rabbi Shimon, nullification by majority is predicated on probabilistic assumptions and is derived from the principle of following the majority.[50] In contrast, Rabbi Yehudah maintains that, since each container holds only fifty measures, if it is not known where the *terumah* fell, neither container on its own generates a significant majority that would define the identity of each unit and nullify the measure of *terumah* that may have fallen into it.

We now turn to another example. Among the items that are not nullified by majority, the sages included spices and leaven, which change the character of the substance in which they are mixed by altering its taste or causing it to ferment: "Anything that leavens, or seasons, or mixes with *terumah*, *orlah*, or *kilayim* of the vineyard is prohibited" (*m. Orlah* 2:4). The status of these agents is stricter than that of normal produce, which is nullified in one part to one hundred. The Mishnah explains:

---

49. A similar dispute appears in another borderline case that likewise seems connected to the question of how to understand nullification by majority:

> Rabbi Yehoshua says: black figs are counted with white figs [if a white fig that is *terumah* fell into a mixture of black and white figs], and white are counted with black.... Rabbi Eliezer prohibits this. Rabbi Akiva says: If it is known what [kind] fell in, then the one [kind] cannot be counted with the other, but if it is not known what [kind] fell in, then the one [kind] can be counted with the other. What is the case? If there were fifty black figs and fifty white, and a black fell in, the black are forbidden, but the white are permitted; and if a white fell in, the white are forbidden and the black are permitted. If it is not known what [kind] fell in, then they can be counted together. (*m. Terumot* 4:8–9)

At first glance, the dispute between Rabbi Eliezer and Rabbi Yehoshua hinges on whether nullification by majority is derived from a probabilistic calculation or is conceptualized as a unit defined by the identity of its majority. Rabbi Yehoshua maintains that the question is about the character of the unit as a whole. It is possible that Rabbi Eliezer agrees with him in principle but maintains that white figs and black figs do not form a single unit for the purposes of nullification. In any event, Rabbi Akiva, for whom nullification in this case depends on not knowing what type of fig fell into the mixed pile of black and white figs, apparently maintains that the question is purely probabilistic.

50. In terms of philosophy of probabilty, which distinguishes between objective and subjective probability, this is a clear case of subjective probability that has no objective basis. From an objective perspective, there is a one in fifty chance that any fruit taken from the pile is *terumah*, whereas from a subjective perspective, since it is not known which pile the *terumah* fell into, there is a one in one hundred chance.

> How so? If leaven of wheat fell into wheat dough and it is sufficient to cause fermentation, whether or not there is enough to nullify it one hundred to one, it is prohibited. (*m. Orlah* 6)

The basic logic of this principle is that a prohibited substance that alters the essential character of a permitted substance into which it was mixed is not nullified. Leaven, which causes dough to rise, is such a case, as is seasoning, which alters the taste and nature of the mixture. As noted, this directive makes sense only against the background of the possibility that forbidden *orlah* and *terumah* can be nullified if they are not leavening agents. If in practice anything prohibited, in any amount, that fell into something permitted would forbid the mixture, there would be no need to create this distinction.

This ruling has ramifications in various real-life contexts. We can imagine cases, even if they are not particularly common, in which forbidden leaven causes the fermentation of permitted dough. The Mishnah, however, goes on to deal with a series of cases that elicit disagreement among the sages, and in which the Mishnah probes deeply into the realm of imaginary halakhah for the purpose of addressing borderline cases with a tenuous connection to behavioral guidance. The next *mishnayot* deal with the following cases:

> If non-sacred leaven fell into dough, and it is sufficient to cause it to ferment, and then the leaven of *terumah* or *kilayim* of the vineyard fell in, and it [too] is sufficient to cause it to ferment, it is prohibited. (*m. Orlah* 8)

This *mishnah* is the transition into the realm of the conceptual and hypothetical. First, non-sacred leaven falls into the dough, and then, before the dough has had a chance to rise, prohibited leaven falls in. Since the forbidden leaven contributes to the fermentation of the dough, the fact that there is also a permissible leavening agent in the mixture, one that is sufficient to cause the dough to rise alone, does not enable the nullification of the forbidden leaven. As usual, the next *mishnah* presents a case that is similar yet different. This time, it will result in a dispute:

> If non-sacred leaven fell into dough and caused it to ferment, and then the leaven of *terumah* or *kilayim* of the vineyard fell in, and it is sufficient to cause it to ferment, it is prohibited. Rabbi Shimon permits. (*m. Orlah* 9)

Unlike in the previous case, here the non-sacred (permitted) leaven managed to cause the dough to rise before the forbidden leaven fell in. According to the sages, this dough is prohibited, but according to Rabbi Shimon, it is permitted. It seems that this borderline case serves to clarify the following concept: Does the fact that the leaven is not nullified stem from its significance—that is, since leaven is an agent that *can* alter the nature of a permitted item, it cannot be nullified? Or, alternatively, is the leaven not nullified because of the actual contribution it makes to this mixture—that is, its presence cannot be nullified in a mixture whose fermentation it caused? The sages viewed a rule that negates the nullification of a leavening agent as an instance of a much broader negation of the nullification of any significant factor. Thus, according to them, even if the dough had already risen by agency of the permitted leaven, it is nevertheless rendered forbidden by the prohibited leaven, which, due to its significance, is not nullified. Rabbi Shimon, on the other hand, adopts the second view. According to him, since the forbidden leaven has no impact on the condition of the already-risen dough, it is nullified, even if it there is enough of it to cause the dough to rise. This case, in which pieces of leaven fell into dough one after another, is not discussed because it is likely to occur, but because it poses and sharpens a conceptual problem.

The Mishnah continues on to another case that serves to exemplify a conceptual conundrum:

> If non-sacred and *terumah* leaven fell into dough, and neither is in sufficient quantity to cause it to ferment, but they combine and cause it to ferment: Rabbi Eliezer says: I follow the last one. But the sages say: whether the prohibited [leaven] fell in first or last, it does not forbid [the dough] unless it is in sufficient quantity to cause it to ferment. (*m. Orlah* 11)[51]

The bone of contention in this *mishnah* is whether the necessary but insufficient contribution of forbidden leaven to the fermentation of dough is enough to prohibit the dough, or whether there must be enough forbidden leaven to cause the entire fermentation. This borderline case forces us to consider how an additive that cannot be nullified is measured: must it be an additive without which fermentation would not be possible, or an additive capable of causing the whole fermentation?

This sequence of increasingly ramified borderline cases, each of which further refines the concept, continues in a later *mishnah*. This case is not merely a borderline case that serves to clarify a conceptual distinction, but a case that generates a seemingly paradoxical result:

> If leaven of *terumah* and *kilayim* of the vineyard fell into dough, and neither is in sufficient quantity to cause it to ferment, but they combine and cause it to ferment: It is forbidden to non-priests but permitted to priests. Rabbi Shimon permits for both non-priests and priests. (*m. Orlah* 14)

Whereas in the previous case, the leaven that enabled the fermentation of the dough was itself a mixture of forbidden and permitted leaven, in the present case, both pieces of leaven that combine to enable the fermenta-

---

51. The next *mishnah*, "Yoezer of Birah was a disciple of the House of Shammai, and he said: 'I asked Rabban Gamliel the Elder standing at the East Gate, and he said that it does not forbid [the dough] unless it is in sufficient quantity to cause it to ferment.'" This indicates that occupation with such borderline cases may have characterized rabbinic circles even while the Temple stood.

tion of the dough are prohibited: one is *terumah* and the other is *kilayim* of the vine. The sages maintain that these bits of leaven combine to form a single quantity of leaven, which in turn renders the dough forbidden. However, since half of the combined leaven is *kilayim* (which is forbidden to all) and half is *terumah* (which is permitted to priests), the dough remains permitted to priests, for, as we saw in the last *mishnah*, the sages maintain that that an insufficient quantity of prohibited leaven does not render the dough forbidden. Therefore, the priests may eat of this dough, because the *terumah* leaven is permitted to them. In contrast, a non-priest, for whom *terumah* is forbidden, may not eat of the dough. Rabbi Shimon maintains that different types of prohibited items (*terumah* and *kilayim*) do not combine into a single quantity of forbidden leaven; forbidden leaven is not nullified only when it is in sufficient quantity and it is forbidden under a single prohibition. Therefore, in the present case, the dough may be eaten by priest and non-priest alike.

The question here is whether the presence of prohibited leaven, in the general sense, is sufficient to negate the possibility of nullification, or whether nullification is prevented by the presence of leaven forbidden under a single, specific prohibition. Aside from the fact that the chances of the *mishnah*'s case ever actually happening are infinitesimal, the very posing of such a case attests to the qualities of halakhic virtuosity, in which the challenge of the Torah scholar is to think up borderline cases that will raise several questions at once—combinations, quantities, priests, and non-priests and will further refine and illuminate the concepts of quantity, nullification, and prohibition. In this sequence of cases, the set of directives that the sages apply to states of uncertainty and mixtures stands as a world unto itself, which develops on terms internal to it, and whose constant refinement through hypothetical borderline cases represents an actualization of halakhah as a world that stands alongside the world. The borderline cases of uncertainty serve as one of the most fertile grounds for the acrobatic thought experiments that expand and develop the web of imagined cases and rules that form the world of halakhah as a realm unto itself that is not exclusively aimed at directing conduct.

Tannaitic literature developed three basic principles for dealing with uncertainties regarding prohibited items: following the majority, *ḥazakah*, and nullification by majority.[52] Close scrutiny of the first appearance of

52. A secondary principle that Tannaitic literature developed to address uncertainty, and which is the subject of its own group of Tannaitic teachings, is formulated in a *mishnah* in *Terumah*: "There are two baskets, one of *terumah* and one of non-sacred produce; a measure of *terumah* fell into one of them, but it is not known into which it fell. I can assume that it had fallen into the *terumah*" (*m. Terumah* 7:5). The Tosefta (*t. Terumot* 6:13–18) broadly develops the various cases where the "I can assume" principle functions to permit uncertainty. This principle also appears in *m. Mikva'ot* 2:3 and *t. Mikva'ot* 2:3.

According to this principle, which is likely derived from the laws of *ḥazakah*, if an object

uncertainty as a realm of halakhic inquiry and of the basic principles for dealing with states of uncertainty show that these principles are not designed to expand awareness of, and anxiety about, prohibition into the realm of the unknown. Rather, in many ways, they are intended to demarcate and limit the destabilizing power of doubt and fear of uncertainty. A return to the very first sources of halakhah, in which the basic templates for facing uncertainty about prohibition were forged, allows us to see the degree of innovation involved not only in making uncertainty an object of inquiry but also in the ways in which uncertainty is confronted. Is the absence of any treatment of uncertainty outside of the sages' circles rooted in a completely different attitude toward it, an attitude that posits that one must avoid all uncertainty when it comes to prohibitions? Do we find echoes within the circles of the sages of this rejected attitude to uncertainty, which put forth an alternative halakhah and reliably reflected a different, perhaps earlier practice that was subsequently rejected? Our attempt to trace the echoes of such a voice in the margins of the sages' halakhah brings us to one of the thorniest issues pertaining to guilt and uncertainty: the tenuous guilt offering (*korban asham talui*).

---

that can forbid an entire mixture fell into one of two units, one of which is already forbidden, and the other of which is permitted, or one that would become forbidden if the prohibited item falls into it, while the other would remain permitted, then one can assume that the item that would cause prohibition fell into the forbidden unit, while the permitted unit remains as it was.

In the Yerushalmi (*y. Terumah* 7:3), Rabbi Yoḥanan and Resh Lakish disagree about how far-reaching this principle is. Resh Lakish limits the *mishnah* to a case where "there is a majority in the second one," that is, that the stockpile of non-sacred produce is larger in quantity than the measure of terumah that may have fallen into it. Had the terumah fallen into this stockpile, it would have been nullified at the biblical level by a regular majority, and it is only by rabbinic decree that it would have been forbidden by anything less than a one-hundred-to-one majority. Thus, according to Resh Lakish, one can assume that the measure of *terumah* fell into the stockpile of *terumah* because even if it had fallen into the non-sacred produce, the mixture would have been forbidden only at the rabbinic level.

Rabbi Yoḥanan understands the *mishnah* according to its straightforward meaning: "even if there is no majority in the second one." Perhaps he maintains that the "I can assume" principle applies even to a biblical prohibition, in which case this is the bone of contention between Rabbi Yoḥanan and Resh Lakish. The Bavli (*b. Yevamot* 82a–b and *Pesaḥim* 10a) limits the applicability of this principle to uncertainties about a rabbinic prohibition, even according to Rabbi Yoḥanan. See the lengthy commentary of Rabbi Shimshon of Sens to *m. Mikva'ot* 2:3.

It goes without saying that the "I can assume" principle, wherein we choose the possibility that the prohibited item fell into the prohibited unit, leaving the permitted unit in its prior state of permissibility, is very far indeed from realist conceptions of prohibitions. From a probabilistic perspective, this idea has no internal logic. It is apparently predicated on extending the concept of *ḥazakah*. Perhaps the boldness of the "I can assume" principle is what caused Resh Lakish to limit it to rabbinic prohibitions and the Bavli to interpret Rabbi Yoḥanan's position accordingly.

V

A study of the sections on sacrificial offerings and sin offerings in Leviticus presents the reader with a complicated exegetical and religious question about guilt and uncertainty. The passage in Leviticus sets forth the law of the sin offering (*korban ḥatat*), which articulates the punishment meted out to one who sins unintentionally:

> If any person from among the populace unwittingly incurs guilt by doing any of the things which by the LORD's commandments ought not to be done, and he realizes his guilt—or the sin of which he is guilty is brought to his knowledge—he shall bring a female goat without blemish as his offering for the sin of which he is guilty.... Thus the priest shall make expiation for him, and he shall be forgiven. (Lev 4:27–31)

The next chapter in Leviticus turns from the sin offering to the guilt offering. Inter alia, one who commits sacrilege must pay back the sacred property he misappropriated, plus one-fifth of its value, and must also bring a ram as a guilt offering. Immediately following the section about the guilt offering for sacrilege is the description of another guilt offering, which the sages termed the "tenuous" guilt offering:

> And when a person sins in regard to any of the LORD's commandments about things not to be done without knowing it, and then realizes his guilt, he shall bear his iniquity. He shall bring to the priest a ram without blemish from the flock, or the equivalent, as a guilt offering. The priest shall make expiation on his behalf for the error that he committed without knowing, and he shall be forgiven. It is a guilt offering; he has incurred guilt before the LORD. (Lev 5:17–19)

The explanation of these verses is not simple at all, and Bible exegetes, both early and late, disagree about their meaning. The passage apparently refers to an offering that greatly resembles the sin offering, though, in contrast to the sin offering, the animal offered is a ram, not a female goat. Moreover, the passage emphasizes in the context of this offering that "it is a guilt offering," which differentiates it from the category of sin offerings.

Jacob Milgrom, in his monumental commentary on Leviticus, contends that these verses relate to the sin of sacrilege that is mentioned in the preceding verses. He draws support for his interpretation from the opening of these verses, "and when" (*ve-im*), which links them to the preceding unit. In Milgrom's view, these verses deal with someone who is concerned that he unknowingly committed sacrilege, and this unresolved uncertainty imposes on him the obligation to bring a guilt offering—a ram—and its sacrifice will atone for the sacrilege he may have committed. However, if he knows for certain that he committed sacrilege, he must repay the principal and the added fifth, as set forth in the preceding verses about the law of sacrilege.[53]

This reading of the verses in Leviticus has certain limitations, as Milgrom himself is aware. Foremost among them is the fact that the verses use inclusive language to describe the sin and do not explicitly state that the subject is someone who is uncertain as to whether he committed the specific sin of sacrilege. The sages adopted a different interpretation of these verses, reading them more broadly in light of their inclusive language. They viewed the guilt offering as a specific branch of the laws of unintentional transgression. The *shogeg*, the bringer of a sin offering, knows, ex post facto, that he committed a sin unintentionally, but the subject of these verses is "without knowing." Thus, these verses refer to the duty to bring an offering for an uncertainty about an unintentional sin.

Thus, for example, these verses refer to someone who eats one of two pieces of meat and then learns that one of the pieces was of the forbidden fat (*ḥelev*), and that he may have eaten it unintentionally. Had he known for certain that he unintentionally ate the forbidden fat, he would have brought a sin offering.[54] The guilt offering is unique in that the person offering it does not know whether he transgressed. For this reason, this is called the "tenuous" guilt offering. If, after bringing the tenuous guilt offering, the person ascertains that he indeed transgressed, he must further bring a sin offering according to the sages. The archetypal examples of scenarios that require a tenuous guilt offering are formulated as follows in Mishnah *Kareitot*:

> If one was uncertain as to whether he ate forbidden fat or not; or even if he ate it and is uncertain as to whether he ate the minimum quantity or not; or if there are permitted fat and forbidden fat before him, and he ate one of them and does not know which of them he ate ... —he brings a tenuous guilt offering. (*m. Kareitot* 4:1)

Another example of uncertainty regarding an unintentional sin appears in an earlier *mishnah*:

---

53. See Jacob Milgrom, *Leviticus 1–16: A New Translation with Introduction and Commentary*, Anchor Bible 3 (New York: Doubleday, 1991), 331–34.

54. In rabbinic halakhah, the sin offering is brought only for sins whose intentional transgression would render the perpetrator liable for excision. Therefore, the guilt offering under discussion is brought for transgressions that would mandate excision if done intentionally and a sin offering if done unwittingly. Based on its proximity to the verses that discuss sacrilege, Rabbi Akiva maintains that a tenuous guilt offering is also brought if it is uncertain whether one unintentionally committed sacrilege. This explains the similarity between Rabbi Akiva's position and the commentary offered by Milgrom. The sages disagreed with Rabbi Akiva, however, because the sin of sacrilege does not carry liability for excision or a sin offering, and, according to them, a tenuous guilt offering is brought only for transgressions that would mandate a sin offering if done unwittingly and excision if done intentionally. See *m. Kareitot* 5:2.

> If [witnesses] say to him: "You ate forbidden fat," he brings a sin offering. If one witness says he ate, and one witness says he did not eat … he brings a tenuous guilt offering. (*m. Kareitot* 3:1)

An uncertainty about an unintentional sin indeed obligates one to bring a sacrifice for atonement, and this section of Leviticus, as interpreted by the sages, expands the realm of sin to uncertainty itself. This expansion of the sin's domain, from unintentional sins that were certainly committed to unintentional sins that may not have been committed, evokes immense legal anxiety, as the heavy shadow of the law extends not only to unintentional transgressions but even to situations in which one is anxious about a sin that he may have committed.

Strains of the anxiety and guilt associated with the tenuous guilt offering appear in the following homily, formulated by Rabbi Yose the Galilean and recorded in *Sifra*:

> "Without knowing it, and then realizes his guilt, he shall bear his iniquity." Rabbi Yose the Galilean says: Scripture punishes one who does not know. If Scripture thus punishes one who does not know, how much more so one who knows! Rabbi Yaakov says: If one eats forbidden fats, he brings a sin offering for a *sela*. If he is in uncertain as to whether or not he has eaten, he brings a guilt offering for two *selaim*. If Scripture thus punishes one for causing an uncertain sin, how much more will be the reward of the doer of a *mitzvah*!? (*Sifra, Dibura De-ḥovah* 12:7–8)[55]

Rabbi Yose the Galilean deduces, based on the obligation of one who is uncertain whether he unintentionally committed a sin to bring a guilt offering, the severity of the punishment for a sin that was committed with certitude. In contrast, and in direct response to Rabbi Yose's position, Rabbi Yaakov maintains that the a-fortiori reasoning should not be applied to deduce the punishment that awaits one who sins, but to deduce the reward that awaits one who performs a commandment. The punishment for the uncertain commission of a transgression is not instructive about the severity of the law; to the contrary, it teaches about the law's great kindness and the reward for abiding by it. If this is the punishment for one who is unsure whether he committed a sin, we can only imagine the reward that awaits one who observes the commandments.[56]

The sages' main approach to understanding the verses about the guilt offering is thus linked to the sense of guilt that comes from being uncer-

---

55. It seems that Rabbi Yaakov comes to refute the a-fortiori derivation of the case where one does not know to the case where one knows based on the fact that the ram brought for a tenuous guilt offering is more expensive than the female goat brought for a sin offering.

56. A comprehensive discussion of this *Sifra* passage and its continuation, in the context of the midrashic polemic against the Pauline critique of the law that imposes the curse of sin and punishment, see Menachem Kister, "Romans 5:12–21 against the Background of Torah Theology and the Hebrew Usage," *Harvard Theological Review* 100 (2007): 391–424.

tain about having unintentionally committed a sin whose punishment would be excision if it had been done on purpose. Alongside this view, however, is an early halakhic tradition that posits a completely different understanding of the guilt offering and that sparks a fundamental debate that gets to the very root of the dread of uncertainty and its meaning. The view that fundamentally differs from the sages' reading in the Mishnah is presented by Rabbi Eliezer as an alternative tradition:

> Rabbi Eliezer says: One may voluntarily donate a tenuous guilt offering every day and at any time he pleases, and such an offering is called "the guilt offering of the pietists." They said of Bava ben Buta that he used to donate a tenuous guilt offering every day, except on the day after the Day of Atonement (Yom Kippur). He used to say: By this Temple! If they would let me, I would bring one, but they say to me: Wait until you enter a state of uncertainty. But the sages say: One brings a tenuous guilt offering only for something that warrants excision if done on purpose and a sin offering if done unintentionally.
>
> Those who are obligated to bring sin offerings and certain-guilt offerings who went through Yom Kippur must [still] bring them after Yom Kippur. Those who owe tenuous guilt offerings are exempt. One who becomes uncertain about whether he committed a sin on Yom Kippur, he is exempt [from the tenuous guilt offering] even if it is getting dark, for any part of the day atones. (*m. Kareitot* 6:3–4).

According to Rabbi Eliezer, a tenuous guilt offering is not brought only when one knows that he has unintentionally committed an act whose sinful status is uncertain. Rather, it is a voluntary offering that one brings in order to atone for possible sins that he does not know about. Such an offering can always be donated because the human condition induces unknown sins about which one bears the burden of guilt. Bava ben Buta, an elder from the academy of Shammai, is mentioned as an extreme precedent for this sort of voluntary guilt offering. He serves as the model pietist, whose fear of sin gnaws at him at all times and whose need for atonement is constant. This pietist, this paragon of guilt, voluntarily brings a guilt offering every day. The *mishnah* reports that the only day that pious Bava ben Buta would refrain from bringing a guilt offering was the day after Yom Kippur—and Bava ben Buta attests that he would have preferred to bring the offering even on that day, so as not to miss even the smallest opportunity to relieve the guilt that weighed on him. According to his testimony, it was the sages who prevented him from doing so, because Yom Kippur atones for unknown sins, and it would seem that no uncertainty would have arisen yet the very next day.

The sages disagree with the position of Rabbi Eliezer, maintaining that a guilt offering is brought only for a real, known uncertainty, not for the possibility of uncertainty that encumbers a person with constant guilt and an uncontrollable urge to gain atonement. This debate between the sages and Rabbi Eliezer highlights a crucial principle in confronting uncertainty. This principle does not guide the way in which uncertainty is resolved but rather defines when uncertainty should be raised altogether. According to the sages, the guilt offering on uncertainty can stem only from a doubt that is anchored in a known event, an event in which a possibility of sin might have occurred, and not from a generalized amorphic doubt whether a sin was committed. In order for a doubt to emerge, a threshold of knowledge has to be passed, in which it is clear to people that they might have transgressed, such as the example in which a piece of meat was eaten and it was clear that one of two possible pieces was not kosher but it was not known which was eaten. Without such known doubt there is no place to raise doubt. The dread of uncertainty is thus curbed and controlled by the sages in locating it within a known and defined domain in contrast to Rabbi Eliezer.

The sages also formulated the novel idea that Yom Kippur itself atones for unknown sins, and that therefore one who did not manage to bring a tenuous guilt offering for the uncertain commission of a sin is exempt from this offering after Yom Kippur. This novel and profound idea is linked by the Talmud to a verse that is notoriously difficult to parse in the description of Yom Kippur, "From all of your sins before God you shall be purified" (Lev 16:30): "Rabbi Elazar said: Scripture states, 'From all of your sins before God...'—[meaning,] a sin of which none but the Omnipresent is aware is atoned by Yom Kippur" (*b. Kareitot* 25b). Yom Kippur releases one from the burden of doubt and uncertainty that can inundate him; those sins that are known only to God, but not to their perpetrator, gain atonement on Yom Kippur.

The dispute between Rabbi Eliezer and the sages about how to understand the tenuous guilt offering reflects completely different religious attitudes toward all that pertains to dread and guilt about uncertainty. The juxtaposition of these different attitudes in this *mishnah* demonstrates how differentiated and varied the religious world of the sages was. The *mishnah* also shows the degree to which such disputes were not disagreements about some detail or another of the halakhic system but essential differences of opinion that reflect vastly different religious sensibilities and worldviews.

We do not possess the full pietistic doctrine of Bava ben Buta and his circle, but it is hard to imagine that pietists who lived in constant fear lest they sin would permit themselves and others to eat a piece of meat of unknown origin based on a bare statistical majority. It is also hard to imagine that such pietists would have eaten three pieces of meat—one of which was forbidden before it got mixed together with two permitted pieces—or that they would have resolved uncertainty by relying on a prior presumption of fitness. We do not know how a circle like this would have contended with uncertainty, but this early attestation, from Temple times, to the existence of "the guilt offering of the pietists" is a reverberation of a doubt-ridden consciousness of sin; it is doubtful that a consciousness like this could have cultivated or approved the basic template for sages' directives for dealing with uncertainty.

It is important to note that this attitude, which opposes the sages' rulings on uncertainty, need not rely on a realist view of prohibitions. A nominalist approach is, as noted, a necessary condition of the sages' teachings about uncertainty, but it is not a sufficient condition. It is likely, and it makes more sense to posit that pure fear of sin—concern even for the mere possibility of violating God's word—and the desire to fulfill one's obligation to the fullest, irrespective of whether the prohibition is based on some dangerous spiritual essence, are what motivated the anxiety about uncertainty and the pietists' guilt offering.[57]

---

57. Tannaitic literature contains additional evidence of this sort of pietistic practice that strives to achieve perfect fulfillment of God's word and commandments. These attestations can provide another window into this kind of pietistic religious consciousness:

> [If a person says,] "[I vow] like the vows of the wicked," he has said nothing, for the wicked do not make vows. "Like the vows of the worthy": Rabbi Yehudah says: He has pledged to be a nazirite, for the early pietists would take vows of nazirism; since the Omnipresent would not cause them to sin unwittingly, they would take vows of nazirism in order to be able to bring an offering. Rabban Shimon ben Gamliel says: "[If a person says,] '[I vow] like the vows of the worthy,' he has not pledged to be a nazirite, for the early pietists did not take vows of nazirism. For if he wanted to bring a burnt offering, he would; if he wanted to bring a peace offering, he would; if he wanted to bring a thanksgiving offering and its four types of bread, he would. They would not take vows of nazirism because they require atonement, as it says: "and he shall make atonement on his behalf, for he sinned against life" (Num 6:11).'" (*t. Nedarim* 1:1)

According to Rabbi Yehudah, the early pietists (*ḥasidim rishonim*) pledged to be nazirites so that they would have the opportunity to bring a sin offering without committing an unwitting transgression. This sort of devotion to the commandments appears in another source, which is likewise about a pietist:

> It happened with a certain pietist that he forgot a sheaf in his field [and thus fulfilled the *mitzvah* of leaving forgotten sheaves for the poor]. He said to his son, "Go sacrifice a bull for a burnt offering and a bull for a peace offering on my behalf." [The son] replied, "Father! Why do you rejoice in this *mitzvah* more than all the *mitzvot* mentioned in the Torah?" He said to him, "The Omnipresent has given us all the *mitzvot* in the Torah to do mindfully, but this one is done unknowingly, for had we done it willfully before the Omnipresent, we would not have this *mitzvah* in hand." [The son] replied, "It says [in the Torah], 'When you reap your harvest [in your field and forget a sheaf in the field, do not turn back to get it; it shall go to the stranger, the fatherless, and the widow—in order that the Lord your God may bless you in all your undertakings]' (Deut 24:19). Scripture establishes a blessing for him. Can we not reason a fortiori? If one who did not intend to gain credit, but did something creditworthy anyway, is given the credit, then certainly one who intends to do something creditworthy [should be given credit]!"

We possess no complete early attestations, but later evidence of reservations about the halakhah's doctrine of uncertainty, as developed in the Mishnah and Tosefta, crops up in the history of halakhah and reflects, in its own way, the ancient anxiety about doubt that is evident from the pietists' guilt offering.

The source of these reservations is found in the Talmud itself, in its description of a practice it attributes to Yeḥezkel, the prophet and priest:

> Then I said, "Ah, Lord God, my person was never defiled; nor have I eaten anything that died of itself or was torn by beasts from my youth until now, nor has foul flesh entered my mouth" (Ezek 4:14). "My person was never defiled"—I never had thoughts during the day that would have led to defilement at night. "Nor have I eaten anything that died of itself or was torn by beasts from my youth until now"—I never ate the flesh of a dying animal. "Nor has foul flesh entered my mouth"—I never ate of an animal on which a sage pronounced a ruling. (*b. Ḥullin* 37b)

According to this homily, the prophet Yeḥezkel was careful never to eat the meat of an animal that required the permissive ruling of a sage to resolve an uncertainty about it. Inspired by the tradition attributed by the Talmud to Yeḥezkel, Rabbi David ibn Abi Zimra (Radbaz), a leading sixteenth-century halakhist, asserted, "Even though it is technically permissible, it is unworthy of holy Israel to put into their bodies something that has a dimension of uncertainty vis-à-vis a prohibition" (*Responsa Radbaz Mikhtav Yad* 8:111). The emphasis in this formulation, which rejects halakhic rulings on uncertainty, is that the sanctity of Israel is desecrated by the insertion of an impure spiritual entity into the body. This motif recurs in a fundamental disagreement between Rabbi Aharon ben Rabbi Gershom and Rabbi Moshe Isserles (Rema). The bone of contention was casks of olive oil that had been greased with lard to reinforce and tighten

---

Similarly:

> "If a person sins by accident ... he shall bring an unblemished ram ..." (Lev 4:27–30). Can we not reason a fortiori? If one who did not intend to sin but sinned [anyway] is considered to have sinned [and must bring a sin offering], then certainly one who intended to sin and indeed sinned [may bring a sin offering]. (*t. Pe'ah* 3:13)

The *ḥasid*'s joy over his forgotten sheaf stemmed from the paradox that this commandment cannot be fulfilled willfully, as any intention would undermine the *mitzvah*'s central element, namely, that these sheaves are "forgotten." Here he has the opportunity to fulfill the *mitzvah* of the forgotten sheaf, and he celebrates this opportunity by offering a bull as a peace offering and a bull as a burnt offering. This aspiration to fulfill all of the *mitzvot* of the Torah is intertwined with the passage about fear of sin and fear of accidental transgression. It is clear from these two attestations that pietistic aspiration to fulfill all of the *mitzvot* is not connected to the nominalism/realism question but rather to the fear of sin and the joy of fulfilling a *mitzvah*. For a broader insightful analysis of piety, caution, and eagerness in the performance of commandments, see Novick, *What Is Good and What God Demands*, 142–48.

them. There was precedent for ruling leniently in such cases in the Ashkenazic halakhic tradition, on the grounds that the lard is nullified as one part in sixty and also imparts foul taste. Rabbi Aharon, who was aware of these precedents, nevertheless inclines toward forbidding the oil in the casks; among his proofs, he cites the practice attributed to the prophet Yeḥezkel: "Yeḥezkel likewise said, 'Nor has foul flesh entered my mouth,' which we expound to mean that he never ate of an animal on which a sage pronounced a ruling. People are very careful about what they put into the body." Rema responds to this stringency angrily, and in a responsum to Rabbi Aharon, he asks sarcastically: "I ask your honored, sagacious excellency whether you refrain from the fish called 'lox'? I have heard many people say that they were told that they are sometimes smeared with lard. Thus, in my opinion, one who is stringent on this matter is simply astonishing" (*Responsa Rema* §53). Halakhic precedent and common practice speak for themselves, and Rema relies on them to attack Rabbi Aharon's ruling.

Rabbi Aharon was quite familiar with Rema's sources and arguments, but his motivating factor was repulsion by the toxic quality of lard; in his words, it is "what they put into the body." The nominalist view, which is deeply embedded in the sages' rules governing uncertainty, does not completely eliminate anxiety about the toxic and repulsive substance of forbidden foods and about its impact on a pure body. This repulsion, which ignores the laws of uncertainty, made its return through Kabbalistic sources, which are riven with the idea that prohibitions and commandments are deeply linked to the real world. Thus, for instance, Rabbi Yeshayahu Horowitz writes in *Shenei Luḥot Ha-brit*:

> *Reishit Ḥokhmah* states (Gate of Sanctity 15:3): "Therefore it is proper for a person to be strict with himself regarding his own food, that it should have no aspect of prohibition at all, for the prophet Yeḥezkel praised himself for never having eaten of an animal on which a sage pronounced a ruling, even if it was permitted, since there was uncertainty that it might be prohibited.... *Ḥovot Ha-levavot* states (Gate of Repentance, chapter 5), 'The pietists would refrain from seventy kinds of permitted things out of fear of consuming one forbidden thing.'" See how far the sanctity of food extends! I have seen lofty people, and they are few—perhaps not even two in any generation—who do not eat anything about which there is a dispute, even though everyone rules in accordance with the permissive view and practices accordingly. (*Shenei Luḥot Ha-brit*, Gate of Letters, The Sanctity of Eating).

This repulsion reflects a deep and primal attitude about the toxic substance of prohibitions and fear of uncertainty. It also reflects, independent of any inherent toxicity, an unrestrained fear of sin, which can be prevented only by the desire to discharge one's obligations with absolute certainty.

It is possible that this later attitude offers a portrayal of the halakhah practiced in the circle of Bava ben Buta and other groups that was rejected by the sages. The obstinate refusal to digest and accept the sages' rules about uncertainty and about rendering decisions based on the principles of a majority, a presumption, or nullification, which undergird those rules, shows, in its own way, the uniqueness and power contained within the initial Tannaitic shaping of attitudes toward uncertainty.

3

Purity and Doubt: Between Strictness and Separation

I

The sages' wide-ranging engagement with matters of uncertainty reaches its full halakhic and conceptual intensity with matters of purity and impurity. Four chapters of the Mishnah of tractate *Taharot* (within the larger Order of *Taharot*) are devoted to rulings pertaining to uncertain states, and these chapters, which constitute something of an independent unit of "Laws of Uncertainties,"[1] include instructions for dealing with uncertain impurities that arise in daily life alongside directives pertaining to imaginary uncertainties that do not arise in real life but which the Mishnah treats with the same level of gravity and meticulousness.[2] To these chapters, stretching from the middle of the third chapter through the end of the sixth, we can add the chapters of the Tosefta that are devoted in their entirety to uncertainties of impurity, as well as individual laws about uncertainty that are scattered liberally throughout the Order of *Taharot*, in the heart of a variety of different subjects.[3] The primary distinction drawn by the chapters of the Mishnah devoted to uncertain impurities establishes a different policy for uncertainties in the private domain versus the public domain. Uncertain purity in a public domain is deemed pure, while in a private domain it is deemed impure. This distinction, which forms the basis for behavioral patterns when one confronts

1. In his analysis of the structure of tractate *Taharot*, Yair Furstenberg defined this section as "tractate of doubts" ("Eating in a State of Purity in the Tannaitic Period: Tractate *Tohorot* and Its Historical and Cultural Contexts (PhD diss., Hebrew University, 2010), 65–66.

2. Zvi, "Introduction to the Mishnah," 60–63.

3. The subject of purity in the Mishnah—its relation to Scripture and early halakhah, the development of tensions, and shifts within rabbinic literature itself—is a broad and complex topic that is treated extensively in works of scholarship. In keeping with the objectives of this book, this chapter will focus on states of uncertainty and rulings about uncertain purity without dealing more broadly with the general issue of purity. The broader issues of purity will be addressed only when they intersect with, and have significant implications for, the laws of uncertainties as they relate to the laws of purity.

uncertain states of purity and impurity, has no precedent in Scripture or in Second Temple literature. Likewise, despite the importance of the distinction between public and private domains in the laws of the Sabbath and tort law, this distinction plays no corresponding role in shaping the directives for cases of uncertainty regarding forbidden foods, pedigree, or monetary matters. The uniqueness of the distinction between public and private domains with respect to purity, in comparison with the laws of purity and impurity as formulated in Scripture and Second Temple literature, and in comparison with the laws governing uncertainty about other areas of halakhah, demands explanation. What is the significance of a guideline that distinguishes between public and private domains, and how did it grow out of the discussion of uncertainties regarding matters of purity and impurity? Why does uncertainty about purity and impurity warrant a circumscribed basis that differs from other areas of halakhah? Additionally, despite its uniqueness, can we identify in this fundamental distinction any continuity with the logic that governs the rulings on uncertainty in the parallel subject of forbidden foods in Tannaitic literature.

The distinction between private and public domains with respect to uncertain impurity is asserted brusquely by the Mishnah: "A case of uncertainty in the private domain is impure until he says, 'I did not touch [it].' A case of uncertainty in the public domain is pure until he says, 'I touched [it]'" (*m. Taharot* 6:6). The difference between the domains does not pertain only to cases where the uncertainty is fifty-fifty but is much broader. In the private domain, as long as there is even the slightest uncertainty, one is rendered impure unless he knows for certain that he touched nothing impure. In contrast, in the public domain, the opposite assertion applies: one is deemed pure as long as he does not know for certain that he touched impurity.[4] According to the same logic, the Mishnah asserts:

> However many uncertainties, and uncertainties upon uncertainties, that you might heap on, it is impure in a private domain and pure in a public domain. How so? If one entered an alleyway and there was impurity in the courtyard, and there is an uncertainty as to whether he entered [the courtyard] or not; there was impurity in a house and there is uncertainty as to whether he entered or did not enter; or even if he entered, if there is uncertainty as to whether [the impurity] was there or not; or even if it was there, if there is uncertainty as to whether there was a sufficient quantity [to render him impure] or not; or even if there was a sufficient quantity, if there is an uncertainty as to whether it was impure or pure; and even if it was impure, if there is an uncertainty as to whether he touched it or not—its uncertainty is impure. (*m. Taharot* 4)

4. See the qualifications of R. Shimshon of Sens in his commentary on *m. Taharot* 6:6.

In the private domain, impurity is rendered even if the uncertainty is not evenly balanced, even when several uncertainties accumulate, making the likelihood of actual impurity much less than 50 percent. This is not true of a public domain.

In the Tosefta, the disparity between a private and public domain is taught as a mirror image, which determines a different set of rulings in each of the domains pertaining to that same state:

> [There are] nine vermin and one frog in a public domain; someone touched one of them and it is unknown which he touched—his uncertainty is deemed pure. If one of them separated from them into a private domain—his uncertainty is deemed impure; to a public domain—his uncertainty is deemed pure. If it was found, we follow the majority. [There are] nine frogs and one vermin in a private domain; someone touched one of them and it is unknown which he touched—his uncertainty is deemed impure. If one of them separated from them into a private domain—his uncertainty is deemed impure; to a public domain—his uncertainty is deemed pure. If it was found, we follow the majority. (*t. Taharot* 6:2, based on MS Vienna)

The Tosefta sharply differentiates the public domain from the private domain. In a public domain, even if most carcasses in a particular group cause impurity (the vermin) and one is ritually pure (the frog),[5] contact with one carcass from the group does not cause impurity as long as the identity of the carcass he touched is unknown. Thus, in the public domain, we do not follow the majority to deem a person impure; rather, we rely on the 10-percent possibility to render him pure in a case of uncertainty. The opposite conclusion is reached in cases of uncertainty in the private domain, where, even if most of the carcasses in the group are pure, contact with any one of them renders him impure, due to the possibility that he may have touched the impure minority. In the private domain, we do not follow the majority to render someone pure, and in the public domain, we do not follow the majority to render someone impure. Moreover, in a case where one of the carcasses in the group separated from the group and entered into a different domain, its status changes in accordance with the status of the domain it entered. That is, a carcass that separated, in a private domain, from a group that was mostly pure but had an impure minority renders one who comes into contact with it is impure due to uncertainty, but if it was moved to the public domain, one who touches it remains pure. Conversely, a carcass from a group in the public domain is deemed pure, but if it separates and is moved to the private domain, it is impure due to uncertainty.[6] The meaning of the rule "Uncertain impurity

---

5. Frogs are not listed in Lev 11:29–30 among the vermin that cause impurity.

6. This Tosefta passage is quoted by the Bavli (*Ketubot* 15a) in support of the distinction between *kavu'a* and *parish*, which was addressed in the previous chapter. However, a straight-

in a private domain is impure and in a public domain is pure" is thus far-reaching.[7] The majoritarian principle, which guides halakhah through uncertainties about forbidden foods, is not valid at all with respect to the domains. We do not follow the majority in a private domain to render something pure, and we do not follow the majority in the public domain to render something impure.[8]

The Tosefta's determination that an object that moves from a private domain to a public domain changes its status from impure to pure and

---

forward reading of this Tosefta passage indicates that the heart of its discussion is the distinction between public and private domains, not the distinction between *kavu'a* and *parish* as the Bavli interprets. The Tosefta itself knows of no such distinction. Moreover, the Tosefta emphasizes that, in a public domain, one does not follow the majority to render something impure, regardless of whether it is *kavu'a* or *parish*. After all, it explicitly asserts, "If one of them separated [*piresh*] from them into a private domain—his uncertainty is deemed impure; to a public domain—his uncertainty is deemed pure." Likewise, in a private domain, one does not follow the majority to render something pure, even in the case of a limb that separated from a group, as the Tosefta asserts, "If one of them separated [*piresh*] from them into a private domain—his uncertainty is deemed impure; to a public domain—his uncertainty is deemed pure." It therefore seems from the Tosefta that in a case of *parish*, the majority is not followed. Rather, the object's status is determined by the domain in which the uncertainty emerged. Rabbi Shimshon of Sens was aware that the Bavli's interpretation of the Tosefta is problematic, and he was forced to explain that, even this case, where "one of them separated [*piresh*]," is a case of *kavu'a*, because the limb that separated was seen at the time of separation. In his words, "We can explain that 'it separated' [*piresh*] means that it separated in our presence; i.e., the uncertainty emerged in its fixed place [*mekom ha-kevi'ut*], and is therefore judged as being fifty-fifty" (Commentary of Rabbi Shimshon of Sens to *Taharot* 5:2).

7. The medieval rabbis disagreed as to whether the rule that "uncertain impurity in a private domain is impure and in a public domain is pure" supersedes the regular rules for deciding uncertainties, like the majority rule. On this, see *Tosafot* to *Ḥullin* 2b, s.v. *"de-leitei,"* which maintains that an impure majority is followed in a public domain, and Naḥmanides in his novellae on *Ḥullin* 2b, s.v. *"ve-im shaḥat,"* which disagrees. The Tosefta clearly goes against the opinion of *Tosafot*.

8. The Tosefta qualifies the distinction between public and private domains when it states, "If it was found, we follow the majority," which apparently should apply in both public and private domains. This addition is problematic, but it can be explained as expressing a different Talmudic principle, *itẓḥazek issura* ("the presence of something prohibited has been established"), to which the Tosefta must add the principle of *itẓḥazek heteira* ("the presence of something permitted has been established"). That is, in a case where it is certain that there is one member from the group that is a pure creature in the public domain, the minority is followed to render the uncertainty pure because the presence of something permitted has been established. In a private domain, in a case where there is one member of the group that can render things impure, the minority is followed to render the uncertainty impure, because the presence of something prohibited has been established. In a case where it was found, where no presence has been established, neither of something permitted nor of something prohibited, we follow the majority in both the public domain and the private domain. It is very likely that this is the explanation of the term "if it was found." In any event, the Tosefta deals not with a distinction between *kavu'a* and *parish* but with a distinction between public and private domains.

vice versa, is also taught in the Mishnah, where it is formulated more sharply and with greater complexity:

> A place that was a private domain, and then became a public domain, and then was turned again into a private domain: while it is a private domain its uncertainty is impure; while it is a public domain its uncertainty is pure. A man who was gravely ill in a private domain, and they took him out into a public domain, and then they returned him to a private domain: while he is in the private domain his uncertainty is impure; while he is in the public domain his uncertainty is pure. Rabbi Shimon says: The public domain interrupts. (*m. Taharot* 6:1)

A person in his death throes, about whom it is uncertain whether he is alive or dead, changes status, from impure to pure, upon being moved from one domain to another, and so on. In the private domain he is considered dead from uncertainty and thus renders impure anyone who touches him; upon being moved to the public domain he is considered alive from uncertainty, and anyone who touches him remains pure. When he returns to the private domain, he is again considered impure. Rabbi Shimon disagrees with the first Tanna of the *mishnah*; in his opinion, it is illogical to claim that the dying person is considered dead while in a private domain but is resurrected and again considered living when moved to the public domain. This is how the Tosefta records R. Shimon's view: "For R. Shimon said: The public domain interrupts retroactively, for one cannot say that he was dead in the private domain and alive in the public domain" (*t. Taharot* 7:1). According to R. Shimon, from the moment that the dying person left the private domain for the public domain, he is retroactively pure even in the private domain, and anyone who came into contact with him in the private domain that he later left is pure. In contrast, when he reenters the private domain, he is considered dead, after he had been considered alive in the public domain. R. Shimon thus limits the paradoxical nature of these halakhic shifts in the status of a dying person upon moving from one domain to another; according to R. Shimon, the halakhic conclusion that a dying person was alive in the public domain after being deemed dead in the private domain simply does not stand to reason.

The distinction drawn in the laws of uncertainty between the public and private domains indicates a nominalist trend in the understanding of impurity.[9] As with respect to uncertainties regarding forbidden foods,

9. On the distinction between nominalism and realism, see pp. 27–28 above. In the context of impurity, see Noam, "On Ritual Contamination," 155–88; Noam, *From Qumran to the Rabbinic Revolution: Conceptions of Impurity* [Hebrew] (Jerusalem: Yad Izhak Ben Zvi, 2010), 221–55; Yair Furstenberg, *Purity and Community in Antiquity: Traditions of the Law from Second Temple Judaism to the Mishnah* [Hebrew] (Jerusalem: Magnes, 2016), 144–55, and the references there in n. 63 to various discussions of the question.

which were discussed in the two previous chapters, looking closely at this question in the context of instructions for uncertainties in matters of purity and impurity points unambiguously toward the nominalist conception. If impurity per se is considered a harmful substance, it is difficult to imagine that different domains impact the harmful nature of the impurity. If impurity were something hazardous that the Torah merely disclosed, the location of the impurity, in one domain or another, should not affect the severity of the harm posed by such a substance. The antirealist tendency in the conception of impurity is especially discernible in how the Mishnah and Tosefta structure their cases, such that the same object goes from impure to pure and back as it crosses from a private to a public domain and back. Changing domains does not alter the features of the object, and certainly the return of the object from a public to a private domain does not restore to it the hazardous property that it had lost, as it were. The distinction between public and private domains indicates that the deeming of something pure or impure is not dictated by realist views of essences that are prior to halakhah, but is established by Tannaitic halakhah in accordance with considerations whose significance I will attempt to elucidate below.

This antirealist view is highlighted not only by the case of an object that is moved from one domain to another but also by another case addressed by the Mishnah. According to the Mishnah, if an object remains in place while the domain that encompasses it changes, for some reason, from a private domain to a public domain, the status of the uncertain object changes from impure to pure, and vice versa:

> A place that was a private domain, and then became a public domain, and then was turned again into a private domain: while it is a private domain its uncertainty is impure; while it is a public domain its uncertainty is pure. (*m. Taharot* 6:1)

Neither the transfer of uncertainties from one domain to another nor a change in the status of the domain itself is a situation that arises often in real life; the purpose of discussing them is not to provide instruction for the rare cases where such scenarios unfold. The Mishnah designs these cases to emphasize the absolute priority of the power of norms and rabbinic law over any supposed essential properties of impurity, and how impurity, as a strictly halakhic concept, changes its state according to broad policy considerations—considerations that, as noted, must still be thoroughly clarified.

It is worth noting that even Rabbi Shimon, who disputes the view of the sages in the Mishnah with respect to a dying person who is moved from one domain to another, does not take a more realist view of impurity. Rather, he believes that there can be no halakhic ruling that a dying person is considered dead in a private domain and then alive again in a public domain. He indeed concludes that the dying person is considered alive when he moves to a public domain, but then he is retroactively treated as having been alive even when he was in the private domain. This retroactive change from impure to pure clearly demonstrates that Rabbi Shimon does not take a realist view of impurity, for a transfer to the public domain should not retroactively alter the degree of danger posed by the object in the private domain before it was moved. The constraint that Rabbi Shimon wished to impose on the ruling of the sages is derived not from a realist view of impurity but from a demand that even a halakhah that is entirely determined by policy decisions and is completely liberated from the constraints of material reality should offer a possible structure that does not rely on the absurd. Halakhah can render a pure object impure, or an impure object pure, without changing any of its intrinsic features. It cannot, however, treat a person as being dead and then alive. Because halakhah changed the status of this person to living after considering him dead, the demands of consistency require changing his past status as well and defining him retroactively as living.[10] The Mishnah expertly designs the unique cases of the transfer of a dying person from one domain to another, and of the changing of the domains themselves, to remove, in one blow, the possibility that impurity is a dangerous substance that the halakhah reveals and to teach that impure status is given over to the sages. Prior essences do not dictate the laws produced in their academy.

II

The distinction between the public and private domains had been accepted by the generation of Yavneh at the latest,[11] and, as noted, it was designed

10. In his *Commentary on the Mishnah,* Maimonides formulated Rabbi Shimon's position as follows:

> For since we have said that one who touched him in the public domain is pure, because there he is presumed to be alive, one who touched him earlier, when he was in a private domain, must be pure, for how can we say that now, in the public domain, he is alive, but earlier, when he was in the private domain, he was already dead? This is impossible. This is what they meant by "the public domain interrupts"; that is, it removes the rule governing the earlier uncertainty in the private domain. (on *Taharot* 6:1)

11. In this regard the Mishnah states:

> There are four cases of uncertainty that Rabbi Yehoshua renders impure and the sages render pure. They are: The impure [person] is standing while the pure [person] passes by; the pure [person] is standing while the impure [person] passes by; the impure [person] is in the private domain and the pure [person] is in the public domain; the pure [person] is in the private domain and the impure [person] is in

as a major, sweeping distinction. Among the Tannaim, however, there were those who opposed the distinction and those who limited it. The view that rejects the assertion that uncertain impurity in a public domain is considered pure appears in the Mishnah as an individual opinion:

> A vermin and a frog in the public domain, and similarly an olive's bulk of a corpse and an olive's bulk of an animal carcass, or a bone from a corpse and a bone from an animal carcass, or a clod of dirt from pure land and a clod from the lands of the gentile nations, a clod from pure land and a clod from a plowed cemetery, or two paths one impure and one pure, if someone walked down one of them and he does not know which one he walked down, or he sheltered over one of them and does not know which one he sheltered over, or he moved one of them and does not know which one he moved, Rabbi Yehoshau[12] deems him impure, but the sages deem him pure. One who said, "I touched this thing and I do not know if it is impure or if it is pure," or "I touched one, but I do not know which of the two I touched"—Rabbi Akiva deems him impure, but the sages deem him pure. Rabbi Yose deems them all impure but deems the path pure, because it is normal for a person to walk but is not normal for a person to touch. (*m. Taharot* 5:1–2)

It emerges clearly from these *mishnayot* that Rabbi Akiva disputes the principle that uncertain impurity in the public domain is deemed pure, and Rabbi Yose limits it to uncertainties that arise when one walks in the

---

> the public domain. [If, in any of these four cases,] there is uncertainty as to whether one [person] touched or did not touch [the other], uncertainty as to whether one [person] sheltered or did not shelter [over the other], [or] uncertainty as to whether one [person] moved or did not move [the other], Rabbi Yehoshua renders [the pure person] impure, and the sages render [the impure person] pure. (*m. Eduyot* 3:7; *Taharot* 6:2)

The disputants accept the distinction between domains and disagree about whether the distinction is applied when the uncertainty arises from the crossing of one border into another. It is interesting to note that the Bavli (*Avodah Zarah* 37b) quotes an Amoraic opinion that attributes the permissive ruling on uncertain impurity in the public domain to a very early stage of Pharisaic halakhah—to Yose ben Yo'ezer, who was known as "Yosef Sharaya"—Joseph the Permissive. The Bavli is addressing the question of which permissive ruling earned Yose ben Yo'ezer his moniker. "Rabbi Naḥman said: He permitted them uncertain impurity in the public domain." Further in the discussion, the Bavli quotes a *baraita* (that appears nowhere else) in support of Rabbi Naḥman's view: "This was also taught [in a *baraita*]: Rabbi Yehudah says: [Yose ben Yo'ezer] drove posts into the ground and said, 'Until here is the public domain; until here is the private domain.'"

Regardless of the Bavli's treatment on its own merits, does the claim that this distinction predates Yavneh really echo the antiquity of this permissive ruling? It is surely significant that the Tannaim and Amoraim identify the permissibility of the public domain with the very first halakhic dictum of the Oral Torah—the halakhah of a Pharisee who was known (criticized?) as "Joseph the Permissive."

12. The right version is Rabbi Akiva as in the Parma manuscript and in the next Mishnah in Kaufmann.

public domain, in which case the uncertainty is rendered pure. With respect to things touched in the public domain, the rule that uncertainties are deemed pure is not asserted.[13] Likewise, it seems that there were those Tannaim who limited the application of the rule to accord with the directives pertaining to other uncertainties relating to impurity:

> If one touched something at night, and it is not known if it was alive or dead, and in the morning he arose and found it dead: Rabbi Meir renders [him] pure; uncertainty in the public domain is pure. But the sages render [him] impure, for all impurities are [rendered] according to the moment they were found. The sages concur with Rabbi Meir that if one saw it alive in the evening, even though he found it dead in the morning, that it is pure, for this is an uncertainty in the public domain. (*t. Taharot* 8:6)

The rule, "all impurities are [rendered] according to moment they were found," is taught in the Mishnah as a clarifying principle for uncertainties regarding purity and impurity. According to this principle, if, for example, a rusted or broken needle, which is not considered a utensil that is susceptible to impurity, is found, we are not concerned that the needle was whole until the moment it was found rusted or broken, and therefore all pure items that came into contact with it are deemed pure. The same principle, that in matters of impurity we follow the state in which something was found, is applied to the converse as well, when the present status is one of impurity.[14] The Mishnah teaches these rules for cases of uncertainty without any relation to the question of whether they take place in a public or private domain, and Tannaim disagree in the Tosefta about whether these principles limit the principle that an uncertainty about impurity in a public domain is considered pure. The sages, in contrast to Rabbi Meir, maintain that the principle that impurity in a public domain is considered pure does not supersede or render superfluous the principle that the state in which something was found is determinative. Rather, they significantly limit the scope of the principle that impurity in a public domain is considered pure.

Despite the dispute about the distinction between public and private domains and attempts to limit its scope, the distinction took shape as a sweeping one through all the discussion of uncertain purity in the Mishnah and Tosefta.[15] It is likely that in the generation of Yavneh some sages,

---

13. In his commentary to *m. Taharot* 5:1, Rabbi Shimshon of Sens, who viewed the distinction between public and private domains as a fundamental premise, interprets Rabbi Akiva's opinion as being limited to the person who walked on the path, not extending to the pure items that he handles.

14. See *m. Taharot* 3:5. See also *t. Taharot* 3:3.

15. The latest evidence of any reservations about the principle that uncertain impurity in the public domain is deemed pure appears in *b. Avodah Zarah* 37b, where Rabbi Yoḥanan opines, "This is the halakhah, but we do not rule accordingly" (*halakhah ve-ein morin ken*), and

including Rabbi Akiva, still disputed it, and other rules for deciding uncertainty and lists of decisions in various cases of uncertainty existed alongside the distinction between public and private domains.[16] The plurality of the various rulings on uncertainty occasionally demands an explicit formulation to qualify one ruling in the face of another, as, for instance, the *ḥazakah* rule was articulated as superseding the rule that distinguishes between domains: "If a *mikveh* was measured and found deficient, all purifications which were made on its bases, whether in a private domain or in a public domain, are retroactively impure" (*m. Mikva'ot* 2:1). In the post-Yavneh generation of Tannaim, the distinction between domains attained pride of place, and by the time the Mishnah in its entirety was edited, the distinction had become dominant.[17]

The distinction, which, as noted, has no precedent in pre-Tannaitic sources, is one of the clearest innovations of the Tannaitic treatment of uncertainty, and so its rationale must be ascertained. A closer look at how the distinction took shape shows that it allows, in practice, for those who are meticulous about purity to be present in the public domain. If uncer-

---

where Rabbi Yannai says that a subject of uncertainty in the public domain should not rely on the permissive ruling but should rather go beyond the letter of the law (*lifnim mi-shurat ha-din*) and immerse to remove impurity.

16. Prima facie, the distinction between uncertainty in a private domain and uncertainty in a public domain should decide every question of uncertainty pertaining to purity and impurity. However, tractate *Taharot* contains quite a few debates about uncertainty that do not hinge on this distinction. It seems that these were formulated before or contemporaneous with the distinction. The sages themselves disagree about how to apply the rule of uncertainty in public and private domains relative to other laws of uncertainty. Thus, for example, *m. Taharot* 4:5 contains an independent list of uncertainties—"For six types of uncertainty, *terumah* is burnt"—at the end of which is a dispute among the sages regarding how this list relates to the question of public and private domains. It thus seems that concurrent with, and perhaps even prior to, the distinction between public and private domains, there were laws of uncertainty organized around other principles and lists. The earliness of these lists of rules about uncertainty can be deduced from the fact that the Mishnah itself explains them. For example, *m. Mikva'ot* 2:3 explains an item from the list of "uncertainties that the sages rendered pure," an independent list that appears in *m. Taharot* 4:7, as do *m. Nazir* 9:2 and 4. An interesting discussion of the attempt to reconcile the independent lists with the principle of distinguishing between public and private domains in the Mishnah can be found in *Tosafot* to *Ketubot* 28b, s.v. "*beit ha-pras.*"

17. As we will see below, *t. Taharot* 6:12 addresses the question of the source and rationale of the distinction between public and private domains. The rule itself appears as a matter of settled and undisputed halakhah, and Ben Zoma and Rabban Shimon ben Gamliel disagree only about the biblical source and rationale. It therefore seems that the distinction was accepted by the generation of Yavneh at the latest, and it was also accepted by the sages in the generation after Yavneh, despite Rabbi Akiva's disputing the principle. The acceptance of this principle is implicit in the words of R. Yose, who seems to be limiting Rabbi Akiva's position to cases of contact in the public domain and denying that they were said with regard to cases of walking within the public domain. Thus, as we will see below, he interprets Rabbi Akiva's view to be consistent with the logic underlying the distinction.

tain impurity in the public domain would render other things impure, a person who is careful to remain pure would never step foot in such a domain.[18] In the public domain, one cannot control contact with passersby, and impurity, which naturally passes from person to person or from object to person, would bar access to the public domain for one who seeks to avoid impurity.

The decision that uncertain impurity in the public domain is deemed pure, thus enabling those who take care to remain pure to be present in the public domain, is especially bold because it undermines the most basic meaning of the idea behind distinguishing purity from impurity. In biblical law, and in other religious traditions, the idea of distinguishing purity from impurity aims to enforce separation and segregation. The contagiousness of impurity prevents contact between the pure and the impure, and the duty to remain in a state of purity is of central significance in the formation of closed, sectarian environments that maintain rigid social castes and strata. The principle, shaped by Tannaitic literature, that deems uncertain impurity in a private domain to be impure and in a public domain to be pure establishes that, in practice, the problem of impurity exists in the private domain, where people are segregated in any event. In a public domain, in contrast, one can walk without concern as long as he is careful not to touch a person or object known to be impure. This directive, an innovation of the Tannaitic literature that distinguishes between domains, thus turns the primary social objective of purity laws on its head. In a private domain, one can control what enters and exits his domain, and he can choose.not to enter the domain of another. These options are not available in the public domain, and once it is established that uncertain impurity in a public domain is deemed pure, it becomes possible for someone who is meticulous about purity to participate in the public domain, where, by its very nature, pedestrians do not know one another.

The distinction between the public and private domains with respect to uncertain purity and impurity thus parallels the distinction between purchasing from a private individual and purchasing in a marketplace in the context of uncertainties about forbidden foods. As we saw in our analysis of directives pertaining to uncertain forbidden foods laws in Tannaitic literature, with respect to purchases from a private entity, we do not

18. Scholars have long disagreed about the scope and nature of the concern with remaining pure, both during and after the Second Temple era. See Adolf Büchler, *The Galilean Am Ha-Aretz* [Hebrew], trans. I. Eldad from German (Jerusalem: Mossad Harav Kook, 1964), 101–12; Gedaliah Alon, "The Bounds of the Laws of Levitical Cleanliness," in *Jews, Judaism, and the Classical World: Studies in Jewish History in the Times of the Second Temple and Talmud*, trans. Israel Abrahams (Jerusalem: Magnes, 1977), 190–234; Vered Noam, "The Bounds of Non-Priestly Purity: A Reassessment" [Hebrew], *Zion* 72 (2007): 127–60. Yair Furstenberg analyzed the question comprehensively and thoroughly in his book *Purity and Community in Antiquity*, esp. chapters 1 and 8.

follow the majority to permit, and the buyer must clarify the nature of the merchandise. In a marketplace, in contrast, we follow the majority, because the market is a place where the source of the merchandise flowing into it cannot be known, so the assertion that we follow the majority, even a bare majority, allows for market transactions to take place in practice. With regard to purity laws, the rule governing uncertainty in the public domain is even more extreme than the one governing uncertain forbidden foods in the market, because, according to the rule of uncertain purity, even if there is an impure majority, it is not considered. One who steps into the public domain is not rendered impure unless he is certain, or almost certain, that he touched something impure. The reason for the difference between the rules of uncertain forbidden foods in the market and uncertain purity in the public domain is rooted in the communicability of impurity, which presents a reality that is more saturated with possibilities of impurity and uncertainty. The possibility of participating in the public domain therefore depends on a more flexible rule for cases of uncertainty, one that broadly enables entry into the realm of massive uncertainty that characterizes the public domain.[19]

Tannaitic literature contains explicit attestation of this sensitivity in a passage that is in line with the logic and policy of purifying uncertainties in the public domain. The Tosefta brings the following story from Temple times:

> Rabbi Shimon ben Azzai said: It happened that bones were found in Jerusalem, in the woodshed, and the sages wanted to render all of Jerusalem impure. Rabbi Yehoshua said to them: It would be shameful and disgraceful for us to deem the home of our forefathers impure. Where are

19. The attempt to come to terms with the possibility of trafficking in the public domain can be detected in other contexts in the Mishnah that have nothing to do with rules of uncertainties. Mishnah *Shekalim* attests to the following traffic patterns:

> Any spittle found in Jerusalem is pure, except [that found] in the upper market—the words of Rabbi Meir. Rabbi Yosah says: During other times of the year, [whatever spittle is found] in the middle [of the road] is deemed impure, [but] at the sides [of the road] is deemed pure. But on festivals, [whatever spittle is found] in the middle [of the road] is deemed pure, [but] at the sides [of the road] is deemed impure, for the minority moves over to the sides. (*m. Shekalim* 8:1)

Saul Lieberman points out the connection between this *mishnah* and the earlier description from the *Letter of Aristeas*: "There are steps too which lead up to the cross roads, and some people are always going up, and others down and they keep as far apart from each other as possible on the road because of those who are bound by the rules of purity, lest they should touch anything which is unlawful" (trans. R. H. Charles, *The Apocrypha and Pseudepigrapha of the Old Testament in English: With Introductions and Critical and Explanatory Notes to the Several Books* [Oxford: Clarendon, 1913], 2:106–7; Lieberman's note appears in his Hebrew translation of the letter (*Meḥkarim Be-Torat Eretz Yisrael*, ed. D. Rosenthal [Jerusalem: Magnes, 1991], 471). The rules that took shape for dealing with general uncertainty deal with the same question but in a more general, sweeping fashion.

> the corpses from the Deluge? Where are those killed by Nebuchadnezzar? Where are those who were killed in war thus far? Rather, they said: Certain [impurity] is deemed impure; uncertain [impurity] is deemed pure. (*t. Eduyot* 3:3)

The discovery of bones in an unexpected place like the woodshed in the northeast corner of the Women's Court on the Temple Mount triggered an attempt by the sages to deem the entire city impure.[20] Rabbi Yehoshua rejects this attempt to declare Jerusalem impure as a disgrace and an embarrassment. Uncertainties like these are self-defeating since they would lead to endless anxieties about the dead from the battles of the distant and not-too-distant past were scattered through the layers of Jerusalem's soil.[21] The defiant question "Where?," which Rabbi Yehoshua levels against those who purported to render the city impure, signifies the hopelessness of trying to create a space where purity is certain. A life of uncertainty was decreed upon those who were meticulous about purity, and the rule "Certain [impurity] is deemed impure; uncertain [impurity] is deemed pure" provides a foothold in spaces where there is no certainty.

In both of these broad realms, forbidden foods and impurity, the rules governing uncertainty do not reflect a paralyzing dread of uncertainty. Rather, in a profound sense, they indicate the opposite: the rules governing uncertainty were created to enable contact and interaction with spaces that invite uncertainty—the market in the case of forbidden foods, and the public domain with respect to purity and impurity. The basic principles that guide halakhic instruction for uncertainty, as it took shape in Tannaitic literature, thus reflect an antisectarian sensibility with respect to purity and impurity—a sensibility that emerges from the sages' rulings

20. See *m. Midot* 2:5: "In the northeast was the chamber of the woodshed, where physically blemished priests would check the wood for worms. Any wood in which a worm was found was unfit for use on the altar."

21. In *b. Zevaḥim* 113a, Rabbi Yehoshua's words—"Where are the corpses from the Deluge? Where are those killed by Nebuchadnezzar?"—are taken as proof that the city was inspected and cleared of corpses and is therefore not suspected of being impure. See Rashi to *b. Zevaḥim*, s.v. *"ayeh harugei Nebuchadnezzar?"*: "He killed therein, [the corpses] were all cleared, and not even one can be found therein. It must have been inspected." It is apparent, however, from the plain meaning of the Tosefta that Rabbi Yehoshua's statement about the corpses from the Deluge and from Nebuchadnezzar does not prove that the city was inspected, but is a sharp, defiant comment on the sages' unending uncertainties. If Rabbi Yehoshua really thought that the city was inspected, it is difficult to explain why he invokes the principle, "Certain [impurity] is deemed impure; uncertain [impurity] is deemed pure," in his defense of Jerusalem's purity.

This Tosefta passage is discussed by Vered Noam in *From Qumran to the Rabbinic Revolution*, 201–3 and n. 66. On the possible connection between this episode and the attempt, described by Josephus, to make the Temple impure by scattering the bones of human corpses on it, see Yael Fisch's discussion in "Bones in the Temple," in *Between Josephus and the Rabbis* [Hebrew], ed. Tal Ilan and Vered Noam (Jerusalem: Yad Ben Zvi, 2017), 485–92.

about uncertainties of forbidden foods as well. With respect to matters of purity, the innovation is even more far-reaching, because enabling one who is meticulous about purity laws to participate in the public domain demands, as noted, a more sweeping law, tendency of to leave things as they are, 169 toward uncertainty than in cases of forbidden foods. Likewise, the rules of conduct in cases of uncertainty about forbidden foods do not reinterpret the most basic distinction between the prohibited and permitted. In contrast, the distinction between public and private domain with respect to purity and impurity redefines the meaning of the very distinction between purity and impurity since, prima facie, the primary meaning of the division between the pure and the impure is to create a barrier and to segregate. By determining that uncertain impurity in the private domain, but not the public domain, is impure, Tannaitic literature, in effect, "privatizes" concern for uncertain purity, limiting it to a space in which one is separated from others in any event and can control the immediate environment.

The continuation of this trend in shaping the rules for uncertain purity finds expression in another, and perhaps identical, rule concerning uncertain purity and impurity:

> If a deaf-mute, a fool, or a minor is found in an alley that has impurity in it, they are presumed to be pure. But anyone fully competent is assumed to be impure. Anyone who does not have sufficient understanding to be questioned is presumed pure when there is uncertainty. (*m. Taharot* 3:6)

This *mishnah* limits the principle that uncertain impurity in a private domain is deemed impure. The principle applies only with respect to persons who can clarify whether they came into contact with impurity. Deaf-mutes, minors, or fools, who do not possess the capacity to answer whether they became impure or not, remain pure in cases of uncertainty. This guideline also reflects a nominalist view, for if impurity is inherently dangerous, it would not matter whether its suspected carrier had the capacity to answer questions about it. The meaning of this distinction is, in reality, an extension of the view that distinguishes between public and private domains. As mentioned, this view is based on the notion that people can control their environment in the private domain but not the public domain. Therefore, uncertain impurity is deemed impure in a private domain.[22]

22. In her important work on purity, Mira Balberg locates the emphasis on the capacity of human control as a defining feature of resolving uncertainty in relation to the emergence of the self and the subject as central to rabbinic conceptions of purity and impurity. According to the reading offered by Balberg, the reality of "objective" impurity as such does not constitute impurity but rather the subjective element of not caring enough about being in a condition of impurity. This is a very fruitful suggestion, but it seems that, if the main concern was the responsiblity put on the subject for being impure, in principle an alternative sectarian position could have been recommended in which the self must create an isolated all-

However, one can only be in control if one can ascertain whether there is impurity. If someone does not have the capacity to answer questions, there can be no ascertainment, and so when it comes to such a person, uncertainty is deemed pure even in the private domain.[23] That the possibility of clarification is the essential element of the distinction emerges from the following discussion in the Tosefta:

> A child that was holding its father's hand or riding on its father's shoulders is deemed impure, since its father can be asked about it. The uncertainty of a deaf-mute, fool, or minor is deemed pure, because they do not have the intelligence to answer questions. Rabbi Shimon said: In this, the letter of the law is lacking. (*t. Taharot* 3:6)[24]

The rule that the uncertainties of one lacking the capacity to answer is deemed pure is not contingent on any of that person's specific qualities, but because it is impossible to ascertain whether that person became impure. Therefore, when a child stays close to its older father, holding his hand or riding on his shoulders, the father can answer the question of whether the child became impure, so in such a case, uncertainty is deemed impure.[25]

The law of the Dead Sea sect did not engage with uncertainty, and its

---

encompssing world that can ensure purity. See Mira Balberg, *Purity, Body, and Self in Early Rabbinic Literature* (Berkeley: University of California Press, 2014), 42–44.

23. Another ruling for a case of uncertainty that limits the rule that uncertain impurity in the private domain is deemed impure appears in a collection of uncertainties about pure items in the Mishnah. It, too, is related to the ability to control and govern the private domain:

> If there is a vermin in the mouth of a weasel and it is walking on loaves of terumah, and it is uncertain whether it touched them or not, its uncertainty is pure.
>
> If there is a vermin in the mouth of a weasel or a carcass in the mouth of a dog, and they passed among pure items, or pure items passed among them, their uncertainty is deemed pure because the impurity has no [fixed] place. If they [the dog or weasel] were picking at them on the ground, and someone says, "I went to that place, but I do not know if I touched [the vermin or the carcass] or not, his uncertainly is deemed impure, because the impurity has a [fixed] place. (*m. Taharot* 4:2-3)

Impurity that is moving and has no fixed place does not render other things impure by virtue of an uncertainty such as this, apparently because it is impossible to control a trafficked space like this.

24. See Rabbi Shimshon of Sens's definition of "have the capacity to answer questions": "If he is asked, 'Did you touch this impurity?' he can answer, 'Yes,' 'No,' or 'I don't know'" (commentary on *m. Taharot* 3:8). Rabbi Shimon's statement "In this, the letter of the law is lacking" demands clarification. Does he disagree with the rule that the uncertainty of one who does not have the intelligence to answer questions is deemed pure? Or does he think that, even when the child is holding the father's hand or riding on his shoulders, the father cannot be asked, and so the uncertainty is deemed pure?

25. As with the distinction between domains, here, too, the question of how the distinction between one who has the intelligence to answer questions and one who does not have this intelligence relates to other rules for deciding uncertainty—such as majority and

isolated sectarian structure was geared toward avoiding friction with doubt. Nevertheless, we have direct evidence from its writings that the sect rejected the distinction between a person who can be questioned and a person who cannot be questioned. This rejection can teach us a great deal about the gap between the sectarian structure and early rabbinic law: "And also concerning the blind [who cannot see: they should keep themselves from all uncleanness,] and uncleaness of [the sin] offering these do not see. [And al]so concerning the deaf who have not heard the law [and the pr]ecept and the purity regulation, and have not [h]eard the precepts of Israel, for whoever neither sees nor hears, does not [k]now how to behave. But these are approaching the pu[ri]ty of the temple" (4Q394 [4QMMT[a]] 8 III, 19–IV, 4).[26] This polemical passage criticizes the practice of allowing the blind and the deaf to enter the temple. It is apparent that the rabbinic exemption of the ones who cannot be questioned from doubtful impurity is a kind of response to this sort of criticism. The sectarian dread of doubt blocks the sacred domain from the entry of people who are incapable of being meticulous about purity and their presence might defile people who come in contact with them.

It is important to note that the policy that emerges from the rules governing uncertainty with respect to purity and impurity in Tannaitic literature cannot be explained by means of the simplistic generalization that the sages tend to be lenient with regard to matters of purity. If that were so, the sages' rulings would be far less interesting than they are. The stringency–leniency axis is not a mold into which all the sages' rulings on

---

ḥazakah—arises. This question seems to be the subject of a Tannaitic dispute. The Mishnah mentions the following cases:

> [If] a young child found at the edge of graveyard with lilies in his hand, and the only lilies are in an impure place, he is pure, for I may say: Someone else picked them and gave them to him. Similarly, the vessels on a donkey [found] among the graves are pure.
>
> [If] a child was found alongside dough, and a piece of it was in his hand: Rabbi Meir considers it pure, and the sages consider it impure, because children touch things. (*m. Taharot* 3:7–8)

It seems that the dispute between the sages and Rabbi Meir is about the degree to which the child's inability to answer questions remains decisive even when the likelihood of impurity is considered very high, as in a case where the child was found next to the dough with a piece of it in his hand. See the formulation of Maimonides:

> When do we say that the uncertainty of someone who does not have the intelligence to answer questions is pure? When [the uncertainty] was balanced and there was no *ḥazakah*. However, if it is known to have a presumption [*ḥazakah*] that it became impure, it is impure. For example, if an impure child was found alongside dough, with a piece of it in his hand, the dough is impure, because children touch things, thus creating a presumption. (*Laws of Other Sources of Impurity* 16:3)

26. *The Dead Sea Scrolls Study Edition*, ed. Florentino García Martínez and Eibert J. C. Tigchelaar, 2 vols. (Leiden: Brill, 1997–1998), 2:793.

uncertainty can be forced, because in the same sense that the sages are lenient with respect to the public domain, they are stringent with respect to the private domain. Moreover, as Mira Balberg showed in her work on purity and impurity in rabbinic law, the entire Order of *Taharot* reflects an expansion of the potential of impurity much further than was called forth in biblical law, which certainly cannot be classified in terms of leniencies and stringencies.[27] The rules governing uncertainty do not simply reflect a tendency toward leniency but institute a complex structure of meticulous observance without segregation. The isolation that the laws of purity requires is primarily observed in private space, not in the public domain. Those who are meticulous about purity will be very selective about whom they host and by whom they are hosted, because uncertainty about purity in the private domain is deemed impure. However, this meticulousness does not require them to separate from the public space and isolate themselves in a private, sectarian space, because uncertain impurity in the public domain is deemed pure.

III

The sages' creative attempt to find a scriptural basis for the distinction between public and private domains in the passage of the "straying wife" (Num 5:11–31) highlights the sheer novelty of the rulings they constituted for deciding uncertainty. The passage of the straying wife is one of three scriptural passages that give instruction for uncertain situations. It establishes that a husband overcome by jealousy for his wife brings her to the Temple, where she undergoes a divine ordeal intended to ascertain whether the husband's suspicions are justified. The sages understood this to mean that the process by which the woman is investigated is based on testimony that she secluded herself with another man; it is this seclusion that forms the evidentiary basis for examining the woman. The sages likewise establish that once the husband has warned his wife, if she subsequently secludes herself with another man, she is sexually prohibited to her husband—out of uncertainty—until the uncertainty is resolved in the Temple. The presumption that seclusion is not part of the husband's suspicion but rather the evidentiary basis for bringing the wife to the Temple for examination, and the assertion that after his warning and her subsequent seclusion, attested to by witnesses, she is forbidden to her husband until after the uncertainty is resolved in the Temple, were innovations of the sages in their exegesis of the scriptural passage. These rulings serve the Midrash in its attempt to base rulings on uncertain purities

27. See Balberg, *Purity, Body, and Self*, 27–39.

and impurities on the precedent of the straying wife's prohibition to her husband, based on uncertainty:

> And from here you extend the ruling to [the impurity caused by a] vermin: If in an instance [i.e., the case of the "straying wife"] where unwillingness is not equated with consent, uncertainty is equated with certainty, then in an instance where unwillingness [i.e., inadvertent contact with vermin] is equated with consent, certainly uncertainty should be equated with certainty! And just as here it refers to a private domain, there, too, it must refer to a private domain. Just as here we are dealing with a subject who has the intelligence to be questioned, there, too, we must be dealing with a subject who has the intelligence to be questioned. Based on this they ruled: Uncertain impurity in the private domain is deemed impure; uncertain impurity in the public domain is deemed pure. Uncertainty of someone with the intelligence to be questioned is impure; uncertainty of one who lacks the intelligence to be questioned is deemed pure. (*Sifrei Bamidbar*, Kahana edition, 28–29)

According to the Midrash, the rule that uncertain impurity in the private domain is deemed impure is derived by equating it to a woman who secluded herself and thus became forbidden out of uncertainty. Just as the woman is forbidden to her husband out of uncertainty, so too, uncertainty about whether one touched an impure object renders one impure. The rule of uncertain impurity is derived a fortiori: touching an impure object renders one impure whether or not one intended to touch it, whereas if a woman is raped, she is not forbidden to her husband. The equation between the prohibition of a woman who secluded herself with another man and uncertain impurity limits the impurity rendered by uncertainty to the private domain, according to the Midrash. Just as the woman is forbidden out of uncertainty only if she secluded herself in a private domain, so too, uncertain impurity renders one who touches it impure only in the private domain, whereas in the public domain, such uncertainty is deemed pure. The Midrash also establishes that just as the woman can be questioned to clarify the uncertainty, so too, an uncertain impurity in the private domain renders impure only one who can be questioned as to whether or not he is impure.

This analogy between the laws of the straying wife and the laws of purity and impurity seems quite contrived at first glance. The woman is forbidden to her husband because of an uncertainty in the private domain, not the public domain, because her seclusion in the private domain with another man makes her suspect. No uncertainty or suspicion about this woman arose in the public domain because she could not have a secret rendezvous or be alone with a man in public. The basic logic that distinguishes between a hiding place and a public place in the case of the straying wife does not exist in the case of impurity. Unlike the case of the straying wife, in the case of purity and impurity, the difference between domains is immaterial to the chances of becoming impure or remaining pure. Moreover, the woman's seclusion with another man, according to the sages' halakhah, itself constitutes a sinful act, because she is inviting the possibility of sin, a consideration that certainly does not apply to a person who may have become impure in the private domain. The artifice of the equation between the straying wife and impurity in the private domain shows that the sages had an independent rationale for distinguishing the private domain from the public with regard to impurity, and they attached their innovation to the scriptural passage in which an uncertainty that emerges only in a private domain renders a woman "impure." This farfetched comparison shows how far the Midrash went to turn uncertain impurity into a question that arises specifically in the context of a person in the private domain, which of course goes against the straightforward meaning of the distinction between pure and impure, whose purpose is to segregate.

Tosefta *Taharot* records a different version of the *midrash* of *Sifrei* and cites another explanation of the source of the distinction between domains:

> They asked Ben Zoma: Why is uncertainty in the private domain deemed impure? He answered them: What is a straying woman to her husband, a certainty or an uncertainty? They said to him: An uncertainty. He said to them: We find that she is forbidden to her husband, and from here you extend the ruling to vermin. Just as here it refers to a private domain, there, too, it refers to a private domain. Just as here we are dealing with a subject who has the intelligence to be questioned, there, too, we must be dealing with a subject who has the intelligence to be questioned. Based on this they ruled: Someone with the intelligence to be questioned—in the private domain, his uncertainty is impure; in the public domain, his uncertainty is deemed pure.
>
> And why is an uncertainty in the public domain deemed pure? He answered them: We find that the public may sacrifice the Paschal offering in a state of impurity as long as most of them are impure. So, if certain impurity is permitted for the public, certainly uncertain impurity is.
>
> Rabban Shimon ben Gamliel says: Why is uncertainty in the private domain deemed impure, while uncertainty in the public domain is deemed pure? Because an individual can be questioned, but the masses cannot be questioned. (*t. Taharot* 6:12)

The Tosefta, which attributes the exegesis of *Sifrei* to Ben Zoma, adds a unique source for the ruling that uncertain impurity in the public domain is deemed pure. This addition seems appropriate because, although the law of the straying wife teaches that uncertain impurity in the private domain is deemed impure, it cannot be derived from there that uncertain impurity in the public domain is deemed pure. In contrast to uncertain impurity in the public domain, where the uncertainty can arise in either the public or private domain, the uncertainty about the straying wife cannot arise in the public domain. The Tosefta therefore brings another, independent source for the rule that uncertain impurity in the public domain is deemed pure, deriving it from a law that permits the Paschal offering in cases where most of the populace is impure: if the Paschal offering can be brought when most of the populace is impure for certain, a fortiori an uncertain impurity in public is deemed permitted to the populace.

This derivation is no less forced than the derivation about the private domain from the episode of the straying wife. The comparison of the Paschal offering to the public domain could be rejected, it seems, if we note that the license to bring the offering when most of the populace is impure is unique to the Paschal offering, which must be brought at a particular time and whose offering supersedes impurity when most of the populace is involved. There is no such consideration, of course, in a regular case of uncertain impurity in the public domain, where there is no commandment that must be fulfilled immediately, forcing the purification of the uncertainty. It seems that the only way to grant the comparison to the Paschal offering any acceptable meaning is by shifting the focus of the license to bring the offering when most of the populace is impure from a duty to perform the Paschal offering at the proper time to a more fundamental idea: that impurity cannot be ascribed to the majority of the populace.[28] Accordingly, the permissibility of bringing the Paschal offering when most of the populace is impure hinges not on the importance of bringing the offering at the proper time superseding the impurity of the masses, but on the more basic claim that there is no room to discern the pure from the impure when most of the populace is impure.[29] With the claim that the majority of the populace cannot become impure, the comparison of the Paschal offering to uncertain impurity in public becomes

---

28. The law that the populace does not defer the Paschal offering to the makeup date (*Pesaḥ Sheni*) if most of its constituents are impure is likewise derived exegetically. See *Sifrei Bamidbar* §70 (Kahana edition, 170); *Sifrei Zuta* on Num 9:7 (Horowitz edition, 259). See also the Tannaitic dispute in *t. Pesaḥim* 8:4–5.

29. The Mishnah teaches the following principle:

> There are [aspects] of public offerings that are not present in individual offerings: Public offerings override the Sabbath and impurity, whereas individual offerings override neither the Sabbath nor impurity. Rabbi Meir said: Are not the High Priest's griddle-offering and the bull he offers on Yom Kippur individual offerings? Yet they override the Sabbath and impurity! Rather, [the reason that certain offerings override the Sabbath and impurity is] because their time is fixed. (*m. Temurah* 2:1)

See also *t. Temurah* 1:16. Perhaps the sages' view is that impurity does not devolve on the populace. On this, see the dispute in *b. Yoma* 6b about whether corpse impurity is "permitted" (*hutrah*) or "overridden" (*deḥuyah*) with respect to the populace. To all indications, this question is the subject of an Amoraic dispute.

clear, because most of the people in the public domain are of uncertain purity. Since impurity cannot be ascribed to an entire populace, there is no room for uncertain impurity in this domain. The claim could have been formulated as follows: The distinction between impure and pure is indeed intended to segregate the pure from the impure, but its role is to separate the pure majority from the impure minority, not vice versa. The claim that most of the populace cannot be impure thus negates the view that distinguishing purity from impurity is intended to define the majority as being impure and to segregate the pure minority from the impure majority. A view that would ascribe impurity to the majority is in fact the foundation of sectarian thinking, where a small minority self-segregates to a pure space, isolated from the majority that it deems impure. Such a minority, like the Dead Sea sect, abandons the Temple and Jerusalem in favor of its own pure encampment, viewing the majority of the populace, as well as the Temple and city, as being impure.[30] Thus, the equation of the Paschal offering by an impure majority to the purification of the public domain from uncertainty is based on the rejection of the idea that an entire populace can be impure and enfold within itself the antisectarian sensibility that undergirds the sages' innovative formulation of the laws of uncertainty.

In addition to Ben Zoma's exegesis, the Tosefta cites Rabban Shimon ben Gamliel, who offers a different source for the distinction between public and private domains. His approach appeals directly to the logic undergirding the principles of uncertain purity without relying on any scriptural precedent: "Rabban Shimon ben Gamliel says: Why is uncertainty in the private domain deemed impure, while uncertainty in the public domain is deemed pure? Because an individual can be questioned, but the masses cannot be questioned." Rabban Shimon ben Gamliel reduces the two major premises governing uncertainty to one by collapsing the distinction between domains into the distinction between those who can be questioned and those who cannot. This identification is based

30. In its literature, the Judean Desert sect describes itself as having separated and segregated themselves from "the people" or from "the majority of the people." For example, in 4QMMT[d]: "[You know that] we separated from the majority of the people and from all their impurities" (4Q397 fragments 14–21, line 7; Elisha Qimron, *The Dead Sea Scrolls: The Hebrew Writings* [Hebrew] [Jerusalem: Yad Ben Zvi, 2013], 2:210); in the Damascus Document: "And thus is the law for the penitents of Israel: Turn from the path of the people in love of God" (CD VIII, 16; Qimron, *Dead Sea Scrolls*, 1:18). On the language of segregation and its features in the literature of the Judean Desert sect, see Adiel Shremer, "Seclusion and Exclusion: The Rhetoric of Separation in Qumran and Tannaitic Literature," in *Rabbinic Perspectives: Rabbinic Literature and the Dead Sea Scrolls; Proceedings of the Eighth International Symposium of the Orion Center for the Study of the Dead Sea Scrolls and Associated Literature, 7–9 January, 2003*, ed. Steven D. Fraade, Aharon Shemesh, and Ruth A. Clements, STDJ 62 (Leiden: Brill, 2006), 127–45.

on the claim that, in the public domain, people cannot really be certain whether they have touched or come into contact with impurity. "The masses cannot be questioned." In contrast, in the private domain, one has real knowledge of who enters and exits, and he can ascertain whether he has become impure. Although Rabban Shimon ben Gamliel does not say this explicitly, it is implied by his claim that the purpose of distinguishing between domains is to enable movement in the public domain, relegating the duty to be careful about uncertain impurity to the private domain alone.

IV

After the Mishnah sharply formulates its central rule for uncertainty—"A case of uncertainty in the private domain is impure until he says, 'I did not touch [it].' A case of uncertainty in the public domain is pure until he says, 'I touched [it]'"—it turns to defining what constitutes a private domain and a public domain with regard to purity: "Which is a public domain?" (*m. Taharot* 6:6). In the ensuing series of *mishnayot*, the definition of domains for the purposes of purity and impurity takes shape, in contrast to and in comparison with their definitions for the purpose of the Sabbath laws. On the Sabbath, a person is prohibited from moving an object from the private domain to the public domain and vice versa. The definition of the public and private domains concerning the Sabbath was therefore a matter of legal importance that was highly developed in Tannaitic literature. The unique articulation of the nature of the public domain for the purpose of the laws of purity, in comparison with and in contrast to the Sabbath, provided by the Mishnah, reflects the idea underlying the rules governing uncertain purity:

> The [narrow, steep, and winding] paths of Beit Gulgul, and those like them, are a private domain with regard to the Sabbath, but a public domain with regard to impurity. Rabbi Elazar says: the paths of Beit Gulgul were only mentioned because they are a private domain with respect to both. The paths that lead to pits, cisterns, caves, and wine presses are each a private domain with respect to the Sabbath, but a public domain with respect to impurity.
>
> A valley in the summer time is a private domain with respect to the Sabbath and a public domain with respect to impurity; and in the rainy season it is a private domain with respect to both.
>
> A basilica is a private domain with respect to the Sabbath, but a public domain with respect to impurity. Rabbi Yehudah says: if one who stands in one entrance can see those who enter and exit through the other entrance, it is a private domain with respect to both; if not, it is a private domain with respect to the Sabbath and a public domain with respect to impurity.

> A forum is a private domain with respect to the Sabbath, but a public domain with respect to impurity, as are the sides. Rabbi Meir says: the sides are a private domain with respect to both.
>
> A colonnade is a private domain with respect to the Sabbath but a public domain with respect to impurity. A courtyard which the masses enter into through and exit from is a private domain with respect to the Sabbath but a public domain with respect to impurity. (*m. Taharot* 6:6–10)

The Mishnah organizes this series of laws by means of a list of places that are considered private domains with respect to the laws of the Sabbath yet are still considered public domains with respect to purity.[31] The common element of all of the spaces enumerated in the Mishnah is that even though, for reasons internal to the halakhot of the Sabbath, they are not considered public domains, the masses can nevertheless be found in such spaces, and there is no way for someone to know for certain whether he will come into contact with impurity. Thus, for example, a basilica is considered a private domain with regard to the Sabbath because it is a closed, walled structure, but since many people visit it, as it is a public building, with regard to purity and impurity it is considered a public domain. The Mishnah mentions the view of Rabbi Yehudah, who maintains that, if one person can see all of the entrances of the basilica at once, and he can tell who is entering and exiting, then this public building is considered a private domain even with respect to purity and impurity. Rabbi Yehudah's qualification isolates the factor that defines a public domain for matters of purity: the inability to observe and know who is coming and going.

Likewise, a courtyard through which the public enters and exits is another obvious example of a space that is not considered a public domain with respect to the Sabbath, as it is surrounded by a fence, yet is still considered a public domain for purity and impurity, because the masses can be found there. The same goes for fenced paths that lead to wells; they are not considered public domains with regard to the Sabbath because they are not open at both ends but lead to one specific place where the path ends. However, since many people frequent and move along these paths, they are considered public domains with respect to purity and impurity.[32] The definition of a public domain for the purposes of purity and impurity is driven by the idea of including one who is pure in the uncertain places so that his movement through the public domain and through public

31. In the Mishnah, spaces are defined as private domains with respect to the Sabbath even if they are considered a *karmelit* (semiprivate domain) with respect to the laws of the Sabbath. The emphasis is therefore that they do not constitute a public domain with respect to the Sabbath. See, on this, the commentary of Rabbi Shimshon of Sens, *m. Taharot* 6:6, s.v. *"reshut ha-yaḥid le-Shabbat."*

32. See also *t. Yoma* 1:3.

gathering places is possible, free of the paralyzing fear of uncertain impurity.[33] The element of motion is emphasized by Rabbi Yose in the Tosefta:

> If vessels are spread out in the public domain, more than ten handbreadths above ground, and someone impure passes by, and it is uncertain whether he moved [the vessels] or not: Rabbi Yaakov deems them impure and Rabbi Yose deems them pure. For Rabbi Yaakov said that anything more than ten handbreadths above ground in a public domain is like a private domain, whereas Rabbi Yose says that anything whose path of travel is in the public domain is deemed pure. (*t. Taharot* 7:2)

Although a space more than ten handbreadths above ground is considered a private domain with regard to the laws of the Sabbath, it is considered a public domain with respect to purity, according to Rabbi Yose, because contact with this space is part of the normal course through the public domain.[34]

The reason for the difference in shaping the definition of domains for the purposes of addressing uncertain purity and impurity, on the one hand, and the Sabbath laws, on the other, leads the Mishnah to enumerate cases where the opposite holds, that is, places that are considered public domains for the Sabbath laws but private domains with respect to purity and impurity:

> If someone climbed to the top of a tree standing in a public domain that has something impure within it, and it is uncertain whether he touched [the impurity] or not, its uncertainty is impure. If someone put his hand into a hole containing something impure, and it is uncertain whether he touched it or did not touch it, its uncertainty is impure. (*m. Taharot* 6:3)

Climbing to the top of a tree and putting one's hand into a hole in the public domain are not part of the typical use of the public domain, so even

---

33. See *t. Taharot* 8:8: "It happened that someone forgot vessels in a synagogue. The incident came before the sages, and they deemed [the synagogue] pure, for it is not an entirely private domain." This passage, though not part of the Mishnah's series of cases that define domains differently for purposes of purity, transmits the same view using a different formulation: "for it is not an entirely private domain."

34. See the words of R. Yose in *m. Taharot* 5:2:

> One who said, "I touched this thing and I do not know if it is impure or if it is pure," or "I touched one, but I do not know which of the two I touched"—Rabbi Akiva deems him impure, but the sages deem him pure. Rabbi Yose deems them all impure but deems the path pure, because it is normal for a person to walk but is not normal for a person to touch.

The definition of the public domain for the purposes of purity is thus more reminiscent of its definition for purposes of damages. Exemptions from liability for damages caused in the public domain are designed to enable normal, familiar movement in that space and thus transfer the cost of damage to the damaged party. See, e.g., *m. Bava Kamma* 3:5; *t. Bava Kamma* 2:11.

though these places are considered public domain with respect to the Sabbath, they are defined as private domains with respect to purity and impurity, and their uncertainty is deemed impure. Maimonides formulated this principle as follows:

> Some places are not the private domain with respect to the Sabbath but are nevertheless the private domain with respect to impurity, because the masses do not utilize them. They are: trees and holes in the public domain, even if they are not four by four [cubits]. (*Mishneh Torah,* Laws of Other Sources of Impurity 20:8)

The potential utility of the public domain is what dictates the parameters of the domain for the purposes of deciding uncertain purity and impurity.

The Mishnah and Tosefta, as usual, address unique situations that serve as precise test cases to clarify when a person crosses the boundary of normal use of the public domain such that with a minor change in action, the environment goes from being a public domain to a private domain.

> A crate in the public domain, ten handbreadths tall, has impurity within it. If it is uncertain whether or not he touched it, he is deemed pure. If he inserted his hand into it, and it is uncertain whether or not he touched it, his uncertainty is deemed impure.... A donkey in the public domain, ten handbreadths tall, has impurity atop it. If it is uncertain whether or not he touched it, his uncertainty is deemed pure. If he extended his hand atop it, and it is uncertain whether or not he touched it, his uncertainty is deemed impure. (*t. Taharot* 7:1)

The rules for uncertainty are meant to enable one to move through the public domain. Therefore, uncertain impurity caused by such movement is deemed pure, whereas placing one's hand inside a box or on top of a donkey represents the cessation of such movement. These actions are not part of the way one traverses the public domain, so uncertainty in such situations is deemed impure. Defining domains to the most subtle level of detail is therefore organized in accordance with the broader conception that forms the foundation of the unusual rules governing uncertainty about purity and impurity. This rule, which enables participation in the public domain, undermines, as we have seen, the basic meaning of the distinction between pure and impure, the heart of which, prima facie, is the idea of segregation.[35]

Such a profound change in the essence of the distinction between purity and impurity is made possible in Tannaitic literature, first and foremost, by liberation from the view of impurity as an intrinsically harmful

35. The attempt to remain meticulous about purity while enabling complex integration into the environment emerges in other areas of the halakhot of purity as well, not only in the laws of uncertainties. Yair Furstenberg addresses this trend in Tannaitic literature (*Purity and Community in Antiquity,* 120–44, 340–44.

metaphysical substance. Had impurity really been considered "poisonous," it would not have been possible to formulate a doctrine of uncertainty like the one produced by the sages. Once the limitations imposed by a dangerous substance were removed, it became possible to entertain various policy considerations that could guide decision making in cases of uncertainty. These policy considerations led to the creation of rules that include those who meticulously maintain purity even in spaces that are saturated with uncertainty, and it is in this policy that a profound shift in the purpose of distinguishing purity from impurity finds expression. We saw a similar structure in uncertainties about forbidden foods, where the nominalist view of prohibition makes possible a way to decide matters of uncertainty based on a simple majority and predicated on the ability to integrate into a different uncertainty-filled space, namely, the marketplace. Nevertheless, it is in the realm of purity and impurity that the sages' teachings on uncertainty reach their greatest and most creative expression.[36] For all of the novelty in following the majority on matters of forbid-

36. In their creative engagement with uncertainty in the realm of purity, as in the realm of prohibited foods, the sages address situations that straddle the border between the practical and the hypothetical. These borderline cases primarily serve an independent theoretical interest through which new questions are raised and new and complex conceptual insights are developed. One of the most spectacular instances of this sort of exercise is the series of *mishnayot* that imagines and discusses cases of uncertainty arising when one walks along a path (*m. Taharot* 5:2-5). The discussion begins with a relatively common case of uncertainty: a person walks along a path and does not know whether there is a grave on that path, or whether the path is impure for other reasons. Under the rule of uncertain impurity in the public domain, the pedestrian is deemed pure. The Mishnah then addresses a less-common case, which opens the door to a wide range of additional cases. In this second case, there are two paths, one of which is certainly impure—though we do not know which—and the pedestrian took one of these paths. The ensuing discussion is about the status of *terumah* that the pedestrian touched after walking on each one of these paths. The pedestrian is clearly impure, because he took both paths. Sometimes, however, each path can be treated as a separate case and each can be determined to have the status of uncertain impurity in a public domain, which is deemed pure. For instance, in a case where a person was deemed pure after traversing the first path, then ate *terumah*, and then traversed the second path and touched other *terumah*, the two traversals are treated as separate cases, and each path is deemed pure on the basis of uncertainty. Conversely, when both *terumot* are still extant, the two traversals are treated as a single case, and since the person is certainly impure, the status of the *terumot* changes. The Mishnah continues developing this discussion by presenting situations where two different people traversed these two paths, creating a paradox in which, under certain conditions, both are deemed pure even though it is obvious that one of them is impure. That is, in a case where each comes to court separately to inquire about their status, the court issues a separate ruling for each one, deeming him pure on account of its being a case of uncertain purity in the public domain—even though it is obvious that one of them is certainly impure:

> Two paths, one impure and one pure: if someone walked down one of them and then prepared pure things, and then his fellow came and walked down the second one and prepared pure things, Rabbi Yehudah says: If each one of them inquired

den foods, the majoritarian principle is supported by certain precedents and statistical logic. In contrast, the distinction between domains in matters of purity and impurity is unprecedented and is free even of considerations of majority and minority. In the public domain, even where most are impure, an uncertainty is deemed pure. The shared antisectarian sensibility that shapes the rules of each of these realms is expressed even more sharply with respect to matters of purity, because it asserts that the fear of uncertainty, which is supposed to create separation and segregation, exists only in the private domain, where one stands apart and is in control. The implication of sectarian existence is the creation of a social environment where there is a blatant attempt to restrict entry into places of rampant uncertainty. The total, all-encompassing environment of sectarian existence is supposed to minimize the interactions that generate uncertainties, and so the sectarian world does not formulate rules for dealing with uncertainty. Rather, such sects try to create environments in which uncertainties do not arise. The rules of governing uncertainty about forbidden foods and impurity alike that are found in Tannaitic literature reflect a complex portrait of an attempt to be as meticulous as possible without enforcing fully separated communal lives. This attempt is characterized by the laws constituted in early rabbinic sources concerning the marketplace and the public domain.

> individually, they are both pure, but if they inquired together, they are impure. Rabbi Yosah says: in either case they are impure. (*m. Taharot* 5:5)

The "two-path" questions that began with Mishnah *Taharot* formed the basis for later, more complex development in the Bavli (*Pesaḥim* 10a and *Niddah* 2a), as well as in the extensive discussions of uncertainty throughout the ages. A prototypical example of later development that emerged from the cases fashioned in these *mishnayot* is the early eighteenth-century treatment of Rabbi Yehudah Rosanes in his *Mishneh La-melekh* commentary on Maimonides's *Mishneh Torah.* He devotes a separate treatise of sorts to the issue in his comments on Laws of Other Sources of Impurity 19:1. Another Tannaitic unit on the laws of uncertainties that is devoted to "two-paths" cases appears in chapter 2 of Tosefta *Mikva'ot*.

4

Lineage, Uncertainty, and the Boundaries of the Community

I

In the chapter of Mishnah *Makhshirin* devoted to the doctrine of uncertainty, which conveys the sages' independent interest in indeterminate states as a self-contained area of halakhah, the following uncertainty arises in a mixed city of Jews and gentiles:

> If he found a baby cast away therein—if the majority is gentiles, it is a gentile; if the majority is Jews, it is a Jew; half-and-half, it is a Jew. Rabbi Yehudah says: We go by the majority of those who cast away [babies]. (*m. Makhshirin* 2:7)

This chapter, which was discussed above, compiles cases of uncertainty from various domains and renders decisions based on a probability-based majority. Inter alia, it addresses the uncertainties related to tragic and all-too-common cases of abandoned children of unknown parentage.[1] The pedigree of the foundling is unknown, and it is uncertain to which community he belongs, so the sages assert that this uncertainty is decided on the basis of the majority. They disagree, however, about which reference group defines the foundling's status. [2]

Aside from these foundlings of unknown parentage, in other contexts Tannaitic sources discuss babies of known maternity but unknown paternity, and an entire chapter of *Mishnah Yevamot* is devoted to babies that were switched at birth. Uncertainties about lineage and ancestry become an acute halakhic problem, as they are enmeshed in a complex web of

1. For the pervasiveness of abandonment of children in late antiquity and in Roman society, see John Boswell, *The Kindness of Strangers: The Abandoment of Children in Western Europe from Late Antiquity to the Renaissance* (1988; repr., Chicago: University of Chicago Press, 1998), 53–137.

2. Rabbi Yehudah's views are stated more explicitly in *t. Makhshirin* 1:7: "Rabbi Yehudah says: If there was one idolatrous woman or one maidservant there, she is suspected of casting [the baby] away."

forbidden sexual relations, laws governing the priestly caste, levirate marriage, and inheritance claims. In addition to uncertainties with regard to specific cases that apply to individuals, questions of uncertainty about ancestry have a broader communal character, because the absorption into families or communities, in the recent or distant past, of those unfit for marriage is liable to cast doubt on the marriageability of future generations. Unlike uncertainty with regard to forbidden foods, here the dark specter of uncertainty takes on a social character with far-reaching implications; it threatens to shred the basic fabric of coexistence, which is predicated on the possibility of family and blood ties.

Within the social, religious, and economic structure in which pedigree confers an important, built-in advantage, the question of ascertaining and verifying pedigree becomes even weightier. This phenomenon induced aggressive attempts to exclude families from membership in the Jewish community: "The Bet Ẓerifa clan was in the Transjordan, and Ben-Ẓion excluded it by force; another was there, and Ben-Ẓion included it" (*m. Eduyot* 8:7). Such phenomena are liable to cast a pall of uncertainty on "unfit" descendants who escaped detection and assimilated. Explicit expressions of uncertain pedigrees appear already at the beginning of the Second Temple, in the book of Ezra. The major concern of the book as a whole with purity of pedigree and "holy seed" begins with the clarification of the ancestry of the families who migrated from Babylonia to Eretz Yisrael with Ezra, and their division into classes based on pedigree. The detailed list of those who ascended with Ezra includes some whose lineage cannot even be traced with certainty to families of Israel: "The following were those who came up from Tel-melah, Tel-harsha, Cherub, Addan, and Immer – they were unable to tell whether their father's house and descent were Israelite" (Ezra 2:59). Alongside these families of dubious Jewish pedigree are other families whose priestly lineage was uncertain:

> Of the sons of the priests, the sons of Habaiah, the sons of Hakkoz, the sons of Barzillai who had married a daughter of Barzillai and had taken his name—these searched for their genealogical records, but they could not be found, so they were disqualified for the priesthood. The Tirshatha ordered them not to eat of the most holy things until a priest with Urim and Thummim should appear. (Ezra 2:61–63)

The priestly families whose lineage had become suspect were disqualified from eating sanctified food, though the expectation was that their status would ultimately be clarified by divine oracle. The prophet Yeḥezkel distinguishes between the Zadokite priestly families, who remained faithful and worthy of serving in the inner sancta of the Temple, and other priestly families, which, in his words, "forsook Me when Israel went astray" (Ezek

44:10) and in the future will be rejected from serving in the inner sancta.[3] This distinction, and the power granted to the priestly class, invited scrutiny of priestly families, and attestations from the Second Temple era show that there were sectarian tensions that cast aspersions on the purity of lineage of the ministering priests and questioned their connection to the right priestly families.[4] In addition, it is likely that, according to the halakhah of the Dead Sea sect, it was forbidden for priests to marry women from Israelite (non-priestly) families.[5] Anxiety about pedigree is reflected in Josephus Flavius's idyllic and apologetic portrayal of the priestly families' careful preservation of genealogies and of the custom of the priestly families to marry only women from known, verified priestly families.[6]

---

3. See also Ezek 40:46. This view persists in Second Temple literature. Ben Sira articulates it thus: "Blessed be the One who chooses the Zadokites to perform the priestly services" (51:21).

4. The Dead Sea sect viewed its leaders as stemming from the Zadokite priestly family and its members as being loyal to that family. Thus, for example, in the Community Rule:

> This is the rule for all members of the community—that is, for such as have declared their readiness to turn away from all evil and to adhere to all that God in His good pleasure has commanded. They are to keep apart from the company of the froward. They are to belong to the community in both doctrinal and an economic sense. They are to abide by the decisions of the sons of Zadok, the same being priests that still keep the Covenant. (1QS V, 1–2; Qimron, *Dead Sea Scrolls*, 1:218; translation is from T. H. Gaster, *The Dead Sea Scriptures*, rev. and enl. ed. [Garden City, NY: Doubleday Anchor, 1964], 54)

Scholars have suggested that the sectarians disqualified the pedigree of the Hasmonean priests. See Daniel R. Schwartz, "On Two Aspects of a Priestly View of Descent at Qumran," in *Archaeology and History in the Dead Sea Scrolls: The New York University Conference in Memory of Yigael Yadin*, ed. Lawrence H. Schiffman, Journal for the Study of Pseudepigrapha Supplement Series 8 (Sheffield: JSOT Press, 1990), 158–66. For a different view, see Menahem Kister, "Studies in 4QMiqṣat Ma'aśe Ha-Torah and Related Texts: Law, Theology, Language and Calendar" [Hebrew], *Tarbiz* 68 (1990): 317–71, here 323 and n. 21.

5. The possible prohibition on marriage between priests and Israelites arises in a fragment of MMT. See Elisha Qimron and John Strugnell, *Qumran Cave 4.V: Miqṣat Ma'ase ha-Torah*, Discoveries in the Judaean Desert 10 (Oxford: Clarendon, 1994), 171–75. The editors maintain that the scroll forbids such marriages. For support of this view, see Christine Hayes, "Intermarriage and Impurity in Ancient Jewish Sources," *Harvard Theological Review* 92 (1999): 25–35. A different understanding of the fragment is presented in Kister ("Studies in 4QMiqṣat Ma'aśe Ha-Torah," 343–47). According to Philo, the high priest may not marry a woman from an Israelite family, but other priests may (*On the Special Laws* 1.22.110–111). Regarding the concern about the pedigree of the high priesthood, see ibid. 1.19.101.

6. Josephus Flavius, *Against Apion* 1.7 (trans. Whiston):

> For our forefathers did not only appoint the best of these priests, and those that attended upon the divine worship, for that design, from the beginning; but made provision that the stock of the priests should continue unmixed, and pure. For he who is partaker of the priesthood, must propagate of a wife of the same nation; without having any regard to money, or any other dignities: but he is to make a

Rabbinic literature itself documents actions to establish priestly lineage at the high court in the Chamber of Hewn Stone: "There they sat and examined the lineages of the priesthood and the Levites. A priest who was found to be unfit would dress in black, shroud himself in black, and leave; one in whom no disqualification was found would dress in white, shroud himself in white, and serve alongside his brothers, the priests. They would declare a holiday, for no unfitness was found in the seed of Aaron" (*t. Ḥagigah* 2:9).[7]

These descriptions by Josephus and in Tannaitic literature of reliable, meticulously kept pedigree scrolls and of mechanisms for orderly investigations do not necessarily provide reliable historical information, but rather they attest to anxiety about lineage and the importance ascribed to solid confirmation of pedigree and status.[8]

The question of genealogical certainty as it pertains to the priesthood originates in two contexts: (1) the need to establish pedigree so as to justify obtaining priestly privilege; and (2) the need, stemming from the priests' concern about marrying those who are unfit to marry priests, to preserve the purity of marriage. As noted, the general concern over lack of fitness

---

> scrutiny, and take his wife's genealogy from the ancient tables; and procure many witnesses to it. And this is our practice, not only in Judea; but wheresoever any body of men of our nation do live: and even there an exact catalogue of our priests' marriages is kept: I mean at Egypt and at Babylon; or in any other place of the rest of the habitable earth, whithersoever our priests are scattered. For they send to Jerusalem the ancient names of their parents in writing, as well as those of their remoter ancestors: and signify who are the witnesses also. But if any war falls out, such as have fallen out a great many of them already, when Antiochus Epiphanes made an invasion upon our country: as also when Pompey the great, and Quintilius Varus did so also: and principally in the wars that have happened in our own times: those priests that survive them compose new tables of genealogy, out of the old records, and examine the circumstances of the women that remain. For still they do not admit of those that have been captives.... But what is the strongest argument of our exact management in this matter is what I am now going to say; that we have the names of our high priests from father to son set down in our records, for the interval of two thousand years. And if any of these have been transgressors of these rules, they are prohibited to present themselves at the altar.

Also see what Josephus wrote of his own priestly pedigree in the first lines of his *Life*.

7. See *m. Middot* 5:4 and Saul Lieberman's comments in *Tosefta Kifshutah: Beitzah–Ḥagigah* (New York: Jewish Theological Seminary, 1962), 1299, regarding scrolls of lineage that were kept in an archive. *Sifrei Bamidbar* §116 describes another tradition about the investigation of priestly pedigree (see Kahana edition, 4:878, lines 62–63 and n. 119). And see *t. Ketubot* 2:3 and 3:1–3, which describe the procedures for accepting testimony about the priesthood and Levites.

8. For a discussion of the historical value of these attestations, see Raphael Yankelevitz, "Mishkalo shel Ha-yiḥus Ha-mishpaḥti Ba-ḥevrah Ha-Yehudit Be-Eretz Yisrael Be-tekufat Ha-Mishnah Ve-haTalmud" [The Significance of Family Pedigree in Palestinian Jewish Society in the Era of the Mishnah and Talmud], in *Uma Ve-toldoteha*, ed. Menahem Stern (Jerusalem: Zalman Shazar Center, 1983), 1:151–62 and n. 13.

to marry was not limited to priestly clans; it was relevant to the broader community as well, and it presents a crisis that penetrates the underlying structure of the texture of communal life. A study of this topic in the Tannaitic and post-Tannaitic literature present us not with a unified, developed teaching but rather with deep fissures that we must disclose with care and caution; these fissures developed out of the sages' attempt to provide a complex structure of directives in an area for which they had no scriptural precedent and which they developed as a significant portion of their great interest in questions of uncertainty.

The fundamental *mishnayot* that form the staging ground for dealing with these questions appear in Mishnah *Kiddushin* 4:1–3:

> Ten pedigrees came up from Babylonia: priests, Levites, Israelites, *ḥalalei* (offspring of priest and a woman unfit to marry a priest), proselytes, manumitted slaves, *mamzerei* (offspring of certain types of forbidden unions), Gibeonites, *shetukei* (those of unknown paternity), and *asufei* (foundlings). Priests, Levites and Israelites may intermarry with one another. Levites, Israelites, *ḥalalei*, proselytes, and manumitted slaves may intermarry with one another. Proselytes, manumitted slaves, *mamzerim*, Gibeonites, *shetukei*, and *asufei* may intermarry with one another.
>
> These are the *shetukin*: Anyone who knows who his mother is but does not know who his father is. An *asufi* is one who is gathered in (*ne'esaf*) from the street and does not know who either his father or his mother is. Abba Shaul would call the *shetukei*, "*bedukei*" (investigated individuals).
>
> All who are forbidden to enter the community [by marriage] may intermarry with one another. Rabbi Yehudah forbids. Rabbi Elazar says: Those of certain status with those of certain status are permitted [to marry]. Those of certain status with those of uncertain status; or those of uncertain status with those of certain status; or those of uncertain status with those of uncertain status are forbidden [to marry]. These are the uncertain statuses: *shetukei*, *asufei*, and Samaritans.

These *mishnayot* mention two groups, the *shetukim* and *asufim*, who are of uncertain lineage.[9] *Shetukim* are of unknown paternity, whereas *asufim* do not know who either parent is. According to the ruling of this *mishnah*,

9. The internal composition of these *mishnayot* is complicated. Epstein (*Introduction to Tannaitic Literature* [Hebrew] [Jerusalem: Magnes, 1957], 54) maintained that the first *mishnah*, which is in Aramaic, is from the Second Temple era. *Mishnayot* 2 and 3 are later; *mishnah* 2 provides an explanation and introduces a dispute related to *mishnah* 1, and *mishnah* 3 seems to be an independent *mishnah* that attaches a later dispute to the earlier *mishnah* 1. It is possible that the Mishnah's redactor wanted to give *mishnah* 1 an aura of antiquity by uncommonly using Aramaic, in which case this *mishnah* should not be ascribed to the early period to which Epstein was inclined to ascribe it. On the arrangement and dating of the mishnayot, see Shaye J. D. Cohen, "The Origins of the Matrimonial Principle in Rabbinic Law," *AJS Review* 10 (1985): 19–53, here 34–35. See also the comprehensive discussion of the possible late dating of *mishnah* 1, contra Epstein, in Michael Satlow, *Jewish Marriage in Antiquity* (Princeton: Princeton University Press, 2001), 148–50.

neither *shetukim* nor *asufim* may marry into the general Jewish community, and the Tannaim disagree about whether they may marry *mamzerim* and whether they may marry one another. Rabbi Elazar is stringent on this matter and forbids them from marrying one another or marrying others who are unfit for marriage. The uncertainty of their status therefore makes their situation even worse than that of *mamzerim*; they are not permitted to marry others who are unfit for marriage, out of concern that they are fit, and they are not permitted to marry those who are fit for marriage, out of concern that they are unfit. These abandoned children can expect a harsh fate, especially according to Rabbi Eliezer, who disqualifies them from marrying anyone and condemns them to barrenness. These children, we can say, have been twice abandoned: first by their parents, and then by the halakhists, some of whom forbid them even from marrying one another.

Other *mishnayot*, from *Ketubot*, address situation of uncertain paternity. These *mishnayot* pose an additional question and record another dispute; the relationship between these *mishnayot* and the *mishnayot* in *Kiddushin* is thorny and complicated:

> If she was pregnant, [and they asked her:] "What is the nature of this fetus?" [And she replied:] "It is by Mr. So-and-so, and he is a priest. Rabban Gamliel and Rabbi Eliezer say: She is believed. Rabbi Yehoshua says: We do not live by [the words of] her mouth. Rather, she is presumed to be pregnant by a Gibeonite or a *mamzer* until she brings evidence for her words.
>
> Rabbi Yose said: It happened that a girl went down to draw water from the spring, and she was raped. Rabbi Yoḥanan ben Nuri said: "If the majority of the townsmen are fit to marry into the priesthood, she may marry into the priesthood." (*m. Ketubot* 1:9–10)

The *mishnah* in *Ketubot* deals with a case of unknown paternity, but it introduces another factor beyond the ones addressed in *Kiddushin*: the woman's credibility to testify about the identity and pedigree of the father of her child. Rabbi Yehoshua maintains that her testimony is not accepted and that she must provide evidence beyond her testimony; as long as no such evidence is brought, we relate to the father as though he were a Gibeonite or a *mamzer*. Rabban Gamliel and Rabbi Eliezer maintain that her testimony is credible, and she thus resolves the uncertainty.[10] This dispute is substantive and has far-reaching ramifications for the future status of the unborn child—a matter that is not explicitly mentioned in Mishnah *Kiddushin*.

The Yerushalmi addresses the relationship between the *mishnah* in *Ketubot* and the *mishnayot* in *Kiddushin*. According to one view in the

---

10. For an analsys of Rabbi Yehoshua's opinion and the attempt to police women's sexuality within the realm of uncertatinty, see Baker, *Rebuilding the House of Israel*, 96–97.

Yerushalmi, the dispute between Rabban Gamliel and Rabbi Yehoshua extends to the *mishnah* in *Kiddushin*: "In the opinion of Rabban Gamliel and Rabbi Eliezer [there are] nine [pedigrees]" (*y. Kiddushin* 4:3; p. 1182, lines 34–35). That is, according to Rabban Gamliel and Rabbi Eliezer, there were not ten pedigrees but only nine, because the mother removes uncertainty from the *shetuki*, and based on her testimony he can be permitted to marry any Jew.

A second view in the Yerushalmi maintains that, even according to Rabban Gamliel and Rabbi Eliezer the category of *shetukei* exists, but only in a case where the mother remains silent (or died) or where she is not sure herself who the father is: "There is a *shetuki* according to Rabban Gamliel and Rabbi Eliezer, and even if she speaks, in a case where she says 'I don't know'" (*y. Ketubot* 1:9, p. 959, lines 39–42).

A third view holds that the mother is believed with respect to herself but not with respect to the fetus: "R. Lazar says: All agree that the offspring is a *shetuki*. But teach as follows: About what are these words said? About the testimony of the woman concerning herself. However, with regard to the offspring, all agree that he is a *shetuki*" (*y. Ketubot* 1.9, p. 959, lines 15–17). Tosefta *Ketubot* seems to adopt this view of Rabbi Yehoshua's disagreement with Rabban Gamliel and Rabbi Eliezer: "About what are these words said? About the testimony of the woman concerning herself. However, with regard to the offspring, all agree that he is a *shetuki*."[11]

The Bavli explains the view of Abba Shaul, who in the Mishnah calls *shetukei*, "*bedukei*," as follows: "We investigate the mother and she says that she had relations with someone who is not unfit, and she is believed." The mother has the power to testify and thus validate the fitness of her child. Later, the law is decided in accordance with Abba Shaul: "Rava says: the law is in accordance with Abba Shaul" (*b. Kiddushin* 74a).

There is thus a dispute among the sages about the status of a child with unknown paternity. According to the plain meaning of the *mishnah*, Rabban Gamliel and Rabbi Eliezer alleviate his situation by deeming the mother's testimony about his status to be reliable, whereas Rabbi Yehoshua rejects the mother's testimony in such cases. It seems, as one view in the Yerushalmi maintained, that Rabbi Yehoshua corroborates the view of the *mishnah* in *Kiddushin*, which disqualifies a child of unknown paternity wholesale, without even mentioning the mother's testimony.

---

11. Rabbi Eliezer's view as presented in the Tosefta limits the dispute of the Mishnah to the question of the woman's status. However, this does not seem to be the straightforward meaning of the Mishnah itself, wherein Rabban Gamliel and Rabbi Eliezer do not distinguish between mother and child. Rabbi Eliezer of the Tosefta, among other things, harmonizes the *mishnah* in *Kiddushin* with the *mishnah* in *Ketubot*. On the straightforward meaning of the *mishnah*, see Robert Brody, *Mishnah and Tosefta Ketubbot: Text, Exegesis, and Redaction* [Hebrew] (Jerusalem: Magnes, 2015), 85; and on the Tosefta passage, see 88 n. 4.

The tragic situation of the abandoned child or the child of unknown paternity according to Rabbi Yehoshua in Mishnah *Kiddushin* is highlighted even further when examined in comparison with the ruling in Mishnah *Makhshirin*. The above-cited *mishnah* in *Makhshirin* establishes that the status of a foundling is determined based on probability: if the majority of locals are Jewish, the child is a Jew. In the *mishnah* in *Kiddushin*, that same abandoned child is indeed Jewish, but, it seems, regardless of the question of probability, he is unfit to marry into the Jewish community.[12] This *mishnah* ignores the question of probability when it comes to the *shetuki*, whose mother is known but whose father is unknown.

It therefore seems that the unfitness of the child of unknown paternity is not connected, at the primary level, to the laws of uncertainties. Consequently, the question of probability does not arise. The unfitness of the *shetuki*, which, as noted, is a matter of Tannaitic dispute, is an attempt to link fertility to a recognized, structured social order.[13] It is no wonder that, in this context, the Tosefta at the beginning of *Kiddushin* emphasizes how structured and recognized marriage is necessary for the ordering of lineage and fertility:

> Rabbi Eliezer ben Yaakov says: If he has relations with multiple women, and it is not known which of them he had relations with, and she has relations with multiple men, and it is not known which of them she had relations with, then we will find that one man will marry his daughter

12. Awareness of this deviation of the status of the *shetuki* from probabilistic, majoritarian considerations emerges from the Bavli's treatment as well: "Rava said: According to the Torah, a *shetuki* is fit [for marriage]. Why? Because most [men] are fit with respect to her, and a minority is disqualified with respect to her" (*b. Kiddushin* 73a). Later in the discussion, the possibility is raised that the concern about the *shetuki* is not that he is himself the child of a mamzer or Gibeonite, which would comport with the view of Rabbi Yehoshua in the *mishnah* about a woman who is pregnant from an unknown man. Rather, the concern about the *shetuki* is that he will marry his paternal sister, because his paternity is unknown. This possibility is rejected, but it shows how the prohibition of the *shetuki*, the child of unknown paternity, is indicative of the rejection of the child born outside the familiar, known order.

13. This is also implicit in the structure of the *mishnah* itself, as *mishnah* 1 includes *shetukim* and *asufim* among those who are forbidden to marry into the main community but who may marry among others who are forbidden, indicating that this *mishnah* does not forbid them because of the uncertainty surrounding them, but because of the very fact that they have no lineage. *Mishnah* 3, however, formulates their status in terms of uncertainty in the words of Rabbi Eliezer:

> Those of certain status with those of certain status are permitted [to marry]. Those of certain status with those of uncertain status; or those of uncertain status with those of certain status; or those of uncertain status with those of uncertain status are forbidden [to marry]. These are the uncertain statuses: *shetukei*, *asufei*, and Samaritans.

This formulation articulates the problem in terms of uncertainty and thus makes their status even worse, forbidding them from marrying one another.

> and another will marry his sister. We will find the whole world becoming *mamzerim*. Of this it is said: "The world was filled with promiscuity [*zimah*]" (Lev 19:29)—'What is he [*zeh mah hu*]?' He is not a priest, nor a Levite, nor an Israelite. (*t. Kiddushin* 1:4)[14]

Concerns about marrying one's daughter or paternal half-sister in cases of unknown paternity go well beyond the familiar considerations of likelihood. They indicate how uncertainties of this sort anchor the structure of fertility within an ordered world of familiar paternity and maternity. A child whose origins are unknown is removed entirely from the pedigreed order.[15]

---

14. And see *Sifra, Kedoshim* 4:3.

15. The question of whether Rabbi Yehoshua ignores probability assumptions in denying the testimony of the mother is explicitly addressed by the Yerushalmi:

> What divides Rabbi Yehoshua and these rabbis? A place where the majority is unfit. However, where the majority is fit, even Rabbi Yehoshua concedes. Rabbi Yaakov bar Aḥa cited in the name of Rabbi Yoḥanan and Rabbi Ila cited in the name of Rabbi Elazar: The dispute applies even where the majority is acceptable; Rabbi Yehoshua maintains that promiscuity seeks out the unfit. (*y. Ketubot* 1:8, p. 959, lines 7–10)

The uncertainty surrounding the *shetuki* of unknown paternity stems from the fact that, since his mother became pregnant outside of the organized framework of marriage, the sexual encounter that resulted in conception is tainted by suspicion of disqualification, regardless of the question of a majority. For this reason, the next *mishnah* in *Ketubot,* which addresses a case where a young woman was raped and there is no context of any premeditated transgression on her part, returns to its reliance on a majority:

> Rabbi Yose said: It happened that a girl went down to draw water from the spring, and she was raped. Rabbi Yoḥanan ben Nuri said: "If the majority of the townsmen are fit to marry into the priesthood, she may marry into the priesthood."

In the patricarchical structures of rabbinic law, a woman who was raped is not "disqualified" from marriage to other Israelite men, but she is disqualified from marrying a priest if she was raped by a man who is unfit for marrying into the priesthood. The Mishnah rules that, in the case in which the rapist is unknown the majority is followed, and if the majority of the townsmen are fit there is no change in the status of the raped woman. The Yerushalmi cites a view that Rabbi Yehoshua would agree with the *mishnah*'s ruling: "Rabbi Yirmiyah [and] Rabbi Ḥama bar Ukva both say in the name of Rabbi Ḥanina in the name of Rabbi Yannai: Rabbi Yehoshua concedes regarding a rape victim. Rabbi Ḥizkiya [and] Rabbi Abbahu in the name of Rabbi Yoḥanan: Rabbi Yehoshua concedes regarding a rape victim" (*y. Ketubot* 1:10, col. 959, lines 44–47). (The Bavli's discussion rejects the straightforward meaning of the *mishnah* that the majority in this case is a regular majority. See *b. Ketubot* 14b–15a.) Similarly, with respect to the *asufi,* the circumstances of the foundling's abandonment raise concern that the abandonment was motivated by sexual transgression. According to this logic, both the Bavli and the Yerushalmi maintain that, if there are clear signs that those who abandoned the child wanted it to survive and live, and to that end they took care of it at the moment of birth or left it in a protected place where it would be found and saved, then the reason for the abandonment was poverty and hunger, not stigma. In such a case, the child is certainly not a possible *mamzer*.

A unique, completely different approach to uncertainties of pedigree appears in *t. Yevamot*:

> If one performs levirate marriage with his sister-in-law and she is found to be pregnant … and it is uncertain whether [the child] was by the first [husband] and full-term or by the second [husband] and premature, that first child is fit to become high priest, but the second child [of the woman with the second husband] is a possible *mamzer* [*mamzer be-safek*]. Rabbi Eliezer ben Yaakov says: There is no such thing as a possible *mamzer*. (*t. Yevamot* 6:2)

The Tosefta deals with a case in which a woman was wed by levirate marriage (*yibum*) within three months of her husband's death. Since she remarried before a pregnancy by her late husband would have become noticeable, it is not known whether she was impregnated by the late husband or by the levir. In such a case, the offspring is fit in every respect, but the levir must divorce her out of uncertainty: it is possible that the child is from the first husband, in which case the woman is not eligible for levirate marriage and is, in fact, forbidden to her late husband's brothers as a matter of incest. The uncertainty about the child's status arises only in a case where another child is born to the woman and the levir, after the birth of the first child. The sages assert that the child is a "possible [*safek*] *mamzer*," as it may be the product of an incestuous relationship. Rabbi Eliezer ben Yaakov disagrees, maintaining that there is no such category as "possible [*safek*] *mamzer*." It seems from the straightforward meaning of his words that this child is fit to marry into the Jewish community.

The Yerushalmi concludes from Rabbi Eliezer ben Yaakov's opinion that, according to him, the categories of *shetuki* and *asufi* do not exist, for they are instances of uncertainty, and there is no such thing as uncertainty when it comes to a *mamzer*:

> We learned there: [If] it is uncertain whether [the child] was by the first [husband] and full-term or by the second [husband] and premature, [the levir] must divorce her, the child is fit, and [the wife and the levir] are obligated to bring a pending guilt offering [*asham talui*].
>
> It was taught: The first [child] is fit to be a priest, and the second is a possible *mamzer*. Rabbi Eliezer ben Yaakov says: There is no such thing as a possible *mamzer*.
>
> Rabbi Eliezer ben Yaakov concedes in the case of possible Samaritans and possible *ḥalalim*, in accordance with what we learned there: "Ten pedigrees came up from Babylonia." According to Rabbi Eliezer ben Yaakov there were eight. According to Rabban Gamliel and Rabbi Eliezer there were nine. According to the sages there were ten. (*y. Kiddushin* 4:3; p. 1182, lines 29–36)[16]

16. In *b. Yevamot* 37a, Rava and Abaye understand the view of Rabbi Eliezer ben Yaakov differently than the Yerushalmi.

Children of unknown paternity and foundlings are common occurrences in various societies, and they attest to the fact that sexuality, fertility, and natality are not completely controlled within the boundaries of the common family. The Tannaitic traditions present a complex spectrum of disagreements over how to deal with these uncertainties, which undermine the regulated structure of pedigree.

An analysis of the views of the sages showed that there are three different approaches. The first view, that of the *mishnah* in *Kiddushin* and of Rabbi Yehoshua, relates to the offspring of unknown paternity and the foundling as existing outside of the legitimate order of pedigree; these individuals may not marry those who are deemed fit, and it is possible that they may not even marry other foundlings or others who are unfit to marry into the main Jewish community. This view clearly deviates from the regular rules of probability because it is apparently interested in linking fertility with a recognized pedigree structure. The second view, that of Rabban Gamliel and Rabbi Eliezer, recognizes the reliability of a woman's testimony about the identity of the fetus's father, thus profoundly changing the status of the child. A third, more expansive view found in Tannaitic literature rejects the idea of uncertainty with respect to the status of *mamzer*. Accordingly, it is only possible to disqualify someone from marriage on the basis of certainty regarding his status. This view has far-reaching implications for everything related to uncertainties of lineage; it will be discussed below at greater length.

The *shetuki* and *asufi* thus became the focus of a substantive dispute between the sages, from the attempt to remove them completely from the system of pedigree and fertility and prohibit them from marrying one another due to their lack of lineage, to viewing them as cases of uncertainty that are subject to leniency by means of various forms of resolution. As we will see below, uncertainties about pedigree became a site of ever-deepening disagreement among the sages.

II

Alongside this complicated attempt to regulate married life and the associated prohibitions under the specter of uncertainty, the sages, as usual, viewed the realm of uncertainty as an independent conceptual matter, which led them to displays of independent judicial virtuosity, free from the directives of halakhic life itself.

A clear example of this is a chapter at the end of *Yevamot* that is devoted, in its entirety, to uncertainties of lineage that have a very tenuous connection to lived reality but are full of conceptual insights and are dizzyingly imaginative. This chapter deals with various cases of babies who were switched at birth and whose parents, consequently, cannot be determined with certainty:

> The offspring of five women got mixed up. The mixed-up children grew up and married women, then died [childless]. Four [levirs, one from each family] perform *ḥaliẓah* (levirate divorce) for one [of the widows] and one performs levirate marriage [with that widow]. He and three others perform *ḥaliẓah* for another [widow], and one performs levirate marriage [with that widow]. Thus, each and every [widow] goes through four *ḥaliẓot* and one levirate marriage. (*m. Yevamot* 11:3)

This *mishnah* addresses a case in which five male children were born to five different mothers and then got mixed up. Each of these mothers has (at least) one positively identified son. The switched babies then grow up and marry. One of them then dies childless, whereupon his widow becomes tied to her late husband's brother. However, she is uncertain as to which of the five sets of brothers, each from a different mother, she is tied, as any set may be her husband's true brothers. The rule is that four brothers, one from each of four mothers, perform *ḥaliẓah* due to this uncertainty, whereupon the fifth may perform levirate marriage. If the fifth man is indeed the brother of the deceased, then he has fulfilled his duty of levirate marriage; if he is not the brother of the deceased, then he is nevertheless permitted to marry the widow because the true levir is one of the four men who performed *ḥaliẓah*. If another of the five mixed-up men dies, the man who married the first widow performs *ḥaliẓah*, and the additional three men from three different mothers likewise perform *ḥaliẓah*, whereupon the remaining brother may perform levirate marriage. And so forth.

Such cases were certainly addressed only because of the complexity of the problem and the creativity and virtuosity of the proposed solutions. This is all the more true of the following *mishnah*:

> A woman's offspring got mixed up with the offspring of her daughter-in-law. The mixed up children grew up, married women, and then died [childless]. The sons of the daughter-in-law perform *ḥaliẓah* but may not perform levirate marriage, for it is uncertain whether she is their brother's wife or their father's brother's wife. The sons of the elder woman (the mother-in-law) may perform either *ḥaliẓah* or levirate marriage, for it is uncertain whether she is their brother's wife or their brother's son's wife.
>
> If the eligible [i.e., non-mixed-up] brothers died, the mixed-up sons perform *ḥaliẓah* but not levirate marriage for the [widows of] the sons of the elder woman, for it is uncertain whether she is their brother's wife or their father's brother's wife. With regard to the [widows of] the sons of the daughter-in-law, one performs *ḥaliẓah* and then the other performs levirate marriage. (*m. Yevamot* 11:4)

In this case and others like it, the sages' engagement with uncertainty is not an attempt to provide an answer to potential eventualities but is an expression of their fondness of halakhic paradoxes and for complex, creative solutions to such hypothetical cases.

In addition to being exercises in complex judicial acrobatics, these borderline cases make significant conceptual contributions, as they acutely exemplify and clarify important principles that have real-life applications. The next *mishnah* deals with such a case:

> If one did not wait three months after [the death of] her husband, remarried, had a baby, and it is not known whether [the child] was by the first [husband] and full-term or by the second [husband] and premature ... if one [husband] was an Israelite and the other a priest, then [the son] may marry a woman who is fit to marry a priest, and he may not defile himself by [coming into contact with] a corpse. However, if he defiled himself, he does not incur forty [lashes]; he may not eat priestly gifts [*terumah*], but if he ate, he does not repay the principal plus a fifth; he does not take a portion [of the priestly gifts] at the granary; he sells *terumah* and keeps the money.... He is exempt [from punishment] if he hits or curses either [of the possible fathers]. (*m. Yevamot* 13:6–7)

From this borderline case of a child whose biological father is one of two men—one a priest and the other an Israelite—and consequently, it is uncertain whether the child is an Israelite or a priest, several important and fundamental principles are derived. The first principle is that, because of the uncertainty, the son is subject to the stringencies of the priesthood as well as the stringencies that apply to an Israelite: like a priest, he may not become defiled through contact with a corpse, but, like an Israelite, he may not eat *terumah*. However, although the uncertainty multiplies prohibitions, it also weakens the severity of the prohibitions, for this child is not punished if he violates these possible transgressions: if he defiles himself through contact with a corpse, he does not receive lashes, and even though he may not eat *terumah*, if he did so, he is not penalized and is not obligated to repay it. This *mishnah* also shows different rulings for uncertainties about ritual matters and uncertainties about monetary matters. Though the son may not eat the *terumah* of his own produce, he may sell it to a priest and keep the money, because it is uncertain whether this *terumah* really belongs to him, and his money cannot be confiscated by virtue of a mere uncertainty. Moreover, this *mishnah* teaches an important principle about punishment. If the son cursed or hit both of his possible fathers, he is nevertheless not punished for transgressing the prohibition against hitting or cursing one's father, even though he hit both and one of them is certainly his father, because punishment of this sort requires that each and every action be certain; to impose punishment, the transgression must be fully individuated.[17]

---

17. The Tosefta differentiates between the following cases: "If he hit one and then hit

By means of this case of uncertainty, the *mishnah* clarifies many areas of instruction for dealing with situations of uncertainty that pertain to the intersection between forbidden foods, monetary matters, and penalties.

III

The cases discussed thus far address uncertainties about the lineage of a particular individual—the foundling and the child of unknown paternity. However, the complications and destabilizing ramifications resulting from uncertainties about lineage go well beyond the individual case and resulted in deep differences of opinion issuing in radically different directives and responses. The established principle with regard to those unfit for marriage by dint of *mamzerut* is that the offspring of a male or female *mamzer* is also a *mamzer,* ad infinitum.[18] The halakhic position according to which "everything follows the disqualification," that is, that the disqualification functions as a "dominant gene" passed on to all offspring, creates a situation in which a few generations of intermingling between the community and those nominally excluded from marriage cast a heavy pall of *mamzerut* over an increasing segment of the community.

The *mishnah,* as we have seen, asserts that ten pedigree statuses migrated from Babylonia, some of which were forbidden to intermarry with one another. It thus indicates that within the Jewish population there were *mamzerim, shetukim,* and *asufim* intermixed, as well as *ḥalalim,* who are excluded from marrying priests. This state of affairs deviates significantly, as noted, from this or that uncertainty in that it casts suspicion on the entire community. The redactor of the Mishnah appends a law to the list of pedigrees that came up from Babylonia—a law that seems to be a reaction to this reality:

> One who marries a woman from a priestly family must investigate four mothers, which are, in fact, eight: Her mother and her mother's mother; her mother's father's mother, and her mother; her father's mother, and

---

the other [or] if he cursed one and then cursed the other, he is exempt. If he hit both together or cursed both together, he is liable. Rabbi Yehudah says: One who hits his father and another together is liable; one who curses his father and another together is liable" (*t. Yevamot* 12:7).

18. The meaning of the term *mamzer* in Scripture is not entirely clear and has been interpreted variously. See Calum M. Carmichael, *The Laws of Deuteronomy* (Ithaca, NY: Cornell University Press, 1974), 173–74. An interpretation from the Second Temple era explains it as an abbreviation of *me-am zar,* "from a foreign nation," that is, the child of a Jewish mother and non-Jewish father. On the scope of the category of *mamzer* itself in rabbinic literature, see Cohen, "Origins of the Matrimonial Principle," 32–34. It seems to emerge from the Mishnah (*m. Yevamot* 7:5) that the child of a Jewish woman and a non-Jewish man is indeed a Jew, albeit a *mamzer,* and this broad concept was narrowed to what became the accepted halakhic ruling. See *m. Yevamot* 4:13 and *t. Kiddushin* 4:15.

> her mother; her father's father's mother, and her mother. Levites and Israelites—another is added to them.
>
> We do not examine beyond the altar, nor beyond the platform, nor beyond the Sanhedrin. Anyone whose fathers were established as public officers or collectors of charity funds may marry into the priesthood, and there is no need to investigate their ancestry. Rabbi Yose says: Even one who was signed as a witness in the old court of Sepphoris. Rabbi Ḥaninah ben Antigonus says: Even one who was inscribed among the king's registers. (*m. Kiddushin* 4:4–5)

Since the Jewish people includes various levels of groups who are unfit to marry, a man who sought to marry a woman had to investigate her lineage. The shadow cast on the seed of Israel as a whole created a need to investigate lineage. The response to these general uncertainties mandates examination, investigation, and an attempt to refine the purity of lineage in the face of intermingling and disqualification.[19]

The Bavli limits such investigations only toward clans that are known to have mingled with disqualified lineages, and it is not known whether a particular descendant of that family inherited that disqualification. In its straightforward meaning, however, it seems that this *mishnah* requires investigation for every future marriage, in order to dispel uncertainty. Moreover, the Yerushalmi has an Amoraic tradition that broadens the duty to investigate beyond the rules posited by the Mishnah.[20]

Another, narrower reading of this *mishnah* contends that it addresses only a priest who wishes to marry: he must investigate the pedigree of his intended wife. The reason for this is that, even though priests are permitted to marry Israelites, Israelites are also permitted to marry those who are unfit to marry priests, such as proselytes and *ḥalalim*. Since such disqualifications do not carry stigmas and are thus not well known among Israelites, priests must thoroughly investigate the women they marry. In the words of the Tosefta on our *mishnah*: "Why did they say that a mixed family [*isah*] is unfit for [marrying into] the priesthood? Because of the

19. The text of this *mishnah* in MS Parma uses the words Levi'ai and Yisra'elai—the same Aramaic plural form as the first *mishnah* in the chapter—for Levites and Israelites. This in turn echoes the Aramaic of the book of Ezra, which describes the migrations from Babylonia and enumerates the various participating clans. This *mishnah* is thus an attempt to connect our *mishnah* to the first *mishnah* in the chapter.

20. See the two dicta that the Bavli cites in the name of Rav: "Rabbi Yehudah said in the name of Rav: These are the words of Rabbi Meir, but the sages say that all families retain a presumption of fitness. Rabbi Ḥama bar Goriya said in the name of Rav: If an objection is raised, it must be investigated" (*b. Kiddushin* 76b). The Yerushalmi brings a different tradition of interpretation of the *mishnah*: "Rabbi Yoḥanan said: This [*mishnah*] is Rabbi Meir ... whereas the sages say that one investigates forever. Rav said: These are the words of Rabbi Meir, but the sages says that one investigates which families marry into the priesthood, and marries accordingly" (*y. Kiddushin* 4:4, col. 1182, lines 38–44).

possible *ḥalalim* that got mixed in; Israelites know the Gibeonites and *mamzerim* among them, but do not know the *ḥalalim* among them" (*t. Kiddushin* 5:3).

This explanation is adopted, inter alios, by Rashi, who maintains that our *mishnah* addresses only a priest who wishes to marry. Later variants of the Mishnah integrate this interpretation into the text itself by changing "Levites and Israelites" (*Levi'im ve-Yisrael*) to "a Levite or Israelite woman" (*Levi'ah ve-Yisraelit*). According to these variants, a priest must investigate fewer generations of the lineage of his intended wife if she is of priestly stock than if she is of Levite or Israelite stock, because Levite and Israelite clans were not as meticulous about maintaining their pedigree. Our *mishnah* is thus addressed only to priests because of the specific concern about proselytes and *ḥalalim*. However, with respect to other marriages, Jewish families have a presumption of fitness that does not require investigation.

Rashi's view notwithstanding, the earlier versions of the *mishnah* have *Levi'im ve-Yisrael* in the text, clearly implying that the duty to investigate applies to priests and Israelites alike. It is possible, however, that the Tosefta's textual tradition comports with the view that the duty to investigate applies only to priests.[21]

Likewise, the question of whether and to what extent the priests must be concerned about clans suspected of having become mixed with individuals who are unfit to marry into the priesthood—clans that are called *isah* (lit., "dough")—itself hinges on a Tannaitic dispute in the Tosefta:

---

21. For a discussion of the text of the *mishnah* and its significance, see Saul Lieberman, *Tosefta Kifshutah: Sotah-Kiddushin* (New York: Jewish Theological Seminary of America, 1973), 974–75. MS Kaufmann has *Levi'im ve-Yisr'* and MS Parma has *Levi'ai ve-Yisra'elai*. These early, authoritative variants indicate that the duty to investigate applies not only to the priests but to Israelites as well. The variant *Levi'ah ve-Yisraelit* is found in MS Leiden, a later manuscript of the Mishnah. An interesting and even difficult outcome of the MS Kaufmann version of this *mishnah* is that Levites and Israelites must be more stringent than priests vis-à-vis the duty to investigate pedigree. There is no difficulty according to those whose text reads *Levi'ah ve-Yisraelit*, as the investigation is broadened when a priest wishes to marry a Levite or Israelite woman since these families are not as meticulous about pedigree as priestly families. This difficulty is raised by the Yerushalmi, whose version of the *mishnah* is identical to that of MS Kaufmann: "Do we not, then, find greater stringency with respect to Israelites than to priests? In either case, the sages imposed a penalty so that a person would stick with his tribe and clan" (*y. Kiddushin*, col. 1183, line 4). Naḥmanides concerns himself with this question and with explaining the Yerushalmi's position in his novellae on *Kiddushin* (76a, s.v. "*U-vaYerushalmi garsinan*"). MS Vienna of the Tosefta has *Levi'ah ve-Yisraelim*, which is an ambiguous formula: The word *Levi'ah* implies that it refers to the duty to investigate that applies to a priest who wishes to marry a Levite woman, yet the word *Yisraelim* implies that the duty to investigate applies to everyone. MS Erfurt has *Levi'ah ve-Yisr'*. The text of MS Vienna is therefore hybrid, though it seems that the word *Levi'ah* in both Tosefta manuscripts constitutes decisive evidence in favor of Lieberman's claim, namely, that according to the Tosefta's tradition, the duty to investigate applies only to the priests.

> What is a mixed family [*isah*]? One in which there is no taint of Gibeonites, *mamzerut*, or royal slaves. Rabbi Meir said: I heard that any [family] in which there is no taint of Gibeonites, *mamzerut*, or royal slaves may marry into the priesthood. Rabbi Shimon ben Lazar says in the name of Rabbi Meir—and Rabbi Shimon ben Menasya would say likewise: Why did they say that a mixed family [*isah*] is unfit for [marrying into] the priesthood? Because of the possible *ḥalalim* that got mixed in; Israelites know the Gibeonites and *mamzerim* among them, but do not know the *ḥalalim* among them. (*t. Kiddushin* 5:2–3)

The Tosefta presents two traditions about what Rabbi Meir said. One maintains that Rabbi Meir held that priests need not be concerned about marrying into a family that is suspected of having assimilated individuals who are unfit to marry into the priesthood, whereas the other tradition maintains that priests may not marry into such families, because since that which disqualifies one from marrying into the priesthood does not disqualify them from marrying an Israelite, they are not singled out and recognized.

The reasoning behind the first view attributed to Rabbi Meir, that a priest need not investigate the pedigree of an Israelite woman he intends to marry, can be found further along in the Tosefta, which states that when a *ḥalalah* (that is, a female *ḥalal*) marries an Israelite, her sons and daughters are not *ḥalalim*; thus, even if an unfit individual got mixed up in an Israelite clan, "Israel is a purification *mikveh* for the priests."[22] According

---

22. In the Yerushalmi, the *mishnah* is ascribed to Rabbi Meir only, and the Amoraim of the first generation disagreed about what the view of the sages was:

> Rabbi Yoḥanan said: This [*mishnah*] is Rabbi Meir, who taught: What *isah* is fit? One that has in it neither *ḥalal*, nor *mamzer*, nor Gibeonite. Rabbi Meir says, the daughter of any [family] that has none of these is fit for [marrying into] the priesthood. However, a family into which it has become embedded is unfit. Rabbi Meir says: Investigate up to four generations, and then permit marriage, whereas the sages say that one investigates forever. Rav said: These are the words of Rabbi Meir, but the sages says that one investigates which families marry into the priesthood, and marries accordingly. (*y. Kiddushin* 4:4, col. 1182, lines 37-44)

Later in the Yerushalmi: "A priest came before Rabbi Yoḥanan and said to him, 'I acted [according to] the *mishnah*; I married a woman from a priestly family and investigated four mothers, which are eight.' He replied, 'If the root is blighted, who will tell you about the head?'" (*y. Kiddushin* 4:4, col. 1182–83, lines 50–53).

The Amoraim disagree about how stringent the sages are vis-à-vis Rabbi Meir. Rabbi Yoḥanan maintains that the sages did not think that "Israel is a *mikveh* for the priests," and the women of a family into which a *ḥalal* got mixed are disqualified from marrying priests, out of uncertainty, for all generations. An investigation of a few generations would not help, because it is possible that the disqualification got mixed in much earlier. Rav suggests a more lenient view, according to which the sages rely on the families who marry into the priesthood, and nothing else is needed. In the Babylonian tradition, the view of the sages was taught as being more lenient than that of Rabbi Meir in the *mishnah*: "Rabbi Yehudah said in the name of Rav: These are the words of Rabbi Meir, but the sages say that all fam-

to this view, there is a major difference between *ḥalalim*, who are unfit to marry into the priesthood, and *mamzerim*. With respect to *mamzerut*, the offspring will always be a *mamzer* if the father or mother is a *mamzer*. With respect to *ḥalalim*, however, our *mishnah* asserts: "If an Israelite married a *ḥalalah*, their daughter is fit to marry into the priesthood" (*m. Kiddushin* 4:3). A *ḥalal* is thus much less "contagious" than a *mamzer*, because when a *ḥalalah* marries an Israelite, her daughters will be fit to marry priests.[23] In addition, the Bavli cites a Tannaitic view that goes even further: "Rabbi Dostai ben Yehudah says: Just as the sons of Israel are a *mikveh* for the purification of *ḥalalot*, so the daughters of Israel are a *mikveh* for the purification of *ḥalalim* (*b. Kiddushin* 77a).

We find a similar dispute about proselyte women. Israelites are permitted to marry proselytes, but it is forbidden for a priest to marry a proselyte woman. This fact would generate the suspicion of disqualification in every Israelite family, and there is a Tannaitic dispute about this:

> Rabbi Yehudah says: The daughter of a male proselyte is like the daughter of a male *ḥalal*. Rabbi Eliezer ben Yaakov says: The daughter of an Israelite man who married a proselyte woman is fit to [marry into] the

---

ilies retain a presumption of fitness" (*b. Kiddushin* 76b). See Lieberman, *Tosefta Kifshutah: Sotah-Kiddushin*, 967, and esp. n. 19, for an explanation of this entire issue.

23. In the Yerushalmi, a dispute about the meaning of this rule arose in the first generation of Amoraim:

> Rav Hamnuna [said] in the name of Rav: "Daughter's daughter's daughter, ad infinitum." Rabbi Yoḥanan [said] in the name of Rabbi Yishmael: "[Scripture states:] 'among his kin.' Just as when 'among his kin' is stated below [Lev 21:4, with regard to corpse impurity], males are forbidden and females are permitted, so too when 'among his kin' is stated here [Lev 21:15], males are forbidden and females permitted." What is the difference between them? If a priest had relations with a divorced woman and sired a son, and the son went and sired a son and daughter: according to Rav, a son, a daughter of a son, a son of a daughter, and a daughter are forbidden; according to Rabbi Yoḥanan, a daughter of a son is forbidden, but the daughter of a daughter is permitted. The *mishnah* disagrees with Rav: "An Israelite who married a *ḥalalah*—his daughter is fit [for marriage to a priest]." He interprets it as [referring to] a *ḥalalah* of her own doing [i.e., who was not born a *ḥalalah* but became one through illicit relations with a priest]. (*y. Kiddushin* 4:6, col. 1183, lines 18–25)

According to Rav, the rule that the daughter of the daughter of a *ḥalal* who married an Israelite is fit to marry into the priesthood is not valid, and in such a case, the daughter's daughter remains disqualified forever. He understands the *mishnah*'s ruling that the daughter of a *ḥalalah* who married an Israelite is fit to marry into the priesthood to refer only to a *ḥalalah* who became unfit by having relations with someone who was disqualified, not by being born to a *ḥalal*; the daughter of a woman born to a *ḥalal* is forbidden to marry into the priesthood. In Rav's conception, the disqualification of a *ḥalal* is almost as contagious as that of a *mamzer*, and it has far-reaching implications for the possibility of priests marrying into Israelite families that intermingled with individuals who are unfit to marry priests. This is the diametric opposite of the position of the Tanna Rabbi Dostai ben Rabbi Yehudah.

> priesthood, but the daughter of a proselyte man who married a proselyte woman is unfit to [marry into] the priesthood.... Rabbi Yose says: Even the daughter of a proselyte man who married a proselyte woman is fit to [marry into] the priesthood. (*m. Kiddushin* 4:7)

The opinions of Rabbi Eliezer ben Yaakov and Rabbi Yose make possible the marriage of priests to Israelite women even though they may not marry *ḥalalot* or proselyte women, for even if an Israelite may marry a proselyte, the daughter of a proselyte man is permitted to marry a priest as long as there is a marriage to an Israelite somewhere in her lineage. The Tosefta's principle that "Israel is a *mikveh* for the priests" therefore allows the descendants of those who are unfit to marry into the priesthood to become eligible to marry into the priesthood. In this, their status is very different from that of the *mamzer*.

It is possible that this fact was the subject of a debate that appears in Mishnah *Eduyot*, which indicates the gap between the sages and the priestly clans who did not accept this principle and who made sure to marry only women from well-known, pedigreed families. These priests forbade themselves from marrying women from *isah*—families into which were mixed, or about which there is suspicion of having been mixed, those who are disqualified from the priesthood:

> Rabbi Yehoshua and Rabbi Yehoshua ben Beteira testified that the widow of *isah* is fit to [marry into] the priesthood; *isah* is fit to defile and purify, to exclude and to include. Rabban Shimon ben Gamliel said: we accept your testimony, but what can we do once Rabban Yoḥanan ben Zakkai decreed that no court can be convened to address this, and the priests heed you with respect to repelling, but not with respect to drawing near. (*m. Eduyot* 8:3)[24]

In these sources, we find certain basic tensions regarding the investigation of lineage precipitated by the fog of uncertainty that ostensibly hovers over the entire congregation:

a. Must an Israelite who marries a woman investigate her lineage, or is it only a priest who must investigate lineage in this manner? It seems from the early versions of the Mishnah that the duty to investigate

---

24. The Yerushalmi attests to the fact that, regarding matters of pedigree, the priests would indeed be far more stringent than required by rabbinic halakhah:

> Rabbi Yosah [and] Rabbi Yassa [said] in the name of Rabbi Yoḥanan; Rabbi Yonah [and] Rabbi Ḥiyyah [said] in the name of Rabbi Yoḥanan: The halakhah accords with Rabbi Yosah [who maintains that the daughter of a proselyte woman, even if her mother married a proselyte man, is fit to marry into the priesthood]. Ḥanin bar Ba [said] in the name of Rav: The halakhah accords with Rabbi Yose, but the priests acted [stringently] according to the view of Rabbi Eliezer ben Yaakov [who maintains that if both parents are proselytes, the daughter may not marry a priest]. (*y. Kiddushin* 4:7, col. 1183, lines 48-50)

applies to Israelites as well, even though the later tendency of Rashi and other medieval halakhists was to claim that the duty to investigate applies only to the priest. In contrast, the Tosefta's textual tradition seems to incline toward a duty of investigation that applies only to the priests.

b. Is this investigation supposed to take place only when there is a known disqualification in the family and if there is no general presumption of fitness, or is there uncertainty in any case that marriage requires investigation? The Bavli tradition attributed to Rav limited our *mishnah* to cases where an objection had been raised. This is in contradistinction to the Yerushalmi's tradition of interpretation, which expands the duty of investigation.

c. Are families that became intermixed with those disqualified from marrying into the priesthood themselves forbidden to the priesthood until their lineage has been ascertained, or not? One of the opinions cited in the name of Rabbi Meir in the Tosefta maintains that a priest may marry a woman from a family that became intermixed with those disqualified from marrying into the priesthood.

The main tensions between Tannaim and between the various possible ways to read the *mishnah* originate in the awareness expressed in the first *mishnah* of the chapter, namely, that the Jews in the age of Ezra included a complex mix of disqualifications, which generated a reality of uncertainty with regard to lineage and marriage.

IV

This priestly anxiety over lineage, about which there is a dispute of transgenerational character regarding the extent of the disqualification of *ḥalalim* and proselytes, becomes much more acute when it comes to *mamzerim*. The descendants of a *mamzer* are defined as *mamzerim*, no matter how many generations have elapsed, and regardless of whether the status is inherited maternally or paternally. The status of *mamzer* broadens the possibility of uncertainty well beyond the narrow priestly circles, since, from a probabilistic perspective, the marriage of a *mamzer* in the distant past is liable to carry the burden of *mamzeret* to later generations, and the uncertainty will touch every Jewish family. The heavy and threatening shadow of this possibility is reflected in a profoundly significant dispute about the messianic era—a debate that echoes dramatically through the history of halakhah:

> In the future, Gibeonites and *mamzerim* will be pure—these are the words of Rabbi Yose. Rabbi Meir says: They will not be pure. Rabbi Yose said to him: Is it not already written, "I will sprinkle purification water on you,

> and you will be purified…"? Rabbi Meir said to him: "…from all your impurities and all your filthiness…" Rabbi Yose replied: What is taught by [the end of the verse, namely,] "I will purify you"? Even from being Gibeonites and from *mamzerut*. (*t. Kiddushin* 5:4)

According to Rabbi Yose, disqualifications that got mixed in will be purified in the future, and therefore there is no need to view the uncertain pedigree that pervades Israel as an indelible stain. This divine act of purification will remove all disqualifications by cleansing them, as one component of the future redemption.[25] Rabbi Yose's position, which regards disqualifications that got mixed into the Jewish community as a reality that will eventually be resolved by the grace of God, Who will cleanse them, was given two explanations by Amoraim: "Rav Huna said in the name of Rabbi Yosef: [If] the law does not accord with Rabbi Yose, in the future, the generations will be despondent" (*y. Kiddushin* 3:13, p. 1182, lines 13–15). The common occurrence of uncertain pedigree is the reason that there must be a more forgiving attitude and an act of purification in the future; without them, many Jews will be found to be unfit for marriage.

Rabbi Yosef's position was formulated similarly in the Bavli:

> Rav Yehudah said in the name of Shmuel: The law accords with Rabbi Yose. Said Rav Yosef: Had not Rav Yehudah said in the name of Shmuel that the law accords with Rabbi Yose, Elijah would come and remove group after group of unfit people. (*b. Kiddushin* 72b)

---

25. This Tosefta passage appears right after another passage that asserts: "Thus, Israel is a *mikveh* for priests, and a maidservant is a *mikveh* for all of those who are disqualified" (5:3). The unique and complex expression "Israel is a *mikveh* for the priests" is connected to the earlier discussion about a *ḥalalah* who married an Israelite, whose daughter is fit to marry a priest. The Israelite is thus a purifying *mikveh* for priests. The next expression, "and a maidservant is a *mikveh* for all of those who are disqualified," relates to a *mishnah* at the end of the third chapter of *Kiddushin*, which quotes a statement of Rabbi Tarfon that enables the purification of a *mamzer*'s offspring by having the *mamzer* marry a maidservant:

> Rabbi Tarfon says: It is possible for *mamzerim* to be purified. How so? A *mamzer* marries a maidservant; the child is a slave. If they were freed, the son becomes a free man. Rabbi Eliezer says: This [child] is a *mamzer* slave. (*m. Kiddushin* 3:13)

A maidservant is thus a *mikveh* for *mamzerim*, a means for the offspring of *mamzerim* to become fit to marry into the community.

The halakhic possibility of purifying *mamzerut* using the marriage mechanism suggested by Rabbi Tarfon is linked, in the editing of the Tosefta, to the much broader purification of in the future messianic era. Rabbi Eliezer, who maintains in the Mishnah that there is no way to purify a *mamzer*, seems to be claiming that *mamzerut* is a status that cannot be changed. There is thus a connection, however indirect, between the disagreement of Rabbi Tarfon and Rabbi Eliezer in the Mishnah and that of Rabbi Yose and Rabbi Meir in the Tosefta.

Another explanation, no less interesting, for the forgiving attitude toward the disqualifications that became intermingled is cited in *Leviticus Rabbah*:

> "And then I considered all of the oppressed" (Eccl 4:1). Ḥanina the tailor interpreted the verse with respect to *mamzerim*. "And then I considered all of the oppressed," these are the *mamzerim*. "Behold the tears of the oppressed"—their mothers transgressed, yet these despondent ones are expelled? His father committed incest, but what has he done? How does it concern him? "There is no one to comfort them"; rather, "there is power in the hand of their oppressor"—this refers to the Great Sanhedrin of Israel, which comes to them with the power of Torah and expels them, based on "A *mamzer* shall not enter into the congregation of the Lord" (Deut 23:3). "There is no one to comfort them"—the Holy One says, "It is incumbent on Me to comfort them." In this world, they have a disqualification, but in the future, said Zechariah, "I see them all like pure gold." For this is symbolized by his vision: "I looked, and behold, a lamp of pure gold" (Zech 4:2). (*Leviticus Rabbah* 32:8, pp. 754–75 [Margaliot ed.])[26]

The reason for permitting the disqualified stems from the injustice inherent in the very concept of "unfitness for marriage," for such unfitness is a price paid by children who were conceived through a transgression committed by their parents, and of which they are innocent. It is God who saves the *mamzer* by purifying him in the future; God is described as the comforter and rescuer of the *mamzer* from his oppressors. The extraordinary thing about this rationale and about the verse from Ecclesiastes that it interprets—"And then I considered all of the oppressed, that are made under the sun; and behold, the tears of the oppressed: There is no one to comfort them, and there is power in the hand of their oppressor, and there is no one to comfort them"—is that God is rescuing the *mamzer* from his oppression at the hands of the rabbinical court, yet the court is applying the law that God Himself gave—"A *mamzer* shall not enter into the congregation of the Lord." God thus takes action against the ruling of the court, in which it imposes the directives that He legislated, yet the court is considered the oppressor because it failed to annul or limit God's own law!

Rabbi Meir, who disagrees with Rabbi Yose in the Tosefta, sees the messianic future in the opposite terms; God will not cleanse the disqualified; rather, on the contrary, God will remove them from Israel and thus cleanse Israel through their expulsion. In the Yerushalmi, Rabbi Meir's words are expanded: "Rabbi Meir says: *Mamzerim* will not be purified in the future, as it is written: 'A *mamzer* shall dwell in Ashdod' (Zech 9:6).

26. See the comment of Margaliot on this text: "The homilist agrees with Rabbi Yose of the previous section: *Mamzerim* will be purified in the future." A thorough discussion of this homily from *Leviticus Rabbah* and its broader context of the series of preceding homilies appears in Tzvi Novick, "'They Come against Them with the Power of the Torah': Rabbinic Reflections on Legal Fiction and Legal Agency," *Studies in Law, Politics and Society* 50, ed. Austin Sarat (2009): 1–18.

Filth is brought to filth, and stench is brought to stench" (*y. Kiddushin* 3:13, p. 1178, lines 7–9). Zechariah's prophecy of redemption, according to this interpretation, includes the removal of that which is not fit; the dirt or filth will be brought to a filthy place. This future discrimination differs fundamentally from Rabbi Yose's view and expresses yearning for a state of pure pedigree, free of uncertainty—a state that can only be accomplished by God, Who knows what is hidden.[27]

These opposing views reflect another, earlier dispute about Elijah the prophet's future role:

> Rabbi Yehoshua said: I received from Rabbi Yoḥanan ben Zakkai, who heard it from his master, and his master from his master—a law to Moses from Sinai—that Elijah is not coming to render pure or impure, to exclude or include, but rather to exclude those who were included by force, and to include those who were excluded by force. The Bet Ẓerifa clan was in the Transjordan, and Ben-Ẓion excluded it by force; another was there, and Ben-Ẓion included it by force. It is such cases that Elijah is coming to render pure or impure, to exclude or include. Rabbi Yehudah says: [He is coming] to include but not to exclude. Rabbi Shimon says: [He is coming] to resolve arguments. The sages say: He is not coming to exclude or include, but to make peace in the world, as it says, "Behold, I will send you Elijah the prophet ... and he shall turn the heart of the fathers to the children, and the heart of the children to their fathers" (Mal 3:23–24). (*m. Eduyot* 8:7)

In Tosefta *Eduyot*, this dispute is taught in this manner:

> The Bet Haẓerifa clan was in the Transjordan, and Ben-Ẓion excluded it by force; another was there, and Ben-Ẓion included it by force. The sages did not want to reveal this about them, but they passed it on to their sons and disciples once every seven years. It is such cases that Elijah is coming to render pure or impure, to exclude or include. Rabbi Meir says: [He is coming] to include but not to exclude. Rabbi Yehudah says: The opposite.[28] Ḥanania ben Arai says: It is written: "The son of an Israelite woman and an Egyptian man went out amidst the Israelites, and the son of the Israelite woman fought with an Israelite man" (Lev 27:10). We can reason a fortiori: if Moses did not wish to disclose the *mamzerim* until they were discovered on their own, Elijah, the disciple of Moses, will certainly not disclose the *mamzerim* until they are discovered on their own. (*t. Eduyot* 3:4)[29]

---

27. See *Avot De-Rabbi Natan*, version 1, chapter 12, p. 27 in the Schechter edition, n. 56.

28. It seems that Rabbi Yehudah means to disagree with Rabbi Meir. According to the former, Elijah will expose those who forced their own inclusion but will not reveal those who were excluded by force. This opposing view apparently maintains that families that were excluded by force have already intermingled with other disqualified individuals.

29. The latter part of this Tosefta passage matches the earlier view that the child of a gentile and a Jewish woman is a *mamzer*. See above, n. 18.

The sages disagree about whether a certain family, whose name is unknown, which was unfit but then rendered fit by force, will be revealed by Elijah in the future. According to the tradition related by Rabbi Yehoshua, the removal of the mask of uncertain lineage is among things that Elijah is promised to fulfill in order to pave the way for the final redemption. In contrast, Rabbi Yehudah maintains that Elijah will disclose who has been excluded unlawfully, but he will not expose disqualified families that became intermingled. The view that maintains that Elijah will reveal the unfit families sees uncertainty of lineage as something that should be fixed by means of exclusion and discrimination; and since this state of affairs casts a heavy shadow of unfitness on the entire congregation, it is partially fixed by the sages, as the Tosefta attests, who secretly pass information about the disqualified from one generation to the next.[30] Rabbi Yehudah, who maintains that Elijah's actions will only include, not exclude, dismisses the possibility of excluding families by revealing their unfit origins in the future, and certainly in the present as well. In Tosefta *Kiddushin*, Rabbi Yose takes a radical step: not only will unfit families that became intermingled not be revealed, but God's grace will cleanse them by sprinkling purifying waters upon them.

In the eschatological prophecies of Malachi, the purification of lineages by the angel of God appears: "But who can endure the day of his coming, and who can hold out when he appears? For he is like a smelter's fire and like fuller's lye. He shall act like a smelter and purger of silver; and he shall purify the descendants of Levi and refine them like gold and silver, so that they shall present offerings in righteousness" (Mal 3:2–3).

A dispute about the meaning of this prophecy arose among the first generation of Amoraim, and this dispute reflects the tension present in the Tannaitic literature:

> Rabbi Ḥama, son of Rabbi Ḥanina, says: When the Holy One, Blessed be He, rests His Divine Presence, He rests it only upon the pedigreed fami-

30. The words of Rabbi Yehoshua in the Mishnah demand explanation:

> Rabbi Yehoshua said: I received from Rabbi Yoḥanan ben Zakkai, who heard it from his master, and his master from his master—a law to Moses from Sinai—that Elijah is not coming to render pure or impure, to exclude or include, but rather to exclude those who were included by force, and to include those who were excluded by force.

This can be explained as limiting the degree to which Elijah will disclose and clarify matters, as Rabbi Yehoshua prefaces his words by saying that Elijah is not coming to render pure or impure, to exclude or include. It seems that Elijah's sole interest is in families that were included or excluded by force; Elijah will not exclude a family that intermingled within the community not by force but by accident. Abaye interprets the *mishnah* in this way when he attempts to limit the broad potential implications of investigations and the keeping of secret pedigree charts. See *b. Kiddushin* 71a: "Abaye said, 'Such as those we know about; but a family that has intermingled has intermingled.'"

lies of Israel, as it is stated: "At that time, says the Lord, I will be the God of all the families of Israel" (Jer 30:25). "Of all Israel" is not stated, rather "of all the families."

"And they shall be my people" … Rabbi Ḥama bar Ḥanina says: When the Holy One purifies tribes, He will purify that of the tribe of Levi first, as it is stated: "He shall act like a smelter and purger of silver; and he shall purify the descendants of Levi and refine them like gold and silver, so that they shall present offerings in righteousness" (Mal 3:3).

Rabbi Yehoshua ben Levi says: Silver (money) purifies *mamzerim*, as it is stated: "He shall act like a smelter and purger of silver."

What is the meaning of "they shall present offerings in righteousness [*tzedakah*]"? Rabbi Yiẓḥak said: The Holy One performed an act of charity [*tzedakah*] for the Jewish people, for once a [disqualified] family has assimilated, it remains assimilated.

The conflict about the interpretation of the verse in Malachi reflects a profound dispute about the reality of intermingled unfit families. One view expects that it will be fixed by purifying it of dross, thus revealing the true, pedigreed families of Israel, to whom God will reveal Himself exclusively. The second view expects divine grace to purify all families.[31]

The Yerushalmi addresses the purification envisioned by the prophet Malachi more narrowly:

Rabbi Yassa [said] in the name of Rabbi Yoḥanan: In the future, God will only attend to [the purification of] the tribe of Levi. Why? "He shall act like a smelter and purger of silver; and he shall purify the descendants of Levi and refine them…." Rabbi Zeurah said: Like a person who drinks from a clean cup. Rabbi Hoshayah said: Because we are Levites, we will lose out?[32] Rabbi Ḥaninah the son of Rabbi Abbahu said: Even in the future, the Holy One will act toward them with charity [*tzedakah*]. Why? "They shall present offerings in righteousness [*tzedakah*]."

Rabbi Yoḥanan said: Any family in which a disqualification has been assimilated is not investigated. Rabbi Shimon ben Lakish said: Our *mishnah* says this: "The Bet Haẓerifa clan was in the Transjordan, and Ben-Ẓion excluded it by force; another was there, and Ben-Ẓion included it by force." Nevertheless, the sages did not want to reveal this about them. Rather, they passed it on to their sons and disciples twice every seven years. Rabbi Yoḥanan said: By the altar! I know of them,[33] and the greatest

31. The words of Rabbi Yehoshua, "Silver purifies *mamzerim*," are bitterly ironic. Silver—money—is not refined and smelted but is a purifying agent (perhaps in the way of ostensibly pedigreed priests who purchased their appointments with silver during the times of the Temple).

32. Another variant appears in the parallel text (*y. Kiddushin* 4a, col. 1181, lines 18–19): "Rabbi Hoshayah said: Because we are not Levites, we will lose out?" This is likely the opposite reaction to that of Rabbi Yoḥanan. Rabbi Yoḥanan, who wishes to save Jewish families, damages them and leaves them with the taint of disqualification.

33. In the parallel source (*y. Kiddushin* 4a, col. 1181, line 27): "Rabbi Yoḥanan said: By

> of the generation have been assimilated into them. (*y. Yevamot* 8:3, col. 871, lines 18–29)

Rabbi Yoḥanan limits the acts of discrimination and refinery to the Levites only, whereas Rabbi Ḥama bar Ḥanina expands it to all of Israel. One of the justifications for purifying *mamzerim* in the future is the terrible communal cost that exposing and excluding them will likely entail: "[If] the law does not accord with Rabbi Yose, in the future, the generations will be despondent." This anxiety, which is projected into the future, obtains a more contemporary and urgent interpretation in the words of Rabbi Yoḥanan. He swears that he knows which families are disqualified, but they have assimilated the generation's leaders, and an attempt to examine and investigate *mamzerim* would turn up those great rabbis. (As we will see below, Rabbi Yoḥanan's disciple, who disagreed with his view that a family that has assimilated a disqualification is not investigated, refused to marry the daughter of Rabbi Yoḥanan because of uncertainties about flawed pedigree.) The severe social ramifications of investigations, whose ultimate consequences are hard to predict, and which can be transformed into a social device for ostracizing and penalizing by spreading rumors and casting accusations, appear in Tannaitic literature as a prohibition and recoil from the disclosure of unfit families: "[If one said:] 'I am a nazirite unless I expose families,' he shall be a nazirite and not expose families" (*t. Nazir* 1:3).[34]

The enormous tension surrounding this very question in Tannaitic literature is revealed through an opposing tradition, which marks and identifies the *mamzer* as an object of distancing and isolation:

> They asked Rabbi Eliezer: Does a *mamzer* inherit? He said to them: Does he perform levirate divorce? [They asked him:] Does he perform levirate divorce? He responded: Does he inherit? [They asked:] Does he inherit? He said: Does he plaster his house? [They asked:] Does he plaster his house? He said: Does he plaster his grave? (*t. Yevamot* 3:1)

Rabbi Eliezer, who rebuffs his students' attempts to find answers to their questions by retorting with different questions, seems to hold that the house of a *mamzer* should be marked with plaster, as should his grave. The Mishnah offers further attestation of a tradition of demarcating and

---

the altar! I know of them, but what can we do? The greatest of the generation have been assimilated into them!" This formulation seems better and sharper than the version in *y. Yevamot*.

34. "It is taught: Anyone who disqualifies [others] is disqualified, and he never speaks in praise of others. And Shmuel said: He disqualifies [others] with his own blemish" (*b. Kiddushin* 70b). The attachment of a pedigree disqualification as a tool in a communal and cultural struggle is known to us from, inter alia, the Maimonidean polemic in 1232, in which a severe pedigree disqualification was attached to the family of Rabbi Yonah Gerondi, and consequently on that of Naḥmanides, who was a cousin of Rabbi Yonah.

attempting to preserve the purity of lineage: "Shimon ben Azzai said: I found a genealogy scroll in Jerusalem, and in it is written: 'So-and-so is a *mamzer* because of adultery'" (*m. Yevamot* 4:13). This attestation, brought in support of Rabbi Shimon's halakhic position, is not necessarily historical evidence of a systematic recording of genealogy tables, but it expresses support, in principle, for marking and cautioning. We are thus witness to a profound tension within Tannaitic literature, between a separatist inclination that labels the *mamzer* a dangerous plague, and the view of *mamzerut* as only a disqualification for marriage, not as something that should be investigated and labeled.[35]

The conflict between the messianic utopia and how it relates to the problem of pedigree is not only an expression of contradictory yearnings for the future. It is significant for how to relate to uncertainty in the here and now. Rabbi Yoḥanan's limiting statements about the future are juxtaposed in the Yerushalmi to another dictum of his: "Any family in which a disqualification has been assimilated is not investigated." In the Bavli, right after the view that maintains that Malachi prophesied about the purification, not the isolation, of the disqualified, the statement of Rabbi Yiẓḥak appears: "The Holy One performed an act of charity for the Jewish people, for once a [disqualified] family has assimilated, it remains assimilated." The messianic image of purifying the disqualified and rendering them fit produces a forgiving attitude with far-reaching halakhic implications with respect to all that pertains to uncertainties of lineage. This image negates investigations, examinations, genealogies, and the general anxiety about pedigree. Another, later expression of this view appears in the Amoraic view that it is permitted by the Torah to marry someone whose *mamzer* status is uncertain—a view that, as we have seen, has its antecedents in Tannaitic literature.[36]

35. See the discussion of the distancing of the *mamzer* in rabbinic literature in Meir Bar-Ilan, "The Attitude toward *Mamzerim* in Jewish Society in Late Antiquity," *Jewish History* 14 (2000): 136–45. Bar-Ilan maintains that Rabbi Eliezer's strict attitude toward the *mamzer* reflects an earlier halakhah, and this attitude gradually becomes more lenient in the later stages of Tannaitic and Amoraic halakhah. It seems, however, that the tension reflected in the sources with respect to this question can be found at different times and in different contexts. It cannot be explained only by time. Thus, for example, we have the stringent position of the late Tanna, Rabbi Meir, vis-à-vis distancing *mamzerim* in the future, the *baraita* in *Avot De-Rabbi Natan* (version 1, 12:8), and the stringent positions of Amoraim from Eretz Yisrael and Babylonia alike. In this context, see Cohen's response to Bar-Ilan: Shaye J. D. Cohen, "Some thoughts on 'The Attitude toward *Mamzerim* in Jewish Society in Late Antiquity,'" *Jewish History* 14 (2000): 171–74.

36. "Rava said: According to the Torah, a *shetuki* is fit [for marriage] … and the Torah said, 'a *mamzer* shall not enter.' A *mamzer* of certain status may not enter, but a *mamzer* of uncertain status may enter the community" (*b. Kiddushin* 73a).

A more problematic but no less fascinating way of removing uncertainties of pedigree without investigations or exclusions is indicative of the same approach:

> They asked Rabbi Eliezer: What is the status of an eleventh-generation *mamzer*? He said to them: Bring me a third-generation, and I will purify him. What is the reasoning of Rabbi Eliezer? Because [*mamzerim*] do not survive. Rabbi Ḥaninah accords with Rabbi Ḥaninah, for Rabbi Ḥaninah said: Once every sixty or seventy years, the Holy One brings something into the world that consumes all *mamzerim*, and it takes untainted individuals along with them, so that sins are not publicized.... Rabbi Ḥunah says: A *mamzer* does not live more than thirty days. When Rabbi Zeira moved here [to Palestine], he heard them calling "*mamzer*" and "*mamzeret*." He said to them: What is this? There goes the statement of Rabbi Huna, for Rabbi Huna said: A *mamzer* does not live more than thirty days. Rabbi Yaakov bar Aḥa said to him: I was with you when Rabbi Abba bar Huna said in the name of Rav: A *mamzer* does not live more than thirty days. When? In a case where it is not publicized; but if it was publicized, he will live. (*y. Kiddushin* 4:1, p. 1181, lines 1–16)

By punishing the *mamzer* and his parents, God frees the community from suspicion and uncertainty about the unfit having gotten mixed in. Without any suspicion or investigation, members of the congregation can marry one another, because *mamzerim* do not survive. As Rabbi Ḥaninah asserts, every sixty or seventy years, the Holy One eliminates them in a plague. This plague also destroys other people, to prevent the identification of the *mamzerim* and the publicizing of transgression.[37] Therefore, according to Rabbi Eliezer, there is no concern about the status of anyone whose lineage is free of *mamzerut* for three generations. *Mamzerut* is never transmitted beyond three generations; that is, it does not survive beyond the period in which it is still possible to investigate. The community is thus freed from the threat of uncertainty. Rabbi Huna, in the name of Rav, cites a far-fetched tradition that completely removes the suspicion of *mamzerut* with the claim that no *mamzer* survives more than thirty days. This view preserves the severity of the prohibition and its deterrent power against those who would commit sexual transgressions: a *mamzer* will not survive. However, it uses that very position to ease concerns about *mamzerut* and to purify the community as it is, regardless of the degree of practical reliability of the solution to the problem.

The idea that a *mamzer* does not survive appears in Second Temple literature, and it originates in the notion that, since he was born in sin, the *mamzer* cannot exist or survive in the world. In this passage, the Amoraim use that same tradition, but they claim that it does not apply to known *mamzerim*. They apply it only to unknown *mamzerim*, and in doing so they

37. Tzvi Novick ("'They Come against Them,'" 1–18) analyzes this source alongside its *Leviticus Rabbah* parallel and in the context of the question of publicizing transgression.

free the community from the threat of uncertainty.[38] The paradoxical form of taking a forgiving attitude toward *mamzerim* by miraculously killing them off is reflected in a story that appears right after Rav Huna's statement that "A *mamzer* does not live more than thirty days":

> In the days of Rabbi Berekhiah, a Babylonian came here [to Palestine], and it was known that he is a *mamzer*. He said to him: "Rabbi, grant me [charity]." He said to him: "Tomorrow, stand up in public, and I will allocate [charity] to you." [Rabbi Berekhiah] came, sat, and expounded. When he finished expounding, he said to them: "Our brothers, give to this man, who is a *mamzer*, one who cannot enter the community." He said to him: "I asked you for temporary sustenance, but you have ruined my life!" He said to him: "I have given you life! For Rabbi Ba bar Huna said in the name of Rav: A *mamzer* does not live more than thirty days. When? In a case where it is not publicized; but if it was publicized, he will live." (*y. Kiddushin* 3:12, p. 1176, lines 12–19)[39]

Rabbi Berekhiah, whom the *mamzer* approached for charity and assistance, organized a public collection on his behalf, which was ostensibly supposed to give the poor man support and supporters. At that public event, however, Rabbi Berekhiah also disclosed his identity as a *mamzer* in public, claiming that he is deserving of more support since he cannot join the community or get married. Thus, as the *mamzer* accuses him, he made him even more despondent, worsening his already precarious situation. Rabbi Berekhiah's response to the Babylonian *mamzer*, who perhaps moved to the Land of Israel so he could disappear in a locale where he was

---

38. See Ecclus 23:36–41 (New American Bible Revised Edition [NABRE] 23:22–26]):

> So it is with the woman unfaithful to her husband, who offers him an heir by another man. First of all, she has disobeyed the law of the Most High; second, she has wronged her husband; third, through her wanton adultery she has brought forth children by another man. Such a woman will be dragged before the assembly, and her punishment will extend to her children. Her children will not take root; her branches will not bring forth fruit. She will leave behind an accursed memory; her disgrace will never be blotted out.

As Moshe Tzvi Segal notes in his edition of Ecclesiasticus/Ben Sira (Jerusalem: Bialik Institute, 1958), this idea has a parallel in the Wisdom of Solomon: "But the children of adulterers will remain without issue, and the progeny of an unlawful bed will disappear" (3:4; NABRE [3:16]). On the use of this idea in Amoraic literature to relieve the problem of uncertainty, see Israel Ta-Shma, "A Mamzer Is Not Alive?" [Hebrew], *Beit Mikra* 34 (1968): 33–36.

39. See the parallel in *Leviticus Rabbah* 32:6–7. The series of dicta in the *Leviticus Rabbah* parallel is better organized because the story of Rabbi Berekhiah appears after the discussion of the words of Rav and his disciple, Rabbi Huna. In contrast, in the Yerushalmi, the story of Rabbi Berekhiah appears right after the words of Rabbi Huna, which are severed from their broader context, while the story of Rabbi Zeira, which serves as the basis for the distinction between a known and an unknown *mamzer*, appears immediately following the story of Rabbi Berekhiah, which is actually premised upon this distinction. In the parallel in *y. Yevamot* 8:3 (col. 870, line 50, and col. 870, line 49–col. 871, line 4), the dicta of Rabbi Ḥaninah and Rabbi Huna appear without the story of Rabbi Berekhiah.

unknown, makes sarcastic, perhaps even cruel, use of a statement whose initial purpose was to protect *mamzerim*. The objective of this statement was that one should not investigate, examine, or announce *mamzerim*, because they will not survive anyway. Rabbi Berekhiah, who opposed the spirit of this assertion, transforms it into a tool for exposing the *mamzer*, for by exposing him, he "saves" him from death—for unknown *mamzerim* do not survive, but a known *mamzer* will live. The attempt to solve the distress of the community and the *mamzer* while deterring and preserving the severity of sexual transgression by "killing" the *mamzer* comes with an unexpected price: someone will want to "save" the *mamzer* by exposing him.

Another view that uses the power of divine providence to spare the community from the burden of uncertainty is expressed in the following words: "Rabbi Yehudah bar Pazi said: 'God settles the lonely at home' (Ps 68:7). Even if a *mamzer* is at one end of the world and a *mamzeret* is at the other end, the Holy One brings them together and makes a match between them" (*y. Kiddushin* 3:12, col. 1176, lines 9–11). The Holy One makes a home for the lonely by making a match between the *mamzer* and *mamzeret*, who are alone and isolated. By doing so, God alleviates the distress of the unfortunate and also removes the cloud of uncertainty from the community, because a *mamzer* will always be matched with a *mamzeret*.[40] The instructive element of this view is that, with the grace of God Who sits and makes matches, it simultaneously resolves two sources of distress that lead to a forgiving view toward *mamzerut*: the fate of the *mamzer* himself, and the cloud of uncertainty that pervades the entire congregation.

The tension between the radically opposing messianic yearnings concerning uncertainty of lineage finds expression in the lineage investigation practices that emerge in Amoraic responses to Mishnah *Kiddushin* —responses that are deeply contentious and divided, like those among the Tannaim. In the first two generations of Babylonian Amoraim, the *mishnah* was interpreted in two conflicting ways: "Rabbi Elazar said: Ezra did not go up from Babylonia before he made it like pure, fine flour" (*b. Kiddushin* 69b); the purification of Babylonia from unfitness is attributed to Ezra, who, according to this dictum, distanced these disqualified individuals and brought them to Eretz Yisrael.

A conception of the superiority of Babylonia over Eretz Yisrael with respect to pedigree emerges from this novel reading of the *mishnah*: "Rabbi Yehudah said in the name of Shmuel: All lands are *isah* compared to Eretz

40. In the Yerushalmi, this dictum appears as a proof that *mamzerim* may marry one another, as against the view, espoused by Rabbi Yehudah in *m. Kiddushin* 4:3, that such a marriage is forbidden. Nevertheless, the purpose of the dictum itself is not to introduce the novel idea that a *mamzer* and a *mamzeret* may marry; rather, it takes this as self-evident. Its interest is to inform the audience of God's kindness; He alleviates the loneliness of *mamzerim* as well as the anxious uncertainty of the rest of the community.

Yisrael, and Eretz Yisrael is *isah* in comparison to Babylonia (*b. Kiddushin* 69b). The question of pedigree becomes an intercommunal political issue with far-reaching halakhic implications, as articulated in another of Shmuel's dicta:

> Shmuel says in the name of an elder: Babylonia retains its presumption of fitness [to marry], until it becomes known to you in what way it became disqualified. Other lands retain their presumption of disqualification, until it becomes known to you in what way it was rendered fit. In Eretz Yisrael, one who has a presumptive status of disqualification is disqualified, and one who has a presumptive status of fitness is fit. (*b. Kiddushin* 71a)[41]

The *mishnah*, in the Bavli's interpretation of it, creates a hierarchy of pedigree that mandates examination and investigation, and the Bavli devotes a long discussion to determining the geographical boundaries of Babylonia, which also demarcate its presumption of fitness. This tradition is reflected in a very sharp narrative about Babylonian sages who refrained from marrying women from Eretz Yisrael for fear of unfitness:

> Zeiri was avoiding Rabbi Yoḥanan, who was telling him to marry his daughter. One day, they were walking along the path, and they arrived at a large puddle of water. Zeiri lifted Rabbi Yoḥanan upon his shoulders and carried him across. [Rabbi Yoḥanan] said to him: Our Torah is fit, but our daughters are unfit? What is your view? If you say it is because we learned in a *mishnah*: Ten pedigrees came up from Babylonia: priests, Levites, etc., is that to say that all of the priests, Levites, and Israelites left? Just as some of these remained, so too some of those [unfit lineages] remained [in Babylonia].
>
> However, this statement of Rabbi Elazar escaped [Rabbi Yoḥanan]: Ezra did not go up from Babylonia before he made it like pure, fine flour. (*b. Kiddushin* 71b)

Rabbi Zeira, the Babylonian student of Rabbi Yoḥanan, who carries him on his shoulders in the manner of a disciple who serves his master, refuses to marry Rabbi Yoḥanan's daughter. Such a marriage was supposed to bolster the disciple's status, as the master recognizes him as being worthy to marry his daughter, yet Rabbi Zeira refuses.

The story frames the exchange between Rabbi Yoḥanan and Rabbi Zeira in a way that simultaneously sharpens Rabbi Zeira's submission to Rabbi Yoḥanan as a disciple who serves his master and the Babylonian sense of supremacy that he arrogates to himself vis-à-vis his master from

41. The transformation of lineage into an arena of intercommunal political conflict finds expression in the attempt to change the presumption of pedigree cited in the Bavli: "In the days of Rabbi [Yehudah the Nasi], they sought to make Babylonia *isah* in comparison to Eretz Yisrael. He said to them, 'You are sticking thorns in my eyes' (*b. Kiddushin* 71a). As Rashi comments, Rabbi Yehudah the Nasi opposed this change because, as a descendant of Hillel, he himself was of Babylonian lineage.

Eretz Yisrael.[42] In response to Rabbi Zeira's refusal, Rabbi Yoḥanan reproves him, saying that even though his Torah is worthy enough to study, his daughter is unfit for marriage. Rabbi Yoḥanan does not attempt to give Eretz Yisrael a presumption of pedigree on the level of Babylonia; rather, he is astonished at the Babylonian sages' supremacist reading of the *mishnah*. If the Babylonians are indeed correct that Ezra purified Babylonia and rendered it fine flour by leading all of the unfit groups to Eretz Yisrael, how is it possible that any priests, Levites, and Israelites, all of which are listed in the *mishnah* among those who migrated from Babylonia, remained in Babylonia? Rather, Rabbi Yoḥanan maintained that "any family in which a disqualification has been assimilated is not investigated," and the attempt to distill from within all of Israel a single group that purports to have purity of lineage is fundamentally baseless.

The Bavli presents us with diametrically opposed responses to the problem of lineage in the first generations of Amoraim from Babylonia and Eretz Yisrael. Alongside repeated attestations to a regime of investigations, presumptions, and boundaries, there is also a principled, consistent position that maintains that a *mamzer* that assimilated is assimilated and that rejects the attempt to create a distinct, internal, pedigreed nobility. An expression of this tension is the different responses to the *mishnah* in *Kiddushin* among the leading Babylonian Amoraim. Rabbi Elazar, as mentioned, held that the *mishnah* attests that "Ezra did not go up from Babylonia before he made it like pure, fine flour." This interpretive position undergirds the Babylonian traditions about the virtues of a regime of inspections and pedigrees. In contrast to this tradition and its variegated ramifications, there is an opposing position that sets our *mishnah* up as the rejected opinion of an individual sage: "Rabbi Yehudah said in the name of Shmuel: These are the words of Rabbi Meir, but the sages say that all lands retain a presumption of fitness" (*b. Kiddushin* 72b).

A similar dictum, designed to cancel the idea of investigation, is directed against the *mishnah* that asserts the scope of lineage investigations: "Rabbi Yehudah said in the name of Rav: These are the words of Rabbi Meir, but the sages say that all families retain a presumption of fitness" (*b. Kiddushin* 76b). This tradition establishes a presumption of fitness that is reflected in a long tradition of Amoraim who maintain that "any family in which a disqualification has been assimilated is not investigated."[43]

42. On Babylonian supremacism vis-à-vis Eretz Yisrael with respect to pedigree and other matters, see Isaiah Gafni, "Expressions and Types of 'Local Patriotism' among the Jews of Sasanian Babylonia," in *Irano-Judaica II: Studies Relating to Jewish Contacts with Persian Culture throughout the Ages*, ed. Shaul Shaked and Amnon Netzer (Jerusalem: Ben-Zvi Institute, 1990), 63–71.

43. Michael Satlow (*Jewish Marriage in Antiquity*, 152–53) and Jeffrey Rubenstein (*The*

Anxieties about uncertainty of lineage and the debates about it are reflected in the following exceptionally powerful story from the Bavli:

> Ulla arrived in Pumbedita, to the house of Rabbi Yehudah. He observed that Rabbi Yitzḥak, the son of Rabbi Yehudah, was grown up but was unmarried. He said to [Rabbi Yehudah]: Why don't you marry a woman to your son? He said back: Who knows whence I can find someone marriageable [who is not of unfit lineage]? He said to him: Do we know where we come from? Perhaps we are from those about whom it is written: "They have ravished the women in Zion, the maidens in the cities of Judah" (Lam 5:11). And if you would say that if a gentile or a slave engaged in sexual intercourse with a Jewish woman, the offspring is fit, perhaps [we come] from those about whom it is written: "Those who lie upon beds of ivory and stretch themselves upon their couches" (Amos 6:4) … [and] Rabbi Abbahu said: This refers to people who eat and drink together, and attach their beds together, and exchange their wives with each other, and befoul their couches with semen that is not theirs. [Rabbi Yehudah] said to [Ulla]: What should we do? He said to him: Go after the silence, like the people of the west [i.e., Eretz Yisrael] investigate: When two people quarrel with each other, they observe which of them becomes silent first, and they say "This one is more pedigreed."

This singular story expresses the notion that suspicion of unfit lineage is self-defeating, as it plagues even those who purport to protect themselves from it. As Ulla says to Rabbi Yehudah, who was paralyzed by anxiety to the point that he hesitates to marry off his son, it is possible that his own ancestors are among those who, the prophet attests, engaged in wife swapping. How did Rabbi Yehudah himself know that his own pedigree was more certain than that of those around him, about which there was uncertainty? The only test of lineage, suggested by Ulla as an alternative to the investigation, doomed to fail, of family history, is connected to the family's moral virtue. This test gives preference to a family that does not bear grudges and is first to work toward reconciliation of disputes. This seems like good marital advice in any case.

The halakhah that determines that *mamzerut* is a trait that passes from one generation to the next, ad infinitum, even if only one parent is a *mamzer*, is supposed to produce real deterrence to sexual transgression. Such a policy engenders an attitude toward *mamzerut* that treats it as

---

Culture of the Babylonian Talmud [Baltimore: Johns Hopkins University Press, 2003], 84) advanced the argument that lineage anxiety and stringency were greater in Babylonia than in Palestine due to the influence of Sassanian culture. See also Adiel Schremer, *Male and Female He Created Them: Jewish Marriage in Late Second Temple Mishnah and Talmud Periods* [Hebrew] (Jerusalem: Schazar Center, 2003), 147–49. For a thorough analysis of the question presenting a different and complex picture, see Yedida Koren, "'Look through Your Books and Make Me a Perfect Match': Talking about Genealogy in Amoraic Palestine and Babylonia," *Journal for the Study of Judaism* 49 (2018): 417–48.

something viral and contagious, as a poisonous substance that cannot be removed. This is expressed in an almost palpable revulsion of the *mamzer* and in turning him into an abomination.

However, this policy is self-defeating, because over time it introduces uncertainty about *mamzer* status into the entire Jewish community, and it magnifies the injustice done to the *mamzer* for a transgression in which he took no part. This state of affairs produced two completely different responses among the Tannaim and the first generations of Amoraim to the problem of uncertain lineage.

The first response takes a forgiving attitude toward a *mamzer* who has assimilated into the community and permits all of these uncertainties from various angles through a series of bold halakhic maneuvers and interpretations, bolstered by messianic yearnings for the future purification of *mamzerim* by God Himself.

The second response, aware of the fragility of pedigree networks, tries to create a regime of investigations, boundaries, and presumptions, in an almost desperate attempt to create pedigreed nobility in a world filled with uncertainties about fitness for marriage. This attempt is accompanied by a messianic expectation of separation and isolation of the disqualified from the rest of the community in the messianic future, when God will be revealed to the pedigreed of the community and will purify and refine them from any unfit elements.

Throughout the history of halakhah, the first approach had primacy, in the main, despite the almost primal intensity of revulsion for the *mamzer*.[44] The large gap between the various opinions about how to act in states of uncertainty about lineage, with all its far-reaching practical implications, is one of the deepest disputes in the history of halakhah, and it comes to the fore already at the first stages of engagement with this question.

V

Uncertainties about lineage are liable to sprout not only from the mingling of those unfit to marry into families but from differences of opinion about the definition of disqualification from marriage in various halakhic traditions. We do not have direct evidence about the pedigree and marriage practice of the Dead Sea sect, but we know that they disagreed with the rabbis with respect to the laws of incest prohibitions. Among the writings

---

44. See Pinchas Shiffman, "Al Yakir ve-al Yastir: Emet Uvdatit ve-Emet Mishpatit be-Ḥashash le-Mamzerut" [Don't Ask, Don't Tell: Factual Truth and Legal Truth in Suspicion of *Mamzerut*], in *Studies in Law and Halakhah: Menachem Elon Memorial Volume*, ed. A. Edrei (Jerusalem: Nevo, 2018), 207–22.

of the sect we find, for example, a view that forbids marriage between an uncle and his niece. They considered such a union to be incest, whereas the rabbis permit and even recommend such a union.[45] It would seem that, after a few generations, a community faithful to the halakhah of the rabbis would become unfit to marry, due to uncertainty, from the perspective of a community that practiced the more restrictive incest code of the Dead Sea sect. Marriage between the two groups would become forbidden, or permitted only after a thorough investigation of several generations and genealogical lists that would render families from that other sect fit to marry. As mentioned, we have no evidence of such sectarian marriage prohibitions, though its absence does not really prove anything.[46]

In contrast, we know of a similar state of affairs in a later period: marriage between Karaites and Rabbanites from the medieval era to our own times. Karaites have a much more restrictive policy than Talmudic halakhah when it comes to incest prohibitions. On the other side of the ledger, halakhists maintain that Karaite divorce proceedings are fundamentally flawed, so Karaite women who remarried after divorce are considered by halakhists to still be married to their first husbands, and their children from their second marriages are thus considered *mamzerim*. It would seem that these groups should forbid their sons and daughters from marrying one another. During the great halakhic controversy about whether it is permitted to marry a Karaite, proof that it is forbidden was adduced from the *mishnah* in *Kiddushin* that we discussed above:

> Rabbi Elazar says: Those of certain status with those of certain status are permitted [to marry]. Those of certain status with those of uncertain status; or those of uncertain status with those of certain status; or those of uncertain status with those of uncertain status are forbidden [to marry]. These are the uncertain statuses: *shetukei*, *asufei*, and Samaritans. (*m. Kiddushin* 4:3)

Samaritans are considered to be unfit out of uncertainty, and according to Rabbi Elazar it is even forbidden for Samaritans to marry one another. In the words of the Tosefta: "So would Rabbi Liezer say: A *mamzer* may not

45. On the difference between rabbinic halakhah and the Dead Sea sect concerning incest prohibitions, see Aharon Shemesh, "Incest Prohibitions in Judean Desert Scrolls and their Importance to the History of Halakhah," *Sidra* 24–25 (2010): 441–57.

46. On genealogical lists in the Dead Sea sect, see Magen Broshi and Ada Yardeni, "On Netinim and False Prophets" [Hebrew], *Tarbiz* 62 (1993): 45–54. It is implied in one of the polemical sections of MMT that, from the perspective of the sectarians, their opponents were rife with promiscuity and were therefore likely unfit for marriage: "And concerning the mixed marriages that are being performed among the people, and they are sons of holy [seed], as is written, Israel is holy" (4QMMT B, 75–76; Qimron, *Dead Sea Scrolls*, 2:209). For additional support for the possibility that the sectarians viewed other groups as unfit for marriage, see Satlow, *Jewish Marriage in Antiquity*, 144 and n. 93.

marry a Samaritan woman, and a Samaritan man may not marry a *mamzeret*. A Samaritan man may not marry a Samaritan woman, and likewise a *shetuki* and a foundling" (*t. Kiddushin* 5:1). The Yerushalmi offers several reasons why Samaritans are considered possible *mamzerim*, and one of them—which was cited to prove that Karaites are disqualified from marriage—was "because they are not knowledgeable about the particulars of writs of divorce" (*y. Gittin* 1:5, p. 1057, lines 10–11).[47]

Procedural differences in marriage and divorce can lead to acute conditions of sectarianism in which disputes are no longer intracommunal disagreements but schisms that rend the community into two different communities. The overcoming of these uncertainties in the case of Karaites is evidence of the refusal of some halakhists, primarily those who lived side by side with Karaites, to create an unbridgeable rift between Rabbanites and Karaites.[48]

Differences in marriage and divorce procedures and the political use of halakhah in the cases of uncertainty that they generate can occasionally be used to define rigid communal boundaries. Marriage bans, whether mutual or unilateral, are the final and irrevocable separation of communities that disagree about the source of halakhic authority. However, this piercing halakhic logic can become an intracommunal problem, occasionally with a local character, within rabbinic circles themselves, in cases of halakhic disagreement about family law. Such cases of uncertainty, and the sectarian potential they contain, are addressed in Mishnah and Tosefta *Yevamot*, which discuss the differences between the House of Shammai and the House of Hillel:

> The House of Shammai permits co-wives to the brothers [for marriage], but the House of Hillel forbids. If they perform *ḥaliẓah,* the House of Shammai disqualifies them from [marrying] priests, but the House of Hillel permits. If they underwent levirate marriage, the House of Shammai considers them fit [to subsequently marry priests], but the House of Hillel disqualifies them. Even though these prohibit and these permit,

47. See *b. Kiddushin* 76a. Regarding the use of the *mishnah* on the Samaritans and the corresponding passage of the Talmud to forbid marriage with Karaites, see the responsum of Rabbi Shimshon quoted in *Beit Yosef, Even Ha-ezer* 4 (at the end). It explains that Karaites are prohibited because their marriages are valid but their divorces are not. Rema (*Even Ha-ezer* 5) explains his decision to forbid marriage with Karaites on the grounds that they are possibly *mamzerim*. A responsum by Rabbi Yeḥezkel Landau makes use of probabilistic decisions from the laws of uncertainties to permit marriage with a Karaite when the marriage does not occur in the place of the Karaite community. The Karaite is considered fit to marry in this case because most Karaites are indeed fit, and this individual separated from the majority. See *Responsa Noda Bi-Yehudah* (first volume), *Even Ha-ezer* 5.

48. See Rabbi Ovadiah Yosef, *Yabi'a Omer* 8, *Even Ha-ezer* 12, which permits marriage with Karaites. It is apparent within the abundance of permissive rationales that appear in the responsum that Rabbi Ovadiah was familiar with the Karaites from his tenure as rabbi of Cairo, and that Karaite solidarity with the Jewish community in general made a profound impression on him.

> these disqualify and these consider fit, the House of Shammai did not refrain from marrying women from the House of Hillel, nor the House of Hillel from the House of Shammai. Regarding all matters of purity and impurity, where these rendered pure and these rendered impure, they did not refrain from using [utensils] the other deemed pure. (*m. Yevamot* 1:6)

The *mishnah* mentions a case in which the Houses of Hillel and Shammai disagreed about the laws of levirate marriage. This is the sort of dispute that can cause a mutual ban on marriage, which would turn the two houses into separate sects. The *mishnah* notes that, despite the disagreement, because of which the two houses were susceptible to viewing one another as disqualified for marriage out of uncertainty, they did not refrain from marrying one another. Likewise, even though the laws of purity and impurity generate, willy-nilly, separation between various groups, the differences of opinion on such matters between the houses did not prevent them from coming into daily, ongoing contact with one another.

The Tosefta lists additional, broader cases of dispute that threatened to dissolve the houses' common fabric of life with respect to marriage:

> Even though the House of Shammai disputed the House of Hillel regarding co-wives, sisters, a woman whose marital status is uncertain, an obsolete bill of divorce, one who betroths a woman with the value of a *perutah*, and one who divorces his wife and then spends the night with her at an inn, the House of Shammai did not refrain from marrying women from the House of Hillel, nor the House of Hillel from the House of Shammai. Rather, they practiced truth and peace between them, as it is stated: "Love truth and peace" (Zech 8:19). Even though these prohibit and these permit, they did not refrain from using [utensils] the other deemed pure, in fulfillment of the verse: "Each man's path is proper in his own eyes, but the Lord weighs the heart" (Prov 21:2). Rabbi Shimon says: They would not refrain from the uncertain, but they would refrain from the certain. (*t. Yevamot* 1:3)

The overcoming of potential schism despite differences in the laws of marriage and divorce is explained with two verses, which signify different reasons. The first verse, "Love truth and peace," gestures toward the need to add peace to truth and to prevent the schism, in the name of truth, of the two houses into two separate sects. This principle of loving peace alongside truth establishes that halakhic truth is bound by the goal of preserving internal harmony. The second verse, "Each man's path is proper in his own eyes, but the Lord weighs the heart," undermines the certainty of truth itself. Even though each person views his path as right and proper, the Holy One examines the purity of the heart. From God's perspective, the intentions of the two houses for the sake of heaven are what is important, whatever the disagreement between them.

Rabbi Shimon's view, which is a minority position in the Tosefta, limits the value of peace to those cases of uncertainty. According to him, in cases where the houses knew for certain that, according to their opinion, a particular man or woman is disqualified from marriage, they would refrain from marrying him or her.[49]

This extraordinary attestation of the value of peace and pure-heartedness in the face of rigid halakhic truth indicates a profound awareness of the possible complications of uncertainties about lineage. In cases where these uncertainties result not from the coincidental assimilation of someone unfit for marriage but from principled halakhic disputes about marriage and divorce procedure or the definition of unfitness, they are liable to generate mutual marriage bans. The renunciation of a rigid and uncompromising stance of pure law, come what may, prevented the trauma of schism and sectarianism within rabbinic circles. The Tosefta tradition attests to a later debate about how far this relinquishment went, and Rabbi Shimon limits it to cases where uncertainty arose.[50]

---

49. For a discussion of the possibility of convivence between the two houses under conditions of disagreement and dispute, see Michael Rotenberg, "Ha-ḥayim Be-tzel Ha-maḥloket: Darkhei Ha-kiyum Ha-meshutaf Be-matzavei Maḥloket She-lo Hukhre'ah Be-mishnat Ḥazal" [In the Shadow of Dispute: Modes of Coexistence in Conditions of Unresolved Dispute in the Teaching of the Sages] (PhD diss., Hebrew University of Jerusalem, 2012).

50. The first generations of Amoraim responded to these traditions, some due to deep reservations and unwillingness to accept their boldness. Both the Yerushalmi and Bavli quote Amoraic traditions that the House of Shammai accepted the established halakhah and in fact practiced according to the House of Hillel, a position that drastically dilutes the innovativeness of the Mishnah and Tosefta. This interpretive stance overcomes the initial challenge from marriage to a *mamzer*, but it is hard to reconcile this with the words of the Tosefta, and especially with Rabbi Shimon's distinction between certain and uncertain *mamzerim*: if the House of Shammai practiced in accordance with the halakhah of the House of Hillel, situations of certainty and uncertainty would not even arise.

Alongside this view a counterposition is maintained in both the Yerushami and Bavli that each of the houses followed their own opinion. As to the question of how the Houses of Shammai and Hillel could do this when the bone of contention between them was *mamzerut*, the Yerushalmi offers the following justification: "The Omnipresent protects, and no such case ever occurred" (*y. Yevamot* 1:6 col. 835, Iine 48). Divine providence is activated to make peace possible while simultaneously preventing uncertainties and the forbidden marriages they precipitate.

The Bavli addresses the same question and provides a different explanation: the Houses of Shammai and Hillel alerted one another in cases where someone was liable to marry one unfit for marriage according to their opinion—"[The House of Hillel and the House of Shammai] in fact always acted [in accordance with their views] because they would inform one another" (*b. Yevamot* 14a). This explanation of Shmuel does not tally with Rabbi Shimon's words in the Tosefta, namely, that the Houses of Shammai and Hillel would not refrain from uncertainties, because in a case where each side provides full disclosure of disqualifications according to the opinion of the other, no uncertainties should have arisen at all. For an extensive and thorough analysis of the position of the relationship between the Tannaitic sources and the Yerushalmi and Bavli in relation to the question of legal pluralism, see Richard Hidary, *Dispute for the Sake of Heaven: Legal Pluralism in the Talmud*, Brown Judaic Studies 353 (Providence, RI: Brown Judaic Studies, 2010), 189–216.

Given the uncertainties that arise from lineage, a question emerges: Is it possible to live together, in full cooperation, with family ties, under conditions of disagreement about marriage and divorce procedures? The prevention of sectarian schism, the threat of which emerges in the context of a regime that is meticulous about pedigree, was explained by means of the value of peace. However, the importance of this value was reinterpreted, and consequently it offered a different answer to the challenge of living together under the looming shadow of uncertainty. The Tanna of our *mishnah* and the first Tanna of the Tosefta maintain that it was the power of peace that made the parties to the dispute willing to marry the *mamzerim* and disqualifications of their disputants. Rabbi Shimon maintains that the weight of this value permits uncertainties but not cases of certainty.

In his important work on the ancient and deeply rooted taboos of incest, Claude Lévi-Strauss claimed that their purpose is to widen blood ties and increase social solidarity. The only way to increase family bonds is by intermarrying with other clans and forging common blood ties. The prohibition of incest, according to Lévi-Strauss, is intended to expand the circle of solidarity and guide the broader structuring of the community. One of the paradoxical results of incest prohibitions, and particularly of the stringent attitude toward uncertainties in this realm, is paradoxically likely to be the ever-increasing limitation of the circle of marriage to a small pedigreed elite with a presumption of fitness. The differences of opinion in this realm within rabbinic literature reflect the inner tension raised by incest prohibitions.

The nature of uncertainty that arises with respect to lineage is that it expands continually, even exponentially. In this, uncertainty of pedigree differs from uncertainty about property, forbidden foods, and all other realms. *Mamzerut* passes from one generation to the next and can plague entire families, like a malignant disease. The divided response to the cloud of uncertainty over lineage is rooted, inter alia, in views of the *mamzer* himself. The continually expanding nature of *mamzerut* can be understood as a means of deterring forbidden sex by reminding those considering it that their descendants will be tainted forever. Within this deterrent framework, the *mamzer* is an innocent victim. Self-defeating uncertainty casts its shadow over the entire community, trapping it in the very prison it constructed to try to deter transgressors. The view that *mamzerut* is solely a deterrent mechanism—and a problematic one at that—strives to minimize the damage that the viral nature of *mamzerut* is liable to cause. It is within the framework of this view that yearnings for the future purification of *mamzerim* find expression. As noted, this view has predominated within halakhah.

Nevertheless, this view has not been able to completely displace the opposing view of the *mamzer*, which is rooted in the fact that the "contagious" nature of *mamzerut* can easily be interpreted as a primal recoiling from a defiling essence, as if the *mamzer* is the carrier of a terrible disease that must be avoided. There are attestations of this dark view in early halakhah, and it has been reawakened at various stages in the history of halakhah.[51] Aside from the creative exegetical maneuvers that accompany the attempt to categorically eliminate uncertainty and its infectious impact from *mamzerut*, the elimination thereof also entails overcoming that essential, primal recoil from the *mamzer*. But it is not easy to overcome this repugnance because it stems, inter alia, from the halakhic formation of the laws of *mamzerut* as a condition that is passed from one generation to the next, forever. By its very nature, any overcoming of this repugnance would be incomplete. It would leave suppressed residue, which will continue to leave its mark.

---

51. See, for example, the harsh formulation of *Responsa Mishneh Halakhot* 17:8:

> If you ask, "What crime has the son done? Does it not say, 'Parents shall not be put to death for children, nor children be put to death for parents' (Deut 24:16)?" ... In my humble opinion, the matter is explained thus: There are physical maladies that a father or mother passes down to their children, even though the son committed no sin and did not bring this malady on himself. Nevertheless, it is reasonable not to marry him. *Shulḥan Arukh, Even Ha-ezer* 2:7 states: "A man should not marry a woman from a family of lepers or epileptics."
>
> Regarding your astonishment at the statement of Maharil, cited by Rema in *Yoreh De'ah* 265:5, that there is a *mitzvah* to publicize that he is a *mamzer*, and that he is also given the name "Ki-dor" so that everyone will understand from his name that he is a *mamzer*, causing him shame his whole life; and the statement in *Responsa Zera Emet* 3:111, cited in *Darkhei Teshuvah* 180:1, that the word "*mamzer*" should be tattooed to his forehead by a gentile, so that it will be well known, and so he cannot go to a place where he is unknown and marry a Jewish woman—how can they not be concerned about the offense to the *mamzer*? He himself wrote that the reason is so that [the *mamzer*] doesn't intermingle among Israel, and regarding anything that pertains to the Jewish people as a whole, the individual is insignificant with respect to the collective. This is akin to someone who is sick with a contagious disease, God forbid; it is surely a *mitzvah* to keep him away from people so that others are not infected with this disease. It happens every day that if someone, God forbid, contracts a contagious disease, he is quarantined from other people so that the disease does not spread and hurt others. Would we say that this insults the diseased? It is only to save others from contracting his disease! Certainly we should have great compassion for the diseased. We should feel his pain and pray for him. But what offense is there? On the contrary, if we do not do so, and he goes among the people, the disease will spread to others, and one who fails to caution the public will have committed a terrible sin. If this applies to a physical malady, then certainly it applies to a spiritual malady. This disease [of *mamzerut*] is contagious, may God save us; [the *mamzer*] is forbidden to marry a Jewish woman, and if he causes a Jewish woman to sin and marry him without informing her, his children and grandchildren will be *mamzerim*.

5

Monetary Law: Possession, Evidence, and Uncertainty

I

Tannaitic literature presents a complex range of uncertain situations pertaining to monetary law, and it offers a variety of rules that are supposed to resolve them. Among the conditions of uncertainty that the Mishnah poses are discussions about a tortious event in which the tortfeasor and the injured party disagree about the extent of the damages or about a found object that both parties claim in its entirety, and there is no additional evidence that would enable a decision in favor of one of the parties. The Mishnah likewise addresses uncertainties about purchase and sale, such as the case, which is subject to dispute in the Mishnah and Tosefta, of a cow that gave birth just as it was sold, and it is not known whether the calf was born before or after the moment of sale and, consequently, whether it belongs to the buyer or seller.

Among the astounding variety of monetary uncertainties that the Mishnah imagines, sculpts, and attunes, there are cases that arise among heirs and between heirs and creditors, such as the exotic case of a house collapsing on its inhabitants, including a husband and wife. It is not known, and it will never be known, who died first—a question with ramifications for the division of their assets between the husband's heirs and the wife's heirs, who are not always the exact same heirs. The Mishnah, as usual, does not waste this opportunity to examine other possible combinations of scenarios in which death is caused by a collapsed house, killing, for example, a father and son or a mother and son. Uncertainty about the order of deaths in these scenarios raises new questions and sometimes requires new solutions.

There is, at first glance, a solid default solution for these uncertainties in cases of monetary law: when in doubt, the advantage should go to the party that is actually in possession of the asset or the party that most recently owned it, unless and until proven otherwise. That is, the burden of proof is on the claimant. In rabbinic parlance, "one who seeks to expropriate from his fellow—[the burden of] proof is upon him" (*ha-motzi me-ḥavero alav ha-re'ayah*). This rule, which, in the history of halakhah, was first formulated in the Mishnah, should have made deliberations about monetary uncertainties relatively simple and brief.[1]

But this is not how things played out in the Tannaitic literature. In their complicated engagements with states of uncertainty, the sages are aware that in some cases there is no prior factual or legal state to which one can return in order to resolve uncertainty. Take, for example, the case of two people who each claim to have found a lost object first, in which there is no prior ownership or prior factual situation that can be relied upon. A similar and even more complex case, where it is likewise impossible to attach any prior factual or legal state, is addressed in a *mishnah* that deals with two people who deposited money with the same trustee: one deposited 100, and the other 200. The trustee does not remember who deposited what, and each party claims to have deposited 200.

Beyond these and similar situations, to which the principle that the burden of proof falls upon the party that wishes to extract money from another cannot extend, there is a profound debate among the sages about the scope and significance of the principle. This all-encompassing and fundamental dispute, which will be at the center of discussion in this chapter, begot different rulings to deal with situations of monetary uncertainty. These different rulings must be mapped out carefully, case by case, by determining the meanings and contexts that led to the various conclusions and the disputes that arose as a result.

I begin the chapter with a complicated example of a discussion of uncertainty in the Mishnah. It will serve as the starting point for our study of these big questions. This example imagines and analyzes cases that arise between a priest and the owner of an animal concerning uncertainties relating to the duty to give male firstborn animals to the priests. A close study and analysis of these cases and the fundamental disagreements about how to resolve them will demonstrate the conceptual depth and sophistication even in the initial phases of the emergence of uncertainty within the history of halakhah:

---

1. Baruch Kehat comprehensively and thoroughly addresses the principle of *ha-motzi me-ḥavero alav ha-re'ayah* in rabbinic literature in his master's thesis and doctoral dissertation ("'The Burden of Proof Lies with the Claimant' in Rabbinic Literature" [Hebrew] [PhD diss., Bar-Ilan University, 2010]; and "'The Burden of Proof Lies with the Claimant' in Tannaitic Sources and Their Interpretation in the Talmuds" [Hebrew] [Master's thesis, Bar-Ilan University, 2006]). For an important discussion of the distinction between the use of the principle of *ha-motzi me-ḥavero alav ha-re'ayah* and the general legal principle of "burden of proof," see Asher Gulak, *The Foundations of Jewish Law* [Hebrew], 4 vols. (Tel Aviv: Dvir, 1922), 4:111–12; Yuval Sinai, "Burden of Persuasion in Civil Cases—A New Model" [Hebrew], *Bar-Ilan Law Studies* 24 (2008): 213–16. Nevertheless, throughout this volume, I use *ha-motzi me-ḥavero alav ha-re'ayah* and "burden of proof" interchangeably for the sake of convenience.

> His ewe had not given birth before and then gave birth to two males, and both heads emerged [from the womb] together: Rabbi Yosah the Galilean says: Both [belong] to the priest, as it is stated: "The males are to God" (Exod 13:12). But the sages say: this is impossible; rather, one belongs to [the owner] and one to the priest.
>
> Rabbi Tarfon says: The priest chooses the better one. Rabbi Akiva says: They appraise and split the difference. The second [offspring] is left to pasture until it develops a blemish, and the priestly gifts are obligatory with respect to it. Rabbi Yose exempts.
>
> If one of [the offspring] died: Rabbi Tarfon says: They divide [the living one]. Rabbi Akiva says: One who seeks to expropriate from his fellow—[the burden of] proof is upon him.
>
> [If the offspring were] one male and one female: the priest gets nothing. (*m. Bekhorot* 2:6)

This *mishnah* presents a complex tiered structure of three uncertain states with respect to the gift of firstborn livestock. The first case addresses a situation in which an animal gave birth to two male offspring simultaneously, and it is uncertain which of them is the firstborn and must be given to the priest. Rabbi Yose the Galilean, who maintains that both offspring are given to the priest, appears first, and the sages dispute him. There are two possible explanations for the view of Rabbi Yose the Galilean: (a) Both offspring born of that birthing are considered firstborns, even if they are born one after another, because it is all part of one birthing—the first; (b) he maintains that the offspring may have been born simultaneously. Rabbi Tarfon says that the priest takes the better and more robust of the two offspring, whereas Rabbi Akiva maintains that the owner of the livestock and the priest split the difference between the value of the offspring (this is apparently the meaning of *meshamnim beineihen*).[2]

In the second case, the animal gave birth to two male offspring, and one of them died. It is not known whether the firstborn was the offspring that died. Rabbi Tarfon says that in such a situation, the owner and the priest split the value of the remaining offspring, whereas Rabbi Akiva rejects this resolution and maintains that unless the priest proves that the firstborn offspring is the one that remains alive, he is not entitled even to half of the value of the living offspring.

---

2. See Hanoch Albeck's explanation of the term *meshamnim* in the supplementary material to his commentary on the Mishnaic Order of *Kodashim* (Tel Aviv: Dvir, 1959), 387–78. *T. Bekhorot* records another tradition that implies that Rabbi Akiva did not think that the priest and the owners split the difference between the value of the offspring, but that the priest takes the offspring of lesser value: "[If] two ewes that had not given birth before then gave birth to two males, he gives both to the priest. A male and a female—[he gives the] male to the priest. Two males and a female—one is his and one is [given] to the priest. Rabbi Tarfon says: The more beautiful of them [is given to the priest]. Rabbi Akiva says: The runt of them [is given to the priest]" (*t. Bekhorot* 2:5). See the Amoraic dispute about Rabbi Akiva's position in *b. Bekhorot* 18a.

In the third case, one male and one female offspring were born, and it is unknown which was the firstborn. In such a case, Rabbi Akiva and Rabbi Tarfon concur that the priest receives nothing unless he proves that the male was born first.

Rabbi Tarfon thus has a different position in each case of uncertainty that this *mishnah* presents. In the first case, he maintains that the priest has the advantage and takes the better of the offspring. In the second case, he asserts that the owner and the priest divide the remaining offspring, and in the third case, he holds that the priest receives nothing.

Rabbi Akiva likewise has different attitudes to states of uncertainty, but he distinguishes only between the first and second cases. In the first case, he asserts that the disputed property must be divided, whereas in the second case, the priest receives nothing without evidence. The same applies to the third case.

It would seem, at first glance, that in all three cases of uncertainty described, the claim of the priest and the claim of the owner of the animal each has a 50-percent likelihood of being correct. What, then, is the source of the different ways of resolving the uncertainty in each case? The answer is rooted in the way that the Mishnah poses the tiered structure of cases of uncertainty. In the first case, we are certain that one of the offspring is a firstborn; the firstborn animal exists, as does the owner's obligation to give it to the priest. However, we do not know which of the two offspring before us is the object of the obligation. In the second case, we are certain that a firstborn male was born, and there was an obligation to give it to the priest; however, now that one of the offspring has died, we no longer know whether the obligation to give it to the priest still exists, because it is possible that the firstborn is the one that died. In the third case, in which male and female offspring were born, we do not know whether there was an obligation to give the firstborn to the priest in the first place, because the firstborn offspring may have been the female.

The *mishnah* astutely structures a tiered series of cases in which the link between the priest's claim and the extant offspring diminishes, and the weakened link is also the source of the different rulings in the different states of uncertainty. In the first case, in which it is clear that the priest is entitled to one of the extant offspring, Rabbi Tarfon argues that, since there is a *mitzvah* for the owner to give the firstborn to the priest, the priest is at an advantage. Rabbi Akiva, however, maintains that they should divide the value of the two offspring.[3] In the second case, where it is

3. The Bavli explained Rabbi Tarfon's reasoning as follows: "What is the reasoning of Rabbi Tarfon? He holds that the healthier [lamb] emerged first" (*b. Bekhorot* 18a). According to this explanation, there is a probabilistic assumption that the better offspring is the one of the pair that emerges first. Therefore, the priest takes the better of the offspring. However, it seems from the case of the aforementioned Tosefta that Rabbi Tarfon has a different reason,

certain that the priest's claim was, at one time, linked to an extant offspring but we do not know whether the link still exists, since one of the offspring died, the priest's situation has worsened. According to Rabbi Tarfon, he receives only half of the value of the living offspring, as opposed to the first case, in which the priest received the more valuable of the offspring. According to Rabbi Akiva, the priest receives nothing, even though in the first case he was entitled to half of his claim. In the third case, it is not certain that there was ever an obligation to give the firstborn to the priest, because the firstborn may have been female. In such a case, even Rabbi Tarfon would agree that the priest is not entitled to anything without evidence.[4]

The purpose of this tiered structuring of states of uncertainty is, inter alia, to define and delimit the power of the rule that the burden of proof is upon the party that seeks to take something away from the other party, which is the apparent default in all cases of uncertainty with respect to monetary claims. The Mishnah articulates this rule as a general principle with respect to firstborns as well: "An uncertain firstborn, whether human or animal, pure or impure, for one who seeks to expropriate from his fellow—the [burden of] proof is upon him" (*m. Taharot* 4:12).

The meaning of this rule is that, in a case of uncertainty, the money is left in the hands of its owners or possessors. However, the *mishnah* in *Bekhorot* in which Rabbi Tarfon and Rabbi Akiva disagree demonstrates that, if the contentions of the claimant "who seeks to take" something out of the other party's possession do not generate a new and unknown legal status of ownership claim, and this ownership claim is anchored in the fact that it has (in the first case) or had (in the second case) a foothold in reality, then the burden of proof is not applied by default to the claimant. The question of whether this foothold must exist presently, as in the first case, or whether it is sufficient that it is certain that it existed at some point, is the subject of dispute between Rabbi Tarfon and Rabbi Akiva with respect to the second case. This *mishnah* teaches that (at least in the case of the obligation to give firstborn male animals to the priest) the imposition of the burden of proof on the priest depends on the degree to which his claim has a foothold in the reality presented.

This *mishnah* allows us to begin clarifying our initial question: Why do the sages deal so extensively with instances of uncertainty? The first

---

because Rabbi Tarfon maintains that the priest takes the better lamb even when the offspring are from two different ewes and we do not know which of the lambs is a firstborn.

4. See Rashi's commentary on this *mishnah* (on *b. Bekhorot* 17b), s.v. "*zakhar u-nekevah*": "'One male and one female: the priest gets nothing' for perhaps the female emerged first, and the burden of proof is on the claimant. Here even Rabbi Tarfon would agree; over there he disagrees because one of them certainly belongs to the priest, so he has strong enough standing to divide evenly. Here, however, his standing is not as strong, for perhaps the question of firstborn is not relevant at all."

answer is related to an essential feature of rabbinic halakhah, namely, its interest in trying to regulate broad areas of life through rules of a high resolution. There is a biblical obligation to give firstborn male livestock to the priest, but, as in tractate *Bekhorot* more generally, the sages were not content with such a general directive, and thus they formulate specific instructions, thereby producing a "tractate." Among the instructions they give are those that address questions of what to do in a case where the priest and the owner do not know which of the offspring is the firstborn.

The attempt to create guidelines for such cases is typical of the efforts associated with the emergence of the halakhah, whose objective is the steady imposition of a system of rules on human action. Some cases of uncertainty, however, are hard to construe as attempts to predetermine the proper response in the event that such a scenario occurs, because the possibility of such a case actually occurring is infinitesimal.

Multiple births are not unusual, and there will likely even be situations in which the animal's owner does not pay attention or otherwise cannot easily discern which of the offspring emerged first. The sages clarify—and disagree about—what he must do in such a case, and what the priest's entitlements are. The second case in our *mishnah,* however, deals with a borderline case that is blatantly uncommon. In this case, two offspring are born at the same time, and the owner does not know which is the firstborn—and, in addition, one of the offspring dies. It is hard to imagine that the sages dealt with such a case in an attempt to predetermine the correct course of action in some future scenario. It seems, rather, that this case serves as an abstract clarification for its own sake, independent of the frequency or infrequency of such a case.

The purpose of this abstract clarification is apparent from the tiered structure of the *mishnah,* which poses varying cases of uncertainty about a firstborn in which the power of the priest's claim gradually diminishes, until, ultimately, he is clearly "one who seeks to take" from his fellow. The specific structure that the *mishnah* creates and the different rulings that apply to each case are meant to demonstrate penetrating conceptual insights of an overtly speculative character. The objective of this *mishnah,* aside from guiding proper behavior in various life circumstances, is independent conceptual elucidation.[5] As with the emergence of halakhah more generally, the sages' increased engagement in rule making relates to two

5. Perhaps no conclusions can be drawn from the discussion in *Bekhorot* about Rabbi Tarfon's view on other states of monetary uncertainty, because in this case, as opposed to other cases of uncertainty, there is a *mitzvah* to give the firstborn to a priest, which can tip the scales. A similar consideration arises in Tannaitic literature with respect to uncertainties regarding mandated gifts to the poor. It seems from the Mishnah's rulings on uncertainties regarding gifts to the poor that the principles are influenced not only by questions of ownership but also by the commandment to give the gifts. For instance:

concurrent themes in rabbinic literature: the goal of one is to guide human life and behavior, and the goal of the second is to construct a noncontingent halakhic universe, alongside the world, engagement and treatment of which are worthwhile pursuits in and of themselves.

II

The status of the burden-of-proof rule and its position with respect to alternative principles of decision making becomes fully clear in another series of cases addressed in the Mishnah. In these cases, the uncertainties lie at the heart of contentions between tortfeasor and injured party, and between buyer and seller:

> If an ox gored a cow, and its offspring was found alongside it, and it is not known whether the cow gave birth before or after it was gored—[the owner of the ox] pays for half the damages to the cow and a quarter of the damages to the offspring. Likewise, if a cow gored an ox and its fetus was found alongside it, and it is not known whether it gave birth before or after it gored—[the owner of the cow] pays half-damages from the ox and a quarter of the damages from the offspring. (*m. Bava Kamma* 5:1)

> If one barters a cow for a donkey, and it gives birth, and likewise if one sells his maidservant, and she gives birth—one party says, "she gave birth before the sale," and the other party says, "it was after my purchase"—they divide [the value of the offspring]. If one had two slaves, one large and one small, or two fields, one large and one small—the buyer says, "I bought the large one," and the other says, "I don't know," [the buyer] is awarded the large one. If the seller says, "I sold the small one," and the other says, "I don't know," [the buyer] has only the small one. One says, "it was the large one," and the other says, "it was the small one," the seller shall take an oath that he sold the small one. If this one and that one say "I don't know"—they divide. (*m. Bava Metzi'a* 8:4)

> [Produce in] ant-holes among the standing crop belong to the field owner. After the harvesters, the upper [produce in the ant-hole] belongs to the poor and the lower belongs to the field owner. Rabbi Meir says: Everything belongs to the poor, since gleanings of uncertain status are [nevertheless considered] gleanings. (*m. Pe'ah* 4:11; see also the parallel text in *Sifre Devarim* §283)

Although, in principle, the owner of the grain is the possessor, the burden-of-proof rule is not applied in this case. The Amoraim debate this *mishnah* in *y. Pe'ah* 4:8: Rabbi Yoḥanan, in contrast to Rabbi Shimon ben Lakish, deems it a minority position. See also the dispute in *b. Ḥullin* 104a. Kehat addresses the fact that the burden-of-proof rule, in the context of the obligation to give gifts to the priests and the poor, is addressed not only to the courts, as is common in legal systems generally, but also to the individual. See Kehat, "'Burden of Proof Lies with the Claimant,'" 456–57.

The *mishnah* in *Bava Kamma* addresses a case of uncertainty wherein we do not know whether the goring of the ox caused the death of the fetus or whether the fetus was stillborn before the ox gored. It is assumed that neither the owner of the ox nor the owner of the cow can provide any information because they were not present at the incident; the offspring, as the *mishnah* states, was "found alongside" the cow, and the *mishnah* asserts that the tortfeasor in this instance pays only half of what would be paid if the damage was certain.

This solution of splitting the difference avoids broad application of the rule placing the burden of proof on the claimant, that is, the party not in possession; the claimant, the injured party, is compensated halfway even without bringing any evidence that the ox indeed caused the death of the offspring. It seems that the *mishnah*'s position is that, when there is uncertainty in a monetary case that does not stem from the parties' claims and is not dependent on them, the principle of division applies. The rule that places the burden of proof on the claimant applies, therefore, only in a case where the uncertainty arises due to the contention of the claimant—that is, in a case where the claimant is, in the most direct, literal sense, "one who seeks to expropriate from his fellow."

A similar approach emerges from the *mishnah* in *Bava Metzi'a*, which presents a more complex set of rules to be followed if uncertainty arises in a case where a cow is bartered for a donkey. In an acquisition by real or symbolic barter (*ḥalipin*), only one object of exchange must be present at the time of the transaction. When that object is transferred from one party to the other, the other object, wherever it is, is acquired by the other party. In the present case, the parties do not know whether the cow gave birth before or after the moment of transaction and, consequently, whether the calf belongs to the original or present owner of the cow. In such a case, the *mishnah* prescribes division of the asset since, as in the case in *Bava Kamma*, the uncertainty is not caused by the claims or contentions of either party, as they provide no information in this matter.[6]

In contrast, in the case of a regular sale, in which the parties dispute the content of the transaction—whether a large or small field was sold—and in which both parties profess to be providing information about the features of the deal, the *mishnah* asserts that the party in possession of the asset is at an advantage, and the parties do not split the difference between

---

6. The unique character of the uncertainties that arise in the *mishnayot* dealing with the seller of a cow that gave birth, and with an ox that gores a cow that was found alongside its fetus is formulated as follows in *Tosafot*: "Without their claims, the court is uncertain, for one can have a case against another person without claims. For example, in the case of an ox that gored a cow or one who bartered a cow for a donkey, since the uncertainty arose on its own, the law is that they should divide it without having to take an oath" (*Tosafot* on *Bava Kamma* 2b, s.v. "*heikha de-ika*").

their claims.[7] In a case where neither party provides information and both claim, "I don't know" (even if the transaction in question was a regular sale, not a barter in which they, in principle, should know what is happening), then, since they are not making any claim and the uncertainty stands alone, the latter part of the *mishnah* asserts that the parties divide the sum that is subject to uncertainty. Neither party is considered to be "expropriating" anything because neither party provides the claim that introduces uncertainty. Consequently, the burden-of-proof principle does not apply to this case either. This *mishnah* thus recognizes the rule placing the burden of proof on the claimant but applies it only in a case where the uncertainty arises due to the differences between the parties' claims.

The Tosefta records a dispute about the same matter:

> If one sells a cow to his fellow, and it was found to be pregnant, and it gave birth: One says, "It gave birth in my possession," and the other is silent, [the one who made a positive claim] wins. If one says, "I do not know," and the other says, "I do not know," they divide it. If one says, "[It gave birth] in my possession," and the other says, "[It gave birth] in my possession," [the one in possession] swears and then does not have to pay, for all those to whom oaths are administered by the Torah exempt themselves from payment by means of the oath; these are the words of Rabbi Meir. Rabbi Yehudah says: The offspring always remains in possession of the seller. And the sages say: One who seeks to expropriate from his fellow—[the burden of] proof is upon him.

The anonymous opinion in the *mishnah* that prescribes division is cited in the *tosefta* in the name of Rabbi Meir. Additionally, the *tosefta* records two opinions of those who dispute Rabbi Meir.[8] Rabbi Yehudah asserts that,

---

7. According to the Mishnah, if one party claims from sure knowledge (*bari*) and the other party makes an unsure claim (*shema*), the sure claim overrides possession. In a case where both parties make sure claims, the seller has the advantage because of the burden-of-proof rule; however, he must take an oath, because he is considered to have partially conceded (*modeh be-miktzat*) to the claimant.

8. J. N. Epstein thought that there is a contradiction between the first part of the *mishnah*, in which both parties make sure claims and the verdict is that they split the disputed sum, and the latter part of the *mishnah*, in which the solution of division applies only in cases where both parties say they do not know. According to Epstein, this *mishnah* is composed of two different sources. The first accords with Sumkhus, who maintains that, even when both parties make sure claims, the disputed sum is divided. The latter part of the *mishnah* accords with Rabbi Meir's view, as formulated in the Tosefta, that division of the disputed sum is imposed only when both parties claim, "I don't know." On this, see Epstein, *Introduction to the Mishnaic Text*, 1:384–85.

It seems that there is no reason to accept contrived solutions that divide the *mishnah* into two separate sources, as Epstein does. In the case where the cow is bartered for a donkey, the parties do not provide any information because, when one is acquiring by barter, the acquired object can be far from where the transaction takes place. The object is not transferred from hand to hand, and the uncertainty does not arise from the claims of the parties.

rather than resolving the case by dividing, the offspring always remains in the possession of the seller; the sages maintain that "one who seeks to expropriate from his fellow—[the burden of] proof is upon him." As Saul Lieberman explained in his commentary on the Tosefta, the sages, who present a third view, maintain that the party in actual possession of the calf, whether buyer or seller, has the advantage.

There are thus three different solutions to the state of uncertainty regarding this money, and the difference between them hinges, inter alia, on three different understandings of the burden-of-proof principle. According to the *mishnah* and Rabbi Meir's view in the *tosefta*, the burden-of-proof principle is relatively narrow, applying only to the laws of claimants and respondents. Therefore, with respect to an uncertainty that does not arise from the claims of the parties, the disputed sum is divided. According to this view, only when the uncertainty arises by virtue of the claimant's contention must he provide proof for his claim. In cases where the uncertainty does not stem from the claimant's contentions, the rule of division of the asset shall be applied. Such a view appears in an early midrashic articulation of the burden-of-proof rule:

> "Judge rightly" (Deut 1:16). One who is right, in his rectitude, makes a claim and brings proof. For example, one dons his cloak, and another says, "it's mine"; one plows with his cow, and another says, "it's mine"; one demonstrates possession over his field, and another says, "it's mine"; one sits in his home, and another says, "it's mine." It is therefore stated: "Judge rightly." One who is right, in his rectitude, makes a claim and brings proof. (*Sifre Deuteronomy* 16; Finkelstein ed. p. 27)

The burden of proof placed on the claimant in such a case stems from the fact that it is he who introduces uncertainty. It is he who, by virtue of his claim, comes to take property away from the party in possession of it. Since he is the one who raises the uncertainty, he bears the burden of

---

This is how Rashi explains our *mishnah*: "For this reason it teaches 'If one barters' and not 'if one sells his cow and it gave birth,' for had he sold it for money, the buyer does not take ownership until he pulls [the acquired animal forward], and once he pulls it, he knows whether or not it has already given birth.... However, when one barters a cow for a donkey, there was no need to pull the cow or the donkey" (s.v. "*ha-maḥlif parah be-ḥamor*"). The language of the first part of the *mishnah*, "one party says," relates not to the parties' eyewitness testimony but to their statements of claim and defense. (Another example wherein "one party says" does not imply a sure claim but only refers to the nature of the claims against one another appears in the next *mishnah*, *Bava Metzi'a* 8:5.) In contrast, in the case of a regular sale, which the Tosefta and the latter part of the *mishnah* address, the objects purchased are transferred from hand to hand, and the parties' claims can be understood to be sure or unsure. In the case of a sale, the uncertainty arises because of the claims made by the parties. Therefore, the rule of division is stated only in cases where both parties say, "I don't know"—that is, when the uncertainty is not rooted in their claims.

proving his claim.[9] Where the uncertainty does not arise due to the claim, or where the uncertainty has a foothold in the acknowledged reality, the burden of proof does not fall on the claimant, and the parties divide the disputed sum.

In contrast, Rabbi Yehudah and the sages present a different, broader conception of the burden-of-proof rule. According to Rabbi Yehudah's view that the offspring is always in the seller's possession, the idea of the burden-of-proof rule is to protect ownership rights. This approach maintains that in order to extract money from its original owners—in this case, the seller—it is necessary to bring evidence that goes well beyond the state of uncertainty; nothing can be taken from him without evidence, not even half the value of the disputed assets. Ownership is something that must be protected; it cannot be taken away on the basis of mere uncertainty. Therefore, the usage of the burden-of-proof rule is much more expansive than the narrow reading that views it as a principle of the laws of claims.

According to the third view in this Tosefta passage, the view of the sages, the burden-of-proof rule does not preserve ownership rights; it preserves the status quo, the present state of affairs. Whoever is in possession of the money at the time of adjudication has the advantage, unless there is evidence for taking the money away from him. The application of the burden-of-proof rule to an independent uncertainty according to which each party's claim is equally likely, such that the preference for the party in possession is not predicated on a probabilistic assertion that in most cases the possessor is the rightful owner and the burden of proof lies with the party that seeks to expropriate the disputed object.[10]

---

9. In his work on the burden-of-proof rule, Baruch Kehat argues that, in Tannaitic literature, this rule is stated only in cases where the uncertainty is objective—that is, the uncertainty arises independently of the parties' claims. In contrast, in a case where one person sues another and the court has no doubts that arise independently of the claimant's suit, the burden-of-proof rule is not applied.

However, it seems that the *Sifre* exposition, though it does not use the formula of *ha-ha-motzi me-ḥavero alav ha-re'ayah*, expresses the same idea even in the context of a claim that is not based on an independent uncertainty. Therefore, there is no reason to limit the use of this rule to cases of objective uncertainty. According to the *Sifre* exposition, a person who claims ownership of an object in another's possession must bring proof in order for his claim to be given weight. This is actually the primary basis of the burden-of-proof principle. Likewise, *t. Shevu'ot* 6:5 brings a case where the principle is activated even though there is no objective basis. In the Tosefta's case, a person claims that a certain landlord hired him for work, and the landlord denies this. In another case, the parties dispute the wages that were set: "However, if he says to him, 'You hired me,' and the other says, 'I did not hire you'; 'I promised you a sela,' and the other says, 'You promised me two,' the one who seeks to expropriate from his fellow—[the burden of] proof is upon him." Kehat addresses this source ("Burden of Proof . . . in Rabbinic Literature," 16–17), but it seems to me that his reading is unnecessarily forced.

10. A quasi-probabilistic view of this principle was articulated by Shalom Albeck in *Evidence in Talmudic Law* [Hebrew] (Ramat Gan: Bar-Ilan University Press, 1987), 324.

In the case where a cow is bartered for a donkey, for example, there is no reason to apply this probabilistic principle. The burden-of-proof rule, according to this view, is not a principle that presumes an evidentiary statistical likelihood that protects ownership rights. It is rather based a conservative principle that the court, under conditions of uncertainty, does not change the status quo that comes before it unless there is substantive proof to change things. Therefore, the offspring remains with the party in possession of it, whether it is the buyer or the seller.[11]

The difference between the second and third approaches (Rabbi Yehudah's approach and the sages' approach) can be expressed not in terms of the difference between protecting ownership and protecting the status quo, but rather as a debate about what is defined as the status quo that bears protection: is the set of legal rights that obtained before the uncertainty what define the status quo, or is the actual state of affairs in the world before us what determines the status quo?[12]

---

11. It is apparent from the formulation of the Tosefta that the expression "one who seeks to expropriate from his fellow—[the burden of] proof is upon him" (*ha-motzi me-ḥavero alav ha-re'ayah*) addresses expropriation from someone who is actually holding onto the asset, as Rabbi Yehudah asserts, "it remains in possession of the seller," and the sages counter with, "one who seeks to expropriate from his fellow—[the burden of] proof is upon him," referring to the person who is in actual possession of the object or asset. In his work on the burden-of-proof rule, Kehat contends that, in the teachings of the Tannaim, the rule refers only to one who is in possession, not to the prior owners of the asset. However, it seems from the language of the Mishnah that the expression is not exclusive to the person in de facto possession but can occasionally also refer to the owner of the asset, as against its de facto possessor:

> A dying person who wrote all of his property over to others, but who withheld even a small amount of land—his gift stands [even if he recovers]. If he did not withhold any amount of land, his gift does not stand. If he did not write [that he was] on his deathbed: he says, "I was on my deathbed," and they say, "He was healthy," he must bring proof that he was on his deathbed—these are the words of Rabbi Meir. But the sages say: "One who seeks to expropriate from his fellow—[the burden of] proof is upon him." (*m. Bava Batra* 9:6)

It seems from this case that, even though the recipients of the gift are already in possession of it, the grantor can claim that it was given only because he thought he was going to die, and that since he recovered, the gift is voided. In such a case, according to the sages of the *mishnah*, the recipients bear the burden of proving that these gifts were not *causa mortis* but were granted by a healthy person and therefore irrevocable—even though the recipients are in possession of the gifts. Apparently, then, the Mishnah invokes the burden-of-proof rule to support prior ownership, not as a principle that gives preference to the party in possession.

It could be claimed that the *mishnah* deals only with a case where the gift has not reached the possession of the grantees, but the *mishnah* does not qualify its statement in this way, and there is no reason to presume that the burden of proof shifts to the recovered grantor in cases where the gift reached the possession of the grantee. See also the dispute as it appears in *t. Bava Batra* 10:11.

12. A similar Tannaitic dispute about the relationship between ownership and possession appears in the Tosefta:

The origins of the conflict between resolution by division and the principle of possession in cases of uncertainty can be found in the earliest stages of Tannaitic literature. The Mishnah presents a series of disputes between the Houses of Shammai and Hillel about how to decide cases of uncertainty—disputes that revolve around the tension between resolution by division and affirmation of possession:

> A house fell down upon [a man] and his father, or upon a man and his heirs, and he was obligated to pay a woman's *ketubah* and a creditor: The father's heirs say, "The son died first and the father died afterward." The creditors say, "The father died first and the son died afterward." The House of Shammai says: Let them split it. The House of Hillel says: The assets remain in possession [of the party holding them].
>
> A house fell upon him and his wife. The husband's heirs say, "The wife died first and the husband died afterward." The wife's heirs say, "The husband died first and the wife died afterward." The House of Shammai says: Let them split it. Beit Hillel says: The assets remain in possession [of the party holding them]: the *ketubah* in possession of the husband's heirs, and the assets that come into and leave [the marriage] with her remains in possession of her father's heirs.
>
> A house fell upon him and his mother. Both [Houses] agree that they split [the assets]. Rabbi Akiva said: I agree here that the assets remain in possession [of the party holding them]. Ben Azzai said to him: We are distressed over the matters in dispute, and you are coming to disagree where all agree? (*m. Bava Batra* 9:8–10)

As in the cases discussed earlier, in the case of the house that fell upon its denizens, it is not the claimant who raises the uncertainty, which would place the burden of proof on him. Rather, the uncertainty arises indepen-

---

> Two women who had not given birth before gave birth, in hiding, to two males must give ten *sela'im* to the priest. If one [of the sons] died within thirty days, the women expropriate [the money from the priest]. Rabbi Yehudah says: If they gave to one priest, they expropriate; if [they gave] to two priests, they cannot expropriate, because one who seeks to expropriate from his fellow—[the burden of] proof is upon him. (*t. Bekhorot* 6:2)

A firstborn son who died within thirty days of birth carries no obligation to redeem him from a priest. If the money had already been given to the priest, he must return it. In the present case, the money for redemption of the two firstborn sons was given by their mothers to two different priests, and one of the sons died within thirty days. However, the circumstances were such that the mothers did not know which of them gave birth to the child who died. According to Rabbi Yehudah, each of the two priests can claim that he received the money for the redemption of the viable child, and the mothers must bring evidence before they can take back the redemption money.

This, too, is a case where prior ownership conflicts with present possession, even if the possession is not of the object of dispute, as in the case of the calf. Rather, it is more abstract; possession is of money given to redeem a firstborn, which the claimant is now trying to reclaim.

dent of the parties. The times of death of the victims are unknown, generating uncertainty vis-à-vis the claims of the various sets of heirs and creditors. Thus, for example, in the first case, a father and son die when a building collapses on them. If the son died first, he never inherited his father's assets, so they all go to the father's heirs. On the other hand, if the father died first, the son inherited the father just before the son himself died, and because the father's assets came into the ownership of the son, the son's creditors can collect from these assets before they are disbursed to the other heirs.

In this case, the contending parties provide no information about the event. Each one presents the order of events that serves his claim—the father's heirs contend that the son died first, and the creditors contend that the father died first. In such cases, the House of Shammai proffers resolution by division of the disputed assets, whereas the House of Hillel leaves the disputed assets with whoever is in possession of them.

The tension regarding how to deal with uncertainty between the Mishnah, which prefers division, and the various opinions in the Tosefta, which prefer ownership or possession, is thus present in the earliest layers of Tannaitic halakhah.[13] It is interesting to note that the redactor of the Mishnah adopted the House of Shammai's preference for division and a narrow understanding of the principle of possession, which relates only to a case in which the claimant introduces uncertainty by means of his claim.[14]

---

13. Baruch Kehat contends that the House of Hillel's view is not based on the burden-of-proof principle because it protects the legal owners of the asset, not its de facto possessor. In Kehat's opinion, the principle that "one who seeks to expropriate from his fellow—[the burden of] proof is upon him" relates only to the protection of de facto possessors of an asset. See Kehat, "Burden of Proof . . . in Rabbinic Literature," 46–51.

It is apparent, however, that there are Tannaitic sources that attest to the use of the burden-of-proof principle with respect to prior owners, not only current possessors. See n. 12 above. Likewise, the view of the House of Hillel is anyway premised on the same burden-of-proof principle, and on this principle they base their opposition to the House of Shammai's solution.

14. As mentioned, the redactor of the Mishnah adopts the view that supports division as the anonymous opinion (*stam*) of the Mishnah and views the burden-of-proof principle as a narrow rule—as in the cases of an ox that gores a cow and the barter of a cow and donkey, and as in the case of a borrowed or rented cow (below, n. 21). One possible exception to this view of the *stam* Mishnah is the case in *m. Bava Kamma* (3:11), which adopts the burden-of-proof principle:

> An ox was chasing after another ox, and it was damaged. This one says "Your ox damaged," and this one says, "No, your ox was injured on a rock," one who seeks to expropriate from his fellow—[the burden of] proof is upon him. If two [oxen] were chasing after one [ox]: this one says, "Your ox damaged," and this one says, "Your ox damaged," both are exempt. If both [oxen] belonged to a single owner, both are liable. If one was large and one was small, and the plaintiff says, "The large one damaged," and the tortfeasor says, "No, the small one damaged"; one was *tam* [= had established no pattern of causing damage] and one was *mu'ad*

A close study of the Bavli's interpretation of this series of *mishnayot* demonstrates that it actually rejects the solution of splitting the disputed sum in the cases of the cow bartered for a donkey and the ox that gored the cow, as they appear in the *mishnah* according to its plain meaning. The Bavli rejects the narrow sense of the burden-of-proof rule that, as we have seen, was established through the redaction of the Mishnah as a major practical principle. This is how the Bavli reinterprets the *mishnah* about the cow bartered for a donkey:

> Why should they divide it? Let us see whose control it is in, and the other is "one who seeks to expropriate from his fellow—[the burden of] proof is upon him."
>
> Rabbi Ḥiya bar Abin said in the name of Shmuel: It is standing in a marsh.
>
> The maidservant as well? She is standing in an alleyway.
>
> So let us place it in the possession of the original owner, and the other is "one who seeks to expropriate from his fellow—[the burden of] proof is upon him."

> [= had established a pattern of causing damage], and the plaintiff says, "The *mu'ad* damaged," while the tortfeasor says, "No, the *tam* damaged": the one who seeks to expropriate from his fellow—[the burden of] proof is upon him. If two [oxen] were damaged, one large and one small, and two [oxen] caused the damage, one large and one small. The plaintiff says, "The large one damaged the large one and the small one damaged the small one," while the tortfeasor says, "No, the small one injured the large one and the large one injured the small one"; [or if] one was *tam* and one was *mu'ad*, and the plaintiff says, "The *mu'ad* damaged the large one and the *tam* damaged the small one," while the tortfeasor says, "No, the *tam* injured the large one and the *mu'ad* injured the small one"—the one who seeks to expropriate from his fellow—[the burden of] proof is upon him.

The uncertainties in this series of cases are resolved in accordance with the burden-of-proof principle, and the Mishnah does not suggest division as a solution.

A distinction between the series of cases can be suggested. In the cases of the barter of a cow for a donkey and of an ox that gores a cow, there was clearly a tortious or transactional act. The uncertainty is about the scope of that act. This uncertainty, as noted, does not depend on the claims of the parties. In contrast, with regard to all of the cases addressed in these *mishnayot* in *Bava Kamma,* the uncertainty is whether there was indeed a tortious act that would generate the specific obligation that the parties are contending about. (In this sense, the cases of the oxen in *Bava Kamma* are akin to the last case of uncertainty addressed in *m. Bekhorot* 2:6—wherein one offspring is male and the other is female—to which the Mishnah applies the burden-of-proof rule; as in this case, it is not certain that the obligations vis-à-vis the firstborn ever applied. In contrast, Rabbi Tarfon does not apply the burden-of-proof rule to a case where it is certain that there was a male firstborn, but its identity is uncertain.) The following distinction could as well have been drawn between the oxen cases and the other *mishnayot.* In the case of the oxen, the parties are attempting to provide information, so the decision is based on the burden-of-proof rule. If both parties would have said, "I don't know," the sum of the damages would have been divided between them. Such a suggestion arises in the Bavli's *sugya* on this *mishnah.*

> Who is [the Tanna of this *mishnah*]? It is Sumkhus, who said: "Money in an uncertain state is to be divided without an oath." (*b. Bava Metzi'a* 101a)

The Bavli proposes two alternatives to *mishnah*'s solution of division, and these alternatives correspond to the two broader conceptions of the burden-of-proof rule as formulated in the Tosefta. The first alternative maintains that the offspring should remain in the possession of whoever possesses it at present, and the other party, whether buyer or seller, bears the burden of proof. The Bavli accepts this principle as a guiding, major principle, and therefore it severely constricts the scope of the *mishnah*'s ruling to a case where the cow is "standing in a marsh," that is, in a location that is under the control of neither buyer nor seller. It is only in such a case, where no party is in possession of the disputed object, that the solution of division is applied. This contrived reading of the *mishnah* stems from the fact that the Bavli views the burden-of-proof rule as a broad principle that governs the outcome of cases of uncertainty.

After positing its contrived reading of the *mishnah*, the Bavli addresses another question: even if the cow is in a marsh and not in the possession of one of the parties, shouldn't the offspring be placed under the control of the seller, who is the original owner, leaving the buyer to bear the burden of proof? The Bavli answers that this *mishnah* represents the minority opinion of Sumkhus, who maintains that money in an uncertain state is to be divided without an oath and does not espouse the expansive view of the burden-of-proof rule.[15]

In its response to the *mishnah*, the Bavli presents the two alternatives that appear in the Tosefta for understanding the burden-of-proof principle and resolving the states of uncertainty: giving ownership to the person who is in possession of it, and leaving it in the hands of the original owner. The Bavli rejects, in practice, the view of the Mishnah's redactor, who proposes division. This response by the Bavli, in which it reinterprets the *mishnah* to accord with a minority opinion, that of Sumkhus, forges a dramatic shift in the way cases of uncertainty are judged; from this point forward in the history of halakhah, the possibility of dividing the disputed monies in cases where one party is in possession or has prior ownership is rejected.[16]

---

15. The medieval commentators discuss whether, once the *mishnah* is attributed to the view of Sumkhus, it is still necessary to restrict its scope to where the cow is "standing in a marsh," or whether even Sumkhus would agree that the asset is not divided in a case where one of the parties is in possession and makes a sure claim. See *Tosafot* on *b. Bava Kamma* 100a, s.v. "*ha*" (quoting Rashbam).

16. The vast majority of medieval commentators rule in accordance with Shmuel that this *mishnah* represents a minority opinion. Therefore, division is rejected as a method of resolving uncertainty. The outlier in this respect is Rashbam, who rules in accordance with Sumkhus because his view is recorded in an anonymous *mishnah*. See Rashbam's commentary to *b. Bava Batra* 92a, s.v. "*le-sheḥitah*."

This reading of the *mishnah* as reflecting a minority opinion follows a Babylonian Amoraic tradition cited by the Talmud in connection with the *mishnah* about an ox that gored a cow and its fetus was found alongside it. This *mishnah*, as we have seen, proposes division of the disputed value to resolve an uncertainty in a monetary case. This proposed solution, it seems, views the burden-of-proof rule as a narrow principle that pertains only to cases in which the uncertainty arises due to the claims of the plaintiff. The Bavli comments on this *mishnah* as follows:

> Rabbi Yehudah said in the name of Shmuel: These are the words of Sumkhus, who says that money in an uncertain state is to be divided without an oath. However, the sages maintain: "This is a major principle of law: one who seeks to expropriate from his fellow—[the burden of] proof is upon him." (*b. Bava Kamma* 46a)

In the first generation of Babylonian Amoraim, the ruling of the redactor of the Mishnah was rejected, and Shmuel relegates this *mishnah* to the status of a rejected minority opinion, establishing the broad understanding of the burden-of-proof rule as the governing halakhic principle.[17]

The Bavli's view reflects the approach of the redactor of the Tosefta, who formulated the anonymous *mishnah* in *Bava Metzi'a* as the minority opinion of Rabbi Meir and the burden-of-proof rule as the (majority) view of the sages. Likewise, the *mishnah* in *Bava Kamma*, which the redactor of the Mishnah presented anonymously (i.e., as the implied majority view), is formulated by the redactor of the Tosefta as the minority opinion of Sumkhus:

> If an ox gored a cow, and its fetus was found alongside it, and it is not known whether the cow gave birth before or after it was gored—Sumkhus says: [the owner of the ox] pays for half the value to the cow and a quarter of the value to the offspring. Likewise, if a cow gored an ox and its offspring was found alongside it, and it is not known whether it gave birth before or after it gored—Sumkhus says: [the owner of the cow] pays half-damages from the ox and a quarter of the damages from the offspring. (*t. Bava Kamma* 5:8)

It is thus apparent that the redactor of the Tosefta rejects the narrow approach to the burden-of-proof principle, the approach that gave rise to the broad use of solutions by division. The Tosefta, like the Bavli after it, maintained that this approach is a minority opinion that stands in opposi-

17. The Bavli also takes this approach in *Bekhorot*, with respect to the *mishnah* discussed above. As we saw, in the first two cases of that *mishnah*, Rabbi Tarfon does not apply the burden-of-proof rule. The Bavli, however, which views this rule as an overriding principle, contrives to significantly narrow the scope of the second case in *b. Bekhorot* 18b.

The Bavli likewise maintains that Rabbi Tarfon holds that the priest takes the better of the offspring, because the healthier of the offspring emerges first.

tion to the broader conception of the burden-of-proof rule, a conception that prefers to leave property in the hands of its owner or possessor. The resolution of monetary uncertainties by division is thus rejected.[18]

The fundamental difference between the Mishnah and the Tosefta can be discerned from another discussion of uncertainty with respect to

---

18. Another case of uncertainty regarding which there is a noticeable difference between the Mishnah and the Tosefta, and wherein the dispute about the nature and scope of the burden-of-proof rule likewise arises, appears in the *mishnah* that precedes the *mishnah* on bartering a cow for a donkey. This *mishnah* addresses a case that relates to the laws of lending and renting:

> If one who borrowed a cow borrowed it for half a day and rented it for half a day, or borrowed it for one day and rented it for the next, or rented one [cow] and borrowed one [cow], and it died, [if] the lender says: "The borrowed one died," [or] "On the day when it was borrowed it died," [or] "During the time when it was borrowed it died," and the other one says: "I don't know," he is liable. [If] the renter says, "It was the rented one that died," [or] "On the day when it was rented it died," [or] "During the time when it was rented it died," and the other says, "I do not know," he is exempt. [If] this one says, "It was [the] borrowed [one]," and this one says, "It was [the] rented [one]," the renter swears that it was the rented one that died. [If] this one says, "I do not know," and this one says, "I do not know," they divide [the disputed value]. (*m. Bava Metzi'a* 8:2)

The uncertainty described here does not arise from the plaintiff's claim, so, consequently, the burden of proof is not upon him. It is known in this case that the cow was borrowed and rented, but it is not known whether the cow died while it was borrowed or rented. This is important information because a borrower, in contrast to a renter, is liable for accidents; if a borrowed cow dies, the borrower is liable, whereas if a rented cow dies, the renter is exempt, because a renter is not liable for accidents. It is apparent from this *mishnah* that the burden-of-proof principle was understood as a narrow principle pertaining to cases where the plaintiff introduces uncertainty by virtue of his claim. The *mishnah* establishes that a sure claim supersedes an unsure claim, irrespective of the principle of placing the burden of proof on the plaintiff. Likewise, where neither party provides information, the *mishnah* imposes division of the disputed value, without restriction by the burden-of-proof rule.

The Tosefta addresses the Mishnah's case differently:

> Whether he borrowed it today and rented it the next day, or rented it today and borrowed it the next day; or whether there were two [cows], one borrowed and one rented: [If] this one says, "I do not know," and this one says, "I do not know," they divide [the disputed value]. [If] this one says, "It was [the] borrowed [one]," and this one says, "It was [the] rented [one]," [the renter] swears that it was the rented one that died, and does not pay, for all oaths in the Torah, one takes the oath and does not pay. These are the words of Rabbi Meir. But the sages say: one who seeks to expropriate from his fellow—[the burden of] proof is upon him. (*t. Bava Metzi'a* 8:22)

The anonymous opinion of the Mishnah is presented in the Tosefta as the minority opinion of Rabbi Meir, whereas the majority opinion is of the sages, who invoke the burden-of-proof rule. As in other cases, the Tosefta takes a different view from the Mishnah with respect to dividing the disputed asset versus invoking the burden-of-proof rule.

monetary claims. Here, too, there is disagreement about a possible solution by division. The first *mishnah* in *Bava Metzi'a* states:

> Two grasp a cloak. This one says, "I found it," and that one says, "I found it." This one says, "It is all mine," and that one says, "It is all mine." This one swears that he owns no less than half of it, and that one swears that he owns no less than half of it, and they divide it.
>
> This one says, "It is all mine," and that one says, "It is half mine." The one who says "It is all mine" swears that he owns no less than three-fourths of it, and the one who says "It is half mine" swears that he owns no less than one-fourth of it. This one takes three-fourths, and that one takes one-fourth. (*m. Bava Metzi'a* 1:1)

The uncertainty in this case, in contrast to the cases of the ox that gored a cow and the barter of a cow and a donkey, stems from the parties' claims. However, since the dispute is about an object that each party claims to have found, neither party has prior ownership, and each is attempting to "take it away" from the other. For this reason, the *mishnah* proposes the division of the object.[19]

In contrast, the parallel Tosefta passage presents a different view:

> Two grasp a cloak. This one takes what is in his grip, and that one takes what is in his grip. When does this apply? When they were both gripping it. However, if it was in the hands of one of them, one who seeks to expropriate from his fellow—[the burden of] proof is upon him. (*t. Bava Metzi'a* 1:1)

The solution proposed in the Tosefta is not division; rather, in cases of uncertainty, the present state of affairs is maintained. Each of the parties receives what he is already holding. If one of the parties is holding the entire cloak, the other party bears the burden of proof and is not entitled to anything. According to the Tosefta, in cases of uncertainty, the court does not intervene and does not change the status quo; in effect, it removes

---

19. In the case of "two grasp a cloak," the solution of dividing the disputed object is accompanied by the obligation of each party to take an oath. In other cases of division—the barter of a cow for a donkey and an ox that gores a cow—there is no reason to impose an oath on the parties because they did not attempt to provide any information about the event, were not present when the uncertainty emerged, or claimed, "I do not know." In contrast, each of the two grasping the cloak is making a positive claim, so it is possible to impose oaths on them.

Regarding the reason for the oath, there is an Amoraic dispute. Rabbi Aḥa maintains that this oath is akin to the oath imposed on one who partially concedes (*modeh be-miktzat*), because there is evidence of a sort that half of the cloak belongs to the other party. Rabbi Yoḥanan maintains that this oath was instituted by the sages to prevent situations wherein someone grabs the cloak of another by force and claims to own the whole thing. On this, see the dispute between Rabbi Ḥiyah and Rabbi Yoḥanan in *y. Bava Metzi'a* 1:1, as well as *b. Bava Metzi'a* 5b.

itself from the case. Moreover, according to the Tosefta, as opposed to the Mishnah, the parties do not swear as to their shares of the cloak, because, in practice, no set of claims and counterclaims has developed.[20]

The Bavli, consistent with its view, rejects the plain meaning of the *mishnah* in favor of a broader conception of the burden-of-proof rule. It limits the ruling of the *mishnah* to a very specific and very rare case:

> Rabbi Taḥlifa bar Ma'arava taught in the presence of Rabbi Abbahu: Two hold onto a cloak. This one takes as far as his hand reaches, and that one takes as far as his hand reaches, and the rest is divided equally. Rabbi Abbahu gestured: And with an oath.
>
> But our *mishnah,* which teaches that they divide it between them and does not teach that each takes as far as his hand reaches—how can it be? Rabbi Papa said: [The *mishnah* applies in a case] where they grasp it by loose threads. (*b. Bava Metzi'a* 7a)

The Mishnah, according to this reading, which shoehorns it into the position of the Tosefta, deals only with a case in which each of the parties holds the hem of the cloak, not its body. The preferred solution of the Tosefta and the Bavli is not division but maintenance of the status quo. One who wishes to alter the present state of affairs and take something away from its present possessor must bring proof. The Babylonian tradition with respect to all of the *mishnayot* we have addressed is to impose the broad principle of the burden of proof on the text of the *mishnah,* despite the fact that the plain meaning of each *mishnah* indicates that the burden-of-proof principle is narrower and more limited—and for this reason the *mishnah* tends to resolve uncertainty by means of division.[21] I will return

---

20. In his commentary on *t. Bava Metzi'a* (*Tosefta Kifshutah: Bava Kamma–Bava Metzi'a* [New York: Jewish Theological Seminary, 1988], 142), Saul Lieberman suggests that the absence of oaths from the solution proposed by the Tosefta is because the Tosefta was formulated before the oath was instituted. This contention presumes that the Mishnah and Tosefta adopted the same solution of dividing the disputed object, and therefore should be reconciled.

However, it seems from the straightforward meaning of the texts that the Tosefta is proposing a completely different solution, very different from division: leaving things as they are, without any court involvement. Consequently, there is no place for any oath. On the distinction between the opinion of the Mishnah and that of the Tosefta, see Yuval Blankovsky, "Essay on Talmudic Interpretation" [Hebrew], 84–90, available at http://www.daat.ac.il/daat/vl/belan-talmud/belan-talmud01.pdf.

21. The solution of division is proposed by the Mishnah in other cases of disputed property, though these cases are not directly connected to the resolution of uncertainty. These *mishnayot* appear around the *mishnah* about the barter of a cow for a donkey. This unit, in the eighth chapter of *Bava Metzi'a* inserted into a chapter about the laws regarding a borrower, brings together several completely different subjects whose organizing principle is division of property that is subject to dispute. This unit, which can be called the "division unit," stretches intermittently from *mishnah* 2 to *mishnah* 8. It begins with the uncertainty as to whether a cow that died was borrowed or rented at the time, which links it to the topic of

to discuss the significance of the debate about the scope of the burden-of-proof rule, and consequently of the possibility of using the division solution in situations of uncertainty pertaining to money. I will analyze the possible rationales for the Bavli to impose the broader view of the burden-of-proof principle on *mishnayot* that resolve cases through division. Before this additional discussion, however, it is worthwhile to gain a fuller picture of the Mishnah's solutions to states of uncertainty.

III

In addition to the solution by division that the Mishnah proposes in cases of uncertainty with monetary implications, it also postulates additional directives in cases of uncertainty that differ in the features of the case and the type of uncertainty to which they give rise:

> If one said to two: I stole a hundred from one of you, and I do not know which of you. Or: The father of one of you deposited a hundred with me, and I do not know which—he gives a hundred to each, for he conceded on his own.
>
> If two deposited with one—this one [deposited] a hundred and that one [deposited] two hundred. This one says, "The two hundred are mine," and that one says, "The two hundred are mine." [The trustee] gives each one a hundred, and the remainder is set aside until Elijah [the prophet] arrives. Rabbi Yose said: In that case, what has the deceiver lost? Rather, everything should be set aside until Elijah arrives. (*m. Bava Metzi'a* 3:3–4)

---

the chapter, namely, laws concerning borrowers. From there, the Mishnah goes on to discuss other topics where uncertainties arise, which are not connected to the topic of the chapter. The last case in the division unit concerns a rental, which is a return to the topic of the latter part of the chapter as well as the next chapter of *Bava Metzi'a*. In between, though, are laws regarding purchases—the barter of a cow for a donkey—that are not connected to the content of the chapter but nevertheless are included in this chapter because they propose the solution of division.

Among the cases discussed in this "division unit," *mishnah* 5 deals with the case of a field owner who sold his olive trees to someone for their wood, but in the meantime the trees grew olives. Each party claims ownership of the olives because they grew by virtue of what he owns: the landowner claims that it was his land that "grew" the olives, and the owner of the trees claims that it was his trees that grew the olives. The *mishnah* asserts that the two parties divide the olives. However, it is likely that the reason for this division is not uncertainty but recognition that the contribution of both the trees and the land to the growth of the olives mandates division in this case.

Another case (*mishnah* 6) that proposes resolution by division concerns a dove that was found midway between two dovecotes. In this case, the solution of division is unexceptional, as it is proffered where there is no prior factual status—of ownership or possession—on whose basis the uncertainty can be resolved.

These *mishnayot* do not propose the solution by division that we saw in cases of uncertainty that we discussed above. The first *mishnah* grants each party the full amount about which there is uncertainty: "he gives a hundred to each." The second *mishnah* withholds from both parties the sum about which there is uncertainty: "the remainder is set aside until Elijah arrives." These two rulings deviate from the principle of division and represent two very different alternative rulings for cases of uncertainty. The reason for this lies in the differences between the features of these cases and the cases of uncertainty for which solution by division was posed.

The second *mishnah,* in which each of the parties claims to have deposited two hundred, the one hundred about which there is uncertainty is not divided among the claimants; rather, it is withheld from both of them. The difference between the ruling of the *mishnah* that divides the cloak between the two that grasp it and claim it in its entirety and the *mishnah* that determines a solution of division in the case of the cow bartered for a donkey, on one hand, and the negation of the possibility of division in the case of the deposit, on the other, derives from the fact that one of the depositors—each of whom claims that he deposited two hundred—is a liar, and division of the disputed money will unjustly give the liar a profit of half the contested sum. In contrast, in the case of the cloak grasped by two, it is possible that each party thinks that he picked up the cloak before his fellow.[22] The present *mishnah,* which posits that the sum that is the subject of uncertainty is withheld from both parties, thus limits the solution by division to cases where such a solution will not profit a liar.

The distinction between these two rulings allows us to sharpen the legal and ethical logic that undergirds the solution of division in cases of uncertainty. It is important to note that, with these rules of conduct for cases of monetary uncertainty, the Mishnah distinguishes between two separate questions. The Mishnah renders decisions that, in absolute terms, do not reflect the "truth" of what should be; it proposes solution by division in cases like the barter of a cow with a donkey and an ox that gored a cow, in which it is obvious that the solution of division does not corre-

---

22. The Talmudic discussion at the beginning of *b. Bava Metzi'a* (3a) examines the relationship between the various rules in the Mishnah regarding situations of uncertainty. It proposes a distinction between cases where one party is certainly deceitful and cases where this is not necessarily so as the basis for the difference between rulings in the case where two grasp a cloak and the case where two parties deposited money with a third. Rabbi Joseph ibn Migash (*Ḥiddushei Ha-Ri Migash* on *Bava Batra* 34b, s.v. "*kol de-alim gevar*") proposes another distinction between the cases, which is related to the fact that, in the case of the depositors, neither party is in possession; the hundred in doubt is in the hands of a trustee, not in the hands of either party, whereas in the case of the cloak, both parties are in possession. According to Rabbi Joseph, the same principle animates the decision in each case: leave things as they are. In the case of the depositors, the asset in dispute is outside the reach of the parties, and there it remains. In the case of the cloak, the parties divide it.

spond to the real state of affairs. The offspring should belong either to the buyer or to the seller; it certainly does not belong to both. The same applies in the case of the goring, though not to the case in which two grasp a cloak, in which it is possible that the two parties picked the cloak up simultaneously. In such cases, the Mishnah proposes a solution by division even though it is not, strictly speaking, "true." In contrast, in the case where it is clear that one of the parties is lying, the solution by division is rejected—as we see from the *mishnah* about two depositors who each claim to have deposited the higher sum.

The rationale for distinguishing between these two types of solution can be explained as follows. In the solution by division proposed in several *mishnayot*, the loss is divided equally between the two parties; everyone loses the same amount. The attractiveness of the solution by division stems from the fact that it minimizes the cost of error by guaranteeing that, in every case, the party that is rightly entitled to the entire sum gets half of it. Nevertheless, the price of limiting the error by dividing the disputed sum results in rewarding the party that deserves nothing by giving him half of the sum he claims. The question of whether to espouse resolution by division, which seems to have sound logic, hinges, inter alia, on the question of whether we are interested in "rewarding" the second party to the claim even though he is entitled to nothing.

In the case of the cow bartered for a donkey, solution by division is more reasonable because the moral standing of the two parties is symmetrical: neither of them is lying, and neither offers any information about the relevant question of when the cow gave birth. A solution by division that grants each party half of the sum subject to uncertainty minimizes the potential cost of error. Likewise, in such cases, there is no reward for a party that is clearly lying, and so, in principle, there is no reason to recoil from such a solution. In contrast, in the case of the two depositors who each claim the right to the whole sum, there is no moral symmetry between the parties: one is lying, and the other speaks the truth. In such a case, solution by division is more problematic because, as noted, even though it ensures that the truth-speaker, who is entitled to the full amount, at least receives half of it, it also always gives the liar half of the sum. Therefore, in such a case, the Mishnah rejects the possibility of division and posits that the disputed sum is withheld from both parties.

The proposed explanation of the difference between the *mishnah* about the barter of a cow for a donkey, which adopts division as the mode of resolution, and the *mishnah* about the two depositors, in which division is rejected as a solution, was built on the premise that, while division minimizes the cost of error by ensuring that the rightful owner of the asset retains half of it, division also guarantees that the other party unjustly obtains half of the asset.

It is possible, however, to understand the solution of the *mishnah* about the two depositors in a different way, which is not based on a local moral judgment about division and its limitations in cases where one of the parties is deceitful. Rather, it is supported by broader policy considerations that ignore the moral aspects of solution by division. According to such an understanding, the Mishnah is interested in creating a rule under which it would not be worthwhile for either party to deceive, for in any event he will not profit from his deceitful attempts. He will not even gain half of what he is attempting to obtain. In cases like these, the court does not merely resolve the immediate problem; it also sets policy. And it stands to reason that, without the burden of setting policy, it would prescribe division in order to minimize the cost of a mistake.

This sort of policy consideration is clearly manifested in the words of Rabbi Yose's dissent. According to this view, in such a case, even the hundred to which each party is entitled is withheld, not just the additional hundred that is disputed. Rabbi Yose, who explains his view with the rationale, "In that case, what has the deceiver lost?," wants to deter the liar by causing him a loss, and to that end, he withholds the entire deposited sum from the parties. However, such a solution perpetrates an injustice against the truth teller, who loses the entire sum to which he is entitled due to the desire to punish the liar.[23] Deciding the uncertain matter in this way takes the long-term ramifications of each and every ruling into account, and its purpose, according to this view, is not just to resolve the conflict in the fairest manner possible but also to generate social norms that will discourage false claims and deceit.

The rejection of the solution by division in the *mishnah* of the two depositors can thus be understood in two different ways. The first is based on moral considerations in evaluating the solution by division and its limitations, and the second is premised on systemic considerations, in which the law attempts to disincentivize deceit[24]—a policy that may come at the expense of justice in the specific case faced by the court.

In addition to the ruling withholding the sum from both parties in the two depositors who each claim to have deposited two hundred, this *mishnah* introduces another ruling, in which each party is granted the entire claimed sum. This ruling likewise deviates from the solution of division:

> If one said to two: I stole a hundred from one of you, and I do not know which of you. Or: The father of one of you deposited a hundred with me,

---

23. Rabbi Yose's solution created an acute problem in game theory. If the halakhah would accord with Rabbi Yose, there is a chance that the party who is telling the truth, knowing that the law may deny him not only the second hundred that is rightfully his, but even the first hundred, will, upon seeing that the liar is claiming two hundred, claim to have deposited only one hundred, so that he may at least salvage half of his money.

24. See Maimonides's explanation of Rabbi Yose's view in his *Commentary on the Mishnah*: "So that the liar among them admits to the truth."

> and I do not know which—he gives a hundred to each, for he conceded on his own. (*m. Bava Metzi'a* 3:3)

The justification for such a ruling in this case stems from the fact that the bailee or thief admits to both parties that he stole from one of them or that one of their fathers deposited something with him, and the parties themselves make no claim. Since neither of them is a liar, and the thief or bailee admits that he is indebted to one of them, though he does not know which, he pays the full sum to each. In this case, we do not adopt the solution of division that would aver that each receives half of the sum. Likewise, we do not adopt the burden-of-proof rule, because neither party is trying to expropriate from the thief or bailee or to make a claim that would require him to bring proof. The uncertainty is introduced by the admission of the thief or bailee, so they must pay each party the full amount. These *mishnayot* thus propose two additional rulings in cases of uncertainty: one ruling withholds the entire disputed sum from both parties, and the second ruling grants each party the entirety of the sum.

A fuller, more complete picture of these additional rulings in cases of uncertainty that deviate from the solution of division can be found in the Mishnah and Tosefta in *Yevamot*:

> If a person betrothed one of five women and it is not known which of them he betrothed, each one saying, "He betrothed me"—he gives a bill of divorce to each one, places [the value of] the *ketubah* between them, and leaves. These are the words of Rabbi Tarfon. Rabbi Akiva says: This is not the way to prevent him from sin; rather he must give a bill of divorce and the *ketubah* to each one.
>
> If a person robbed one of five people but it is not known from whom he stole, and each one says, "He robbed me"—he places the stolen object among them and leaves. These are the words of Rabbi Tarfon. Rabbi Akiva says: This is not the way to prevent him from sin; rather he must pay the sum robbed to each one. (*m. Yevamot* 15:7)

> If a person betrothed one of five women, and it is not known which of them he betrothed, and each one says, "He betrothed me"; [or] if a person made a purchase from one of five people and it is not known from whom he purchased, and each one says, "He bought from me"—Rabbi Shimon ben Lazar says: Rabbi Tarfon and Rabbi Akiva did not disagree about a person who betrothed one of five women, and it is not known which of them he betrothed; [they agree that] he places [the value of] the *ketubah* between them and leaves. About what did they disagree? About a case where he copulated.
>
> And they did not disagree that if one bought from one of five people but does not know from whom he bought, that he places the purchase price object among them and leaves. About what did they disagree? About one who stole. Rabbi Tarfon concedes that one who says to two people: "I robbed one of you of a sum of money, but I don't know who," or: "The father of one of you deposited a sum with me, but I don't know

who," that he gives the sum to each of them, for he admitted it on his own. (*t. Yevamot* 14:3)

The Mishnah presents a dispute between Rabbi Akiva and Rabbi Tarfon regarding a case where five people claim to have been robbed by one person, and he indeed stole from one of them but does not know whom he robbed. Rabbi Akiva maintains that he must pay the full amount to each of them, whereas Rabbi Tarfon maintains that the thief is required only to place the stolen amount among the five claimants, who must then settle the debate among themselves. Rabbi Shimon ben Elazar qualifies and limits Rabbi Akiva's opinion to only cases where a person has an obligation to make restitution for his transgression and return the stolen object to its owner. Where there was a transgression, the thief must dispel all uncertainty and pay each of the five. However, if the uncertainty was not generated by his transgression, as in the case of one who purchased an object but does not know from which of five vendors he purchased it, Rabbi Akiva concedes that he leaves the purchase amount with them and lets them sort it out.[25]

Rabbi Tarfon maintains that, even one who stole from one of five people must likewise repay the stolen amount to the group and let them sort it out. Since all five are certain in their claims, four of them are lying, and there is no obligation to pay each of them. Rather, he returns the stolen sum to them collectively and thus discharges his obligation to repay what he stole.

In contrast, in a case where the parties do not sue the thief, and the uncertainty arises from the thief's own admission that he does not know which of the five people he robbed, Rabbi Tarfon concedes to Rabbi Akiva that he must pay each of them. This position deviates from the burden-of-proof rule that is applied in cases of uncertainty, and this deviation stems from the same narrow reading of this rule in the Mishnah, for as in other cases in the Mishnah, the uncertainty is generated not by the claims of the claimant or claimants, but by the admission of the thief or bailee.[26] The burden of proof is not imposed on these parties because they do not seek to expropriate money by virtue of their claims; therefore, in such a case,

25. The question of the relationship between the anonymous first opinion in the Tosefta passage and the corresponding *mishnah* in *Yevamot* is complicated. On this, see Saul Lieberman, *Tosefta Kifshutah: Yevamot-Ketubot* (New York: Jewish Theological Seminary, 1967), 196.

26. The *mishnah* in the third chapter of *Bava Metzi'a*—"If one said to two: I stole a hundred from one of you, and I do not know which of you. Or: The father of one of you deposited a hundred with me, and I do not know which—he gives a hundred to each, for he conceded on his own"—accords with the opinion of Rabbi Tarfon, as explained and articulated by Rabbi Shimon ben Elazar in the Tosefta. According to Rabbi Akiva, the thief should pay the full amount to each party, even if he did not admit of his own accord, but they made claims on him.

the principle that places the burden of proof on the claimant does not apply.[27]

At this stage of clarifying the various alternatives to the solution of division in the Mishnah and Tosefta, we can more thoroughly reexamine the views that emerge in Tannaitic literature. The Mishnah and Tosefta present us with an expansive engagement with uncertainty in monetary cases and with an attempt to govern these states of uncertainty. At the heart of this attempt is a fundamental debate about the proper position to take vis-à-vis monetary uncertainty. Tannaitic literature offers a complex series of rulings on how to behave under such circumstances: division of the disputed sum among the parties; leaving things as they are before us and leaving assets in the possession of those who hold them (the *muḥzak*); giving preference to the known prior owner of the assets (the *mara kamma*); keeping the disputed monies outside of the grasp of both claimants (until Elijah arrives); and giving the entire claimed sum to each of the claimants. This complicated proliferation of directives originates in conceptual depth

---

27. Following its principled position, the Bavli rereads the *mishnah* from a different perspective on deciding cases of uncertainty with respect to money—a perspective that assigns decisive value to the burden-of-proof rule. The Bavli (*Bava Metzi'a* 37a), challenges the *mishnah* that asserts that the robber or bailee must pay both parties and maintains that this solution opposes the principle that one may not take money from its owner on the basis of an uncertainty. This challenge, which presumes, as the Bavli does, the broader definition of the burden-of-proof rule, leads the discussion in the Bavli to conclude that the robber and bailee of the *mishnah* do not compensate both parties as a matter of law, but because they want to fulfill their duty toward God. It is not possible to obligate them to pay, because money cannot be expropriated on the basis of an uncertainty. Therefore, the basis for the *mishnah*'s assertion that the robber or bailee must pay both parties in full is the fact that a transgression was committed, and the transgressor wishes to fulfill his duties toward God.

This view presumes that a bailee who admits that two depositors left different sums with him and he does not know who deposited what has transgressed, as a thief has transgressed, because he had a duty to differentiate and remember who deposited two hundred. Therefore, he must pay both parties. If the bailee indeed bears such responsibility, and this is the reason that both parties are paid in full—the Bavli asks—why does the next *mishnah* state that a bailee who is sued by two depositors must repay one hundred to each of them and leave the disputed amount for Elijah to resolve? It would seem that the bailee has an obligation to know who deposited what, and he therefore should have to pay both.

According to the plain meaning of the *mishnah*, there is no contradiction between the cases. In the first case, the uncertainty arises from the bailee's admission, whereas, in the second case, the uncertainty is caused by the competing claims of the parties. However, the Bavli, which rejects this approach (in Rava's name), must posit that the *mishnah*'s two cases of depositors relate to vastly different sets of circumstances. The first case describes how each party makes his deposit separately, wherefore the bailee was obligated to know exactly who deposited what. In the second case, however, the deposit was made by both parties simultaneously, and since the depositors were not careful about their deposit, the bailee was absolved of the duty to clarify who deposited what.

To defend its expansive view of possession as ownership and of the burden-of-proof rule, the Bavli reads the *mishnah* as referring to one who seeks to fulfill his duty toward God and must draw a forced distinction between the *mishnah*'s two cases of deposits.

and sophistication, wherein a change in the features of an uncertainty changes the method of its resolution.

Likewise, the multiplicity of directives in the *mishnah* stems, inter alia, from a narrow reading of what would seem to be the default for cases of uncertainty: "one who seeks to expropriate from his fellow—[the burden of] proof is upon him." The Mishnah views this principle as one form of solution to states of uncertainty with respect to money, but it does not view it as the exclusive or dominant solution. In contrast, the Bavli, in accordance with what the redaction of the Tosefta indicates as the most acceptable approach, imperiously squelches the Mishnah's multiplicity and brings it in line with a single central principle: "one who seeks to expropriate from his fellow—[the burden of] proof is upon him."

In attempting to understand this fundamental dispute, we are faced with a question: What is the source of the Tosefta's, and later the Bavli's, tendency to subordinate all questions of uncertainty to the burden-of-proof rule? It would seem that the prior state of affairs, the status quo—whether the legal status quo of prior ownership or the actual status quo of possession—does not provide all of the information necessary to resolve the uncertainty. Absent such information, and in a case where the uncertainty arises independent of the parties' claims, the solution of division, offered by the Mishnah, would seem fair, as it limits the cost of error in judgment by evenly distributing potential loss and guaranteeing that the rightful owner receives half of what is justly his.

The reasons for the debate about the solution of division hinge on an understanding of the alternatives presented in the Tosefta. One alternative to division was to leave the prior order of ownership as it is. In such a case, the burden-of-proof rule is intended to protect ownership rights. The meaning of the rule is that we do not take money away from someone based on an uncertainty, even if the uncertainty is very real. Ownership is meant to be stable and unassailable absent evidence that goes well beyond the mere raising of uncertainty.

The second alternative to division presented in the Tosefta is to leave the present state of possession as it is, without changing it. The logic behind the position that rules in favor of preserving the status quo stems from the deeper function of law vis-à-vis uncertainty in a broader sense. This logic obtains even vis-à-vis the first alternative to division, namely, preserving the prior order of ownership.[28]

---

28. Eventually, in the seventeenth and eighteenth centuries, the question of possession versus ownership became the center of an acute halakhic debate between Rabbi Shabbetai Kohen (author of *Siftei Kohen*, or "*Shakh*"), in his book *Tekafo Kohen*, and Rabbi Yehuda Kahana Heller, in his book *Kuntres Ha-sfeikot*. On this debate and its roots, see Tikochinsky, "'*Kuntres HaSfekot*,'" 1–44.

Law represents an attempt to make the world predictable and expected. Human beings need to presume that they will attain a certain degree of security when forecasting the behavior of those with whom they sign contracts, to whom they transfer assets, by whom they are injured, whether by accident or purposefully, and to whom they cause injury. The ability to plan our lives in the most basic sense hinges on a level of certainty and stability in a world that is fundamentally unpredictable, changing, and unstable. The law as an attempt to create a space where things are predictable enables, inter alia, the division of labor and coordination between parties, which in turn enable cooperation and synchronization.

The tendency to leave things as they are when facing an uncertainty about monetary questions is thus an echo of the deeper principle of law as a way to regulate a shared existence. Law's role of enabling prediction and planning does not only pertain to the notion that the law should be known in advance or that its directives should apply consistently across similar instances; more than that, the law should have an inherent tendency to leave things as they are as long as there is no compelling reason to change them. This should be an independent general principle.[29]

Law also has another, contrasting role: to narrow the gap between the "is" and the "ought" by trying to impose a certain moral order on a complicated reality. In the case of uncertainty under discussion, the gap between the "is" and the "ought" is expressed in the fact that the sum "ought" to go, in full, to the just party, but in reality, we do not know which of the parties is on the side of justice. Narrowing the gap would mean dividing the sum so that the just party at least gets half of what he is entitled to.

---

29. There may be other rationales that are linked to the preference for the status quo. One of them relates to the indirect costs of deciding. Since the legal system entails operating costs, it prefers not to intervene unless sufficient evidence has been brought before it. This rationale does not appear in Mishnaic or Talmudic literature, but it carries weight in other legal systems. Another possible rationale is the idea that, absent just cause, the court does not deem itself authorized to act, especially when such an action entails the coercion of one of the parties. In such cases, the issue is not just preference of inaction over action but refraining from coercing one of the parties, as coercion of this sort must be accompanied by a decisive reason.

One of the ways of testing the motivations underlying support for the status quo hinges on whether the court's preference for the status quo is expressed in its recusal from the matter entirely or in the active validation of the ownership status quo. This distinction emerges from the understanding of the Talmudic passage (*b. Bava Metzi'a* 1a-b) dealing with a case where one party attempts to change the status quo and create new facts by seizing the disputed property. The question that emerges from such an incident is whether the court removes the property from the hands of the one who seized it. For a discussion of this passage and the distinction with respect to the meaning of preserving the status quo, see Elitzur Bar-Asher and Yair Furstenberg, "A Reexamination of the Talmudical Discussion *'teqafo kohen'*" [Hebrew], *Sinai* 125 (2000): 48–80.

Law's goal of bringing the "is" closer to the "ought" is sometimes in tension with the other goal, of making the world stable and predictable. It is possible that this fundamental tension is discernible in the dispute about the weight that should be ascribed to the status quo when contending with states of uncertainty—and, consequently, the degree to which the burden-of-proof principle is an exclusive arbiter when ruling on uncertain states.

6

Doubt and Vagueness

I

Legal systems tend to structure their concepts as binary distinctions—between guilty and not guilty, valid and not valid, alive and dead, sane and insane, minor and adult, and so on—which do not tolerate intermediate states, gradual transitions, and ragged edges. These classifications generally appear in law as comprehensive, clear-cut categories whose members are supposed to belong completely to one class or the other.[1]

Like any legal system, Tannaitic literature develops such categories, but it uniquely gives rise to uncertainties that flourish when binary legal categories are undermined. This undermining produces a range of intermediate stages and gradual transitions that provide fertile ground for the cultivation of rules governing uncertainty within Tannaitic literature. These uncertainties do not necessarily pertain to specific areas of law, like purity, forbidden foods, pedigree, or property. Rather, they take shape in the Mishnah and Tosefta through examination of the very possibility of constructing a rigid conceptual system.

One of the clearest and most important instances of borderline-based uncertainty developed in Tannaitic literature regards the transition from day to night. There are far-reaching halakhic implications for determining when the day ends and the night begins, so presumably a halakhic system, or any legal system, would attempt to determine and mark the transitional moment clearly and sharply. Law, for instance, has a strong interest in determining the precise date on which a loan was repaid in a case where a delinquent payment carries monetary penalties. However,

---

1. For a discussion of the binary character of legal categories and the attempt to challenge them, see Larry Alexander, "Scalar Properties, Binary Judgments," *Journal of Applied Philosophy* 25.2 (2008): 85–104. For an interesting attempt to defend the binary nature of legal categories, see Leo Katz, *Why Is Law So Perverse?* (Chicago: University of Chicago Press, 2011), 139–84. See also the response to Leo Katz in Adam J. Kolber, "Smoothing Vague Laws," in *Vagueness and Law: Philosophical and Legal Perspectives*, ed. Geert Keil and Ralf Poscher (Oxford: Oxford University Press, 2016), 275–98.

the transition from day to night is elusive: Does the day end when it begins to grow dark, or does it end only when the sunlight is completely gone? The transition from light to dark is a prolonged process, as we are aware. Is it possible, during this gradual transition from light to darkness, to identify a specific moment at which day becomes night?

This challenge to the clearly binary division of night and day led the sages to develop the concept of a transitional time, which they call *bein ha-shemashot* (twilight; lit., "between the suns"), during which light gives way to darkness and about which it cannot be said that it belongs to the outgoing day or incoming night with any degree of certainty. This temporal unit produced a broad arena of uncertainty that the sages brought to bear in various halakhic contexts. For example, the Mishnah uses this transitional time to discuss rare halakhic contingencies:

> An infant may be circumcised on the eighth, the ninth, the tenth, the eleventh, or the twelfth [day after birth], but no earlier or later. How so? Under normal conditions, he is circumcised on the eighth; if he was born at twilight [*bein ha-shemashot*], he is circumcised on the ninth; at twilight of the eve of the Sabbath, he is circumcised on the tenth; if a festival immediately follows the Sabbath, he is circumcised on the eleventh; if [the Sabbath is immediately followed by] two days of Rosh Hashanah, he is circumcised on the twelfth. (*m. Shabbat* 19:6)

It is well known that the sages maintained that the circumcision of a baby on the eighth day after birth overrides the Sabbath. However, a circumcision that had been postponed from its proper time, to the ninth day, for instance, does not override the Sabbath and is further postponed until the following Sunday. The circumcision of a baby who was born during *bein ha-shemashot* at the onset of the Sabbath does not override the next Sabbath, for it is uncertain whether the baby's eighth day is Friday, in which case his circumcision would not override the Sabbath, or the Sabbath, in which case it would. Given this uncertainty, the Sabbath is not overridden, and the circumcision is postponed until Sunday. Similarly, if the baby was born during *bein ha-shemashot* at the onset of the Sabbath and the next Sabbath is followed immediately by a festival, the child's circumcision is postponed by another day, until Monday, for Sunday is certainly not the eighth day and therefore circumcision does not override the prohibition of certain types of labor on festivals. If the Sabbath is followed by the two days of Rosh Hashanah, then the circumcision is postponed by three days. Thus, the uncertainty generated when a baby is born during *bein ha-shemashot* at the onset of the Sabbath produces several uncommon halakhic eventualities wherein a baby cannot be circumcised until several days after his eighth day. As in other cases involving uncertainty, these situations give rise to borderline cases that can produce unexpected halakhic results, which the Mishnah is more than happy to examine and catalog.

In addition to these exotic cases, *bein ha-shemashot*, as a time when it is not certain whether it is day or night, has far-reaching implications for the question of the onset of the Sabbath and the laws of the Sabbath:

> If it is uncertain whether it is dark or not, one may not tithe [produce that is] certain[ly untithed]; and one may not immerse vessels [in a *mikveh*]; and one may not light the lamps. One may [however] tithe *demai*; and one may make an *eruv*, and one may bury hot food [to insulate it]. (*m. Shabbat* 2:7)

The Mishnah uses the term "uncertain whether it is dark" (*safeik ḥashekhah*) to denote an intermediate time with a different halakhic status than the week as well as the Sabbath. Several activities that are forbidden on the Sabbath remain permitted when it is "uncertain whether it is dark"—such as tithing *demai* and insulating hot food—because the lesser degree of severity of these prohibited actions on the Sabbath means that they were not deemed forbidden at a time that may or may not be the Sabbath.

These intermediate stages are typically the sites of disagreement, and the Tosefta cites another opinion about *bein ha-shemashot* on the eve of the Sabbath:

> Rabbi Shimon ben Lazar stated a general rule: Any [Sabbath violation] that warrants excision if done on purpose and a sin-offering if done unintentionally may not be done during *bein ha-shemashot*. [And anything that does not warrant excision if done on purpose or a sin-offering if done unintentionally may be done during *bein ha-shemashot*.] (*t. Shabbat* 2:8)

Whereas the Tanna of the *mishnah* characterizes *bein ha-shemashot* of the Sabbath eve by means of several unsystematic examples of relatively minor infractions that are permitted at that time, Rabbi Shimon ben Elazar poses an essential distinction: forms of labor on the Sabbath punishable by Torah law are forbidden during *bein ha-shemashot*, whereas activities like immersing vessels, which are not prohibited by the Torah but which the sages forbade for various reasons, are permitted during *bein ha-shemashot*. Tannaitic literature thus develops a new concept of "uncertain Sabbath," demonstrating that there is no clear, abrupt differentiation of sacred time from profane time.[2]

---

2. Uncertainty concerning the beginning of Shabbat had an impact on the halakhah of the Dead Sea sect, as is apparent from the following passage in the Damascus Document: "Concerning the Sabbath to guard it according to its precept: Let no man do work on the sixth day from the time when the sphere of the sun is distant from the gate by its fullness; for that is what is said: 'Guard the Sabbath day to make it holy'" (CD X, 14–17). As Aharon Shemesh pointed out, this time added to the Sabbath is not considered an uncertain time with its own unique halakhic standing. Starting the Sabbath earlier is rather derived from the verse itself as a way of guarding the Sabbath so it will not be violated. Needless to say, a further explication of its unique status as an uncertain period of the day and nignt and the unique rules that apply to it do not appear in the writings of the sect. See Aharon Shemesh,

The nature of the uncertainty presented by *bein ha-shemashot* can be understood in three different ways. The first is that the intermediate time between light and darkness is a sort of mixture of night and day, containing something of both. The existence of this intermediate time reflects the view that the transition from day to night is not abrupt. According to this view, the problem with the categories "day" and "night" when applied to the gradual transition to darkness is that they are not mutually exclusive. The twenty-four-hour cycle cannot be divided into times that are "day" and times that are "night," because there are transitional times that are both day and night.[3]

According to the second understanding, *bein ha-shemashot* is either entirely day or entirely night, but we are unable to definitively place it on either side of the temporal barrier. Day and night are mutually exclusive, but they are not defined and delineated clearly enough to enable us to assign these transitional times to one of them.

According to the third understanding, during *bein ha-shemashot* there is a single distinct moment of transition from day to night, but the moment is elusive, and we are incapable of defining it. Accordingly, day transitions to night at some moment between sunset and darkness, but our inability to identify this moment places the entire temporal unit in a state of uncertainty. The third understanding does not undermine the fundamental binarity of day and night, but it does question our ability to ascertain the moment where one transitions to the other. All we can do is demarcate a broader temporal unit within which this momentary transitional event takes place.

A closer look at additional developments of the laws of *bein ha-shemashot* in the Mishnah shows that these different possible ways of understanding the nature of the uncertainty of *bein ha-shemashot* were the subject of a Tannaitic dispute:

> The Sabbath and Yom Kippur [fell on consecutive days] and one performed forbidden labor during *bein ha-shemashot* [between the days] and does not know on which day he acted: Rabbi Eliezer deems [him] liable for a sin offering, but Rabbi Yehoshua exempts. Rabbi Yose said: They do not disagree about one who did prohibited labor during *bein ha-shemashot*, who is exempt, for I can say that he performed part of the forbidden act on one day and part on the following day. About what do they disagree? About one who did a prohibited act during the day, but does not know whether he did it on the Sabbath or on Yom Kippur; or where

---

Halakhah in the Making: The Development of Jewish Law from Qumran to the Rabbis, Taubman Lectures in Jewish Studies (Berkeley: University of California Press, 2009), 74–75.

3. A similar question would pertain at the time of transition from night to day, between dawn and sunrise, with halakhic implications for obligations, like the daily burnt offering and morning prayers, which can be discharged only during the day.

> he did a prohibited act but does not know what category of forbidden labor he violated—Rabbi Eliezer deems [him] liable for a sin offering, but Rabbi Yehoshua exempts. (*m. Kareitot* 4:3)

People who unwittingly performed *melakhah,* one of the categories of labor prohibited on the Sabbath, during *bein ha-shemashot* between the Sabbath and Yom Kippur, do not know whether they committed their transgression on the Sabbath or on Yom Kippur, and they have no way of precisely defining which prohibition they unwittingly violated. Did they transgress the prohibition of *melakhah* on Yom Kippur or the prohibition against *melakhah* on the Sabbath? According to Rabbi Eliezer, since clearly, in any case, they unwittingly transgressed the prohibition on *melakhah,* whether on the Sabbath or Yom Kippur, they must bring a sin offering. In contrast, Rabbi Yehoshua maintains that they must know for certain which prohibition they transgressed in order to be liable for a sin offering, and since they transgressed during *bein ha-shemashot,* they cannot bring a sin offering for this.

Rabbi Yose disputes the first Tanna of the *mishnah*'s account of the disagreement between Rabbi Eliezer and Rabbi Yehoshua. According to Rabbi Yose, if a transgression was inadvertently committed during *bein ha-shemashot,* even Rabbi Eliezer concedes that no sin offering is brought, as it is possible that the transition from the Sabbath to Yom Kippur occurred during the commission of the transgression, in which case half of the prohibited act was done on the Sabbath and half on Yom Kippur. According to Rabbi Yose, in such a case, the perpetrator of the transgression would be exempt from a sin offering, for in order to be liable, the entire act must be committed on one of the two days, and there is no way of knowing whether this indeed happened.

The Tosefta exemplifies Rabbi Yose's position by means of the *melakhah* of writing. To be liable for writing on the Sabbath, the perpetrator must write at least two letters. In the present case, it is possible that the moment of transition from day to night took place after the writing of the first letter and before the writing of the second. It would thus emerge that the writer did not perform a complete *melakhah* on either day, the Sabbath or Yom Kippur. The clear implication of Rabbi Yose's position is that the transition from day to night is binary and instantaneous. However, the moment of transition is elusive and cannot be determined, and it is therefore possible that it occurred during the commission of the *melakhah.*[4]

---

4. See the version of the Tosefta:

> If Yom Kippur coincided with Friday and one performed forbidden labor during *bein ha-shemashot*: Rabbi Eliezer deems [him] liable for a sin offering, but Rabbi Yehoshua exempts. Rabbi Yose said: I do not accept the words of Rabbi Eliezer here, for I can say that one who wrote two letters, one on the Sabbath and one on Yom Kippur, is exempt, for two days cannot combine in the case of one *melakhah.*

The Tanna who taught this *mishnah* disagrees with Rabbi Yose and has a different understanding of the uncertainty generated by the state of *bein ha-shemashot*. According to this Tanna, there is no abrupt transition from day to night during *bein ha-shemashot*. The uncertainty of *bein ha-shemashot* is whether this interval belongs entirely to the outgoing day or entirely to the incoming night. This alternative conception of the uncertainty posed by *bein ha-shemashot* emerges from the way the dispute between Rabbi Eliezer and Rabbi Yehoshua is presented in *Sifra*, where the rationales of the various disputants are added:

> "Wherein he has sinned" (Lev 4:23): What does "in it" teach? Whence do we derive ... Sabbath and Yom Kippur, and one performed forbidden labor during *bein ha-shemashot* and did not know on which of them he performed it: Rabbi Eliezer deems [him] liable for a sin offering, but Rabbi Yehoshua exempts. Rabbi Eliezer said to him: Take your pick! ... If he desecrated the Sabbath, he is liable, and if he desecrated Yom Kippur he is liable! Rabbi Yehoshua replied: It is written: "wherein he has sinned in it"—this teaches that he is not liable until it is known to him wherein he sinned. (*Sifra, Ḥovah*, section 5, chapter 5, MS Vatican 66).

According to the claim in *Sifra, bein ha-shemashot* belongs either to the previous day or to the next day, and Rabbi Eliezer therefore maintains that one who performs a *melakhah* during *bein ha-shemashot* as Shabbat gives way to Yom Kippur is liable for a sin offering, because he definitely did a forbidden *melakhah,* whether on the Sabbath or Yom Kippur. Rabbi Yehoshua maintains that, since the person performing the *melakhah* does not know exactly what prohibition he is violating—the prohibition on *melakhah* on the Sabbath or on Yom Kippur—he cannot be held liable to bring a sin offering. Rabbi Yehoshua links his unique notion that a sin offering obligation requires definite knowledge to his exegesis of the verse, "Or he is made to know of the sin wherein he has sinned in it" (Lev 4:23), which teaches that the sin must be definite and known.

> They said to him: [The *melakhah*] of the final hammer blow will demonstrate [that Rabbi Eliezer's position applies]. He replied to them: He lifted it on the Sabbath and brought it down on Yom Kippur." (*t. Kareitot* 2:15)

Unlike in the Mishnah's tradition, here Rabbi Yose does not offer an alternative understanding of the dispute between Rabbi Eliezer and Rabbi Yehoshua. Rather, he disputes the view of Rabbi Eliezer. It is apparent that the counterexample of the final hammer blow (*makeh be-fatish*), which is directed against Rabbi Yose in the Tosefta, purports to describe an act that cannot be divided into two distinct events that cumulatively constitute the *melakhah,* such as the writing of two letters. Rabbi Eliezer's opinion can still be applied to such an indivisible act. Rabbi Yose's response is that even the final hammer blow can be divided in half, for according to him, the *melakhah* of striking with the hammer must encompass the entire process of lifting the hammer and bringing it down—a process that can be divided into two phases that can theoretically happen on different days. Thus, the hammer can be lifted on Yom Kippur and brought down on the Sabbath.

Another Tannaitic source, *Mekhilta De-Rabbi Yishmael*, records the expounding of a different verse, from which a third position on the nature of *bein ha-shemashot* emerges:

> "Whoever does any *melakhah* on it will be put to death" (Exod 35:2). "On it" and not "on it and its neighbor," so if Yom Kippur coincides with the eve of the Sabbath and one did *melakhah* during *bein ha-shemashot*, I would think that he should be liable. Therefore it teaches, "whoever does any *melakhah* on it will be put to death"; "on it" and not "on it and its neighbor." (*Mekhilta De-Rabbi Yishmael, Mesekhta De-Shabta, Vayakhel* 1, Horowitz edition, p. 346)

This expounding seems to indicate that *bein ha-shemashot* is a transitional interval that belongs both to the outgoing day and the incoming night; one who performs *melakhah* during this period is considered as one who performed *melakhah* "on it and its neighbor." Therefore, one who performed *melakhah* during this period cannot be punished, as he did not commit the act at a time that clearly belongs to one of the days on which such *melakhah* is prohibited. *Bein ha-shemashot* is not some elusive moment between day and night, as Rabbi Yose maintains, nor is it an interval about which we are uncertain whether it is entirely day or entirely night. Rather, it seems from the language of the *Mekhilta* that *bein ha-shemashot* belongs simultaneously to the outgoing day and the incoming night, because the transition from day to night is gradual. The various Tannaitic sources indicate that, whereas the sages defined *bein ha-shemashot* as a time that produces uncertainty, they disagreed about the nature of this uncertainty. Defining the transition from day to night is especially important with respect to the onset and completion of the Sabbath and festivals, and, as we have seen, the Tannaitic sources develop and address various cases that allow them not only to establish *bein ha-shemashot* as a time of uncertainty but also to investigate the nature of the uncertainty.[5]

---

5. The Mishnah addresses additional potential implications of *bein ha-shemashot* in other contexts where the question of the transition from day to night has halakhic significance. Another discussion of uncertainty that produces the intermediate temporal category of *bein ha-shemashot* appears in the Mishnah of tractate *Zavin*. A person who experiences an abnormal genital discharge (*zivah*) twice in one day or on consecutive days is considered impure, having contracted *zav* impurity. To return to purity, the person must count seven days free of any discharge and then immerse. If the person experienced *zivah* three times in one day or on three consecutive days, then becoming pure, in addition to seven clean days and immersion, mandates a sacrificial offering. The question of *bein ha-shemashot* in the context of seeing an abnormal flow appears in the following *mishnah*:

> If one saw a [discharge] during the day and another during *bein ha-shemashot*, [or] one during *bein ha-shemashot* and one the next day, if it is known that part of the sighting was during the day and part was the next day, there is certainty with regard to a sacrifice and with regard to impurity [i.e., the person is impure and must bring a sacrifice]. If there is uncertainty whether part of the sighting was

The Bavli quotes a Tannaitic source that lays out the various possibilities for understanding the time of *bein ha-shemashot*:

> The sages taught: It is uncertain whether *bein ha-shemashot* is of the day or of the night; it is uncertain whether it is completely day, and it is uncertain whether it is completely night, so [the sages] impose the stringencies of both days upon it. And what is twilight? From when the sun sets, as long as the eastern face of the sky is reddened. If the lower segment of the sky has lost its color, and the upper segment has not yet lost its color, it is *bein ha-shemashot*. If the upper segment has lost its color, and its color equals that of the lower one, it is night. These are the words Rabbi Yehuda. Rabbi Neḥemiah says: [*Bein ha-shemashot* is], counting from sunset, the time it takes a person to walk half a *mil*. Rabbi Yose says: *Bein ha-shemashot* is like the blink of an eye. One enters, the other leaves, and it is impossible to ascertain it. (*b. Shabbat* 34b)

> today and part was the next day, there is certainty with regard to impurity but uncertainty with regard to the sacrifice. If he saw on two [consecutive] days during *bein ha-shemashot*, there is uncertainty with regard to both impurity and sacrifice. If he saw one [discharge] during *bein ha-shemashot*, there is uncertainty with regard to impurity. (*m. Zavim* 1:6)

According to this *mishnah*, a single discharge can be considered as two discharges if it occurs on two different days. (Under normal circumstances where a discharge takes place on a single day, the second discharge is considered a separate event only if there was sufficient time to immerse and towel off the entire body in between the two discharges.) The transition from day to night "splits" a single discharge into two. Therefore, a person who saw a single discharge is not yet considered impure, but if the sighting was during *bein ha-shemashot*, then there is uncertainty as to whether he is impure, because the transition from day to night may have occurred just as he was experiencing the discharge, which means that, in effect, he experienced two discharges. Likewise, if a person saw two discharges during *bein ha-shemashot* of consecutive days, he has an uncertain status with respect to the sacrificial offering, since it is possible that there were three separate sightings.

This *mishnah* accords with the view of Rabbi Yose as it appears in *Kareitot*, namely, that the transition from day to night is binary and instantaneous, though the moment of transition cannot be ascertained. In Tosefta *Zavim* 1:12, our *mishnah* is taught explicitly in Rabbi Yose's name:

> Rabbi Yose agrees that if he saw one during *bein ha-shemashot*, even if there was not enough time to immerse and towel off, there are two sightings because the two days split it. And so would Rabbi Yose say: If one saw a [discharge] during *bein ha-shemashot*, there is uncertainty with regard to impurity and he is exempt from an offering. If he saw on two [consecutive] days during *bein ha-shemashot*, there is uncertainty with regard to both impurity and sacrifice. [If one saw] a discharge at a time of certainty and two during *bein ha-shemashot*, or two at a time of certainty, there is certainty with regard to impurity and uncertainty with regard to the sacrifice. Two [at times of certainty] and one during *bein ha-shemashot*, or two during *bein ha-shemashot* and one at a time of certainty, [there is certainty] with respect to impurity and certainty with respect to the sacrifice.

See also *y. Berakhot* 1:1, fol. 2, col. 2, lines 19–20.

The *baraita* begins by positing two possible understandings of the nature of uncertainty generated by *bein ha-shemashot*: Is it a transitional time that has something of both day and night and thus belongs to both days? Or is it a time about which we are uncertain whether it belongs entirely to the incoming night or entirely to the outgoing day?[6] These two views fit with a conception of *bein ha-shemashot* as a time interval that Rabbi Yehudah and Rabbi Nehemiah demarcate in different ways. Rabbi Yehudah demarcates *bein ha-shemashot* by means of changes in the hues of the sky during the process that lasts from sunset until darkness. Rabbi Nehemiah liberates the definition from the difficulties likely to arise from the identification of light and dark hues; instead, he prescribes an amount of time dictated by a walking distance: starting at sunset, *bein ha-shemashot* lasts for the time it takes to walk half a *mil*.[7] Rabbi Yose, in contrast to Rabbi Yehudah and Rabbi Nehemiah, views *bein ha-shemashot* not as a period of time but as an elusive moment, the blink of an eye, when day becomes night. Rabbi Yose explains the nature of the uncertainty in a completely

---

6. A possible halakhic difference between these two possibilities, namely, whether *bein ha-shemashot* is either entirely day or entirely night, or *bein ha-shemashot* is both day and night, is likely to appear in the context of the two cases brought in the Yerushalmi:

> Rabbi Yose bar Bon inquired: If you say that two [stars] is uncertain, if someone saw two stars on the eve of the Sabbath, and people cautioned him, and he performed a *melakhah*, and then he saw two stars at the end of the Sabbath, and people cautioned him, and he performed a *melakhah*, then take your pick: If the former was during the day, then so was the latter, and he should liable for the latter. If the latter was at night, then the former was also at night, and he should be liable for the former. If he saw two stars on the eve of the Sabbath and harvested half of a date, then in the morning harvested half a date, and then saw two stars at the end of the Sabbath and harvested a date, then take your pick: If the former was during the day, then so was the latter; that of the morning should combine with that of the end of the Sabbath, and he should liable for the latter. If the latter was at night, then the former was also at night; that of the morning should combine with that of the eve of the Sabbath, and he should be liable for the former. (*y. Berakhot* 1:1, col, 1, lines 28–38)

These cases presume that *bein ha-shemashot* is either entirely day or entirely night. Therefore, one who performed *melakhah* on the eve of the Sabbath and at the end of the Sabbath has certainly desecrated the Sabbath. However, if we would maintain that *bein ha-shemashot* is neither day nor night but a gradual transition from day to night that contains elements of both, then we could say that such a person is not liable, because he never performed a *melakhah* at a time that was fully Sabbath.

7. An alternate method of demarcating the duration of *bein ha-shemashot* appears in the Yerushalmi:

> Rabbi Pinḥas in the name of Rabbi Abba bar Papa: One star is certainly day. Two is uncertain. Three is certainly night.... On the eve of the Sabbath, if he saw one star and performed *melakhah*, he is exempt. Two [stars], he brings a tenuous guilt offering. Three [stars], he brings a sin offering. At the end of the Sabbath, if he saw one star and performed *melakhah*, he brings a sin offering. Two, he brings a tenuous guilt offering. Three, he is exempt. (*y. Berakhot* 1:1, col. 1, lines 22–28)

different way than the first two views, and, as we have seen, this has ramifications for how to rule on uncertainties pertaining to *bein ha-shemashot*.

Philosophers, over time, have thoroughly analyzed the idea of vagueness. Among other things, they have addressed whether the source of vagueness is epistemic—that is, whether it stems from our capacity to identify the phenomenon—or whether it stems from the phenomenon itself. One of the most common examples in philosophical literature about vagueness is the "heap of sand" concept. At what point, from the moment that grains of sand begin to accumulate, does the growing collection of grains become an object that can be called a "heap"?

There are two philosophical positions on this. The first is that the concept of a "heap" is itself a concept with vague margins. Therefore, there will be no specific transitional point at which the addition of a single grain will transform the collection of grains into a heap. The vagueness, as it were, lies in the heap itself. Other philosophers, most prominently Timothy Williamson, contend that there is indeed a single grain of sand that causes the transformation of this collection of grains into a heap. However, we cannot identify it precisely; the problem lies in our ability to ascertain things, not in the things themselves.[8]

This philosophical debate resonates with the Tannaitic treatment of the *bein ha-shemashot* problem. Rabbi Yose's position is similar to the epistemic position, which maintains that there is indeed a real, specific moment at which day becomes night, but that we cannot identify it. On the other hand, positions that view *bein ha-shemashot* as an interval that undermines the binarity of the transition would take the view that vagueness is inherent in the very transition from day to night, in the gradual, complex process of darkening.

The emergence of the vagueness question in Tannaitic literature is not motivated by independent interest in quasi-logical paradoxes, which provided the background for the problem's emergence in Stoic philosophical literature.[9] The formation of the uncertain halakhic condition of *bein ha-shemashot* and the investigation of its character are undertaken by examining the vague state of *bein ha-shemashot* in various halakhic contexts. The sages' halakhic creativity allows them to construct uncertain cases involving *bein ha-shemashot*, in which the theoretical and speculative alternatives for understanding the concept of vagueness will have real-world implications in the field of halakhah.

---

8. See Timothy Williamson, *Vagueness*, Problems of Philosophy (London: Routledge, 1994).

9. For an extensive analysis of vagueness in Stoic philosophy, see Susanne Bodsien, "Chrysipppus and the Epistemic Theory of Vagueness," *Proceedings of the Aristotelian Society* 102 (2002): 217–38.

Borderline cases like *bein ha-shemashot* produce halakhic exceptions that Tannaitic literature probes and develops. Let us return to the case of circumcision, with which we began this discussion. The standard circumcision takes place on the eighth day and is postponed only when the state of the baby's health does not warrant circumcision on time. The standard time of circumcision is so deeply entrenched, according to the teachings of the rabbis, that, if the eighth day coincides with the Sabbath, circumcision overrides the severe prohibition of performing *melakhah* on the Sabbath.[10] The Mishnah introduces *bein ha-shemashot* as a borderline situation that produces exceptions to the rule of circumcision on the eighth day; the halakhic ramification of a male baby's birth during *bein ha-shemashot* at the onset of the Sabbath is that the circumcision is postponed until the tenth day and sometimes even the eleventh or twelfth.

The interesting element in this series of deviations from the proper time of circumcision is that the postponement in such cases is not due to constraints imposed by external factors, such as the baby's health. The constraint that forces the postponement of circumcision is internal to the system of rules, and the halakhic exceptions produced in such cases derive from the borderline state of *bein ha-shemashot*. Identification of a legal exception and the ability to formulate it and deal with it are the clearest signs of a Torah scholar's virtuosity. Dwelling on borderline cases such as *bein ha-shemashot* ensures the proliferation of exceptions and sometimes even halakhic paradoxes, like those that appear in Mishnah *Kareitot* with respect to one who performs *melakhah* during *bein ha-shemashot* between Yom Kippur and the Sabbath.

Another case in which a halakhic exception was developed in the borderline conditions of *bein ha-shemashot* emerges in a *mishnah* that deals with menstrual and *zav* impurities. However, this *mishnah* contains a rare moment of critical counter-reaction against the very engagement with such borderline cases. The Mishnah constructs two different halakhic frameworks of purity and impurity, one for blood that originates in a woman's regular menstrual cycle (*niddah*) and one for blood that originates in a flow that is not linked to the menstrual cycle (*zivah*). Tannaitic

10. There is a view in Second Temple halakhah that the verse "On the eighth day, the flesh of his foreskin shall be circumcised" (Lev 12:3) establishes that the baby must be circumcised by, not on, the eighth day, and circumcision therefore does not override the Sabbath. This view finds expression in the book of Jubilees: "Anyone who is born and the flesh of his foreskin not circumcised by the eighth day is not among the children of the covenant that our God made with Abraham" (Jub. 15:26). See Menahem Kister, "Concerning the History of the Essenes: A Study of the Animal Apocalypse, the Book of Jubilees and the Damascus Document" [Hebrew], *Tarbiz* 56 (1987): 1–18, here 6–7 n. 26; see also Aharon Shemesh, *The History of the Halakhic Concept 'Piku'aḥ Nefesh Doḥ Shabbat'*" [Hebrew], *Tarbiz* 80 (2012): 8–9.

literature addresses the question of determining when blood is deemed to be menstrual and when it is deemed to be unrelated to the menstrual cycle. One of the most significant factors in differentiating *niddah* from *zivah* blood stems from the assumption that menstruation generally lasts about seven days, so if a woman sees blood more than seven days from when she gets her period, it is likely that this blood is not menstrual blood but the blood of *zivah*. According to the sages, there are at least eleven days between the end of one *niddah*-cycle and the beginning of the next, so a blood flow during this interval is likely, under specific circumstances, to produce the halakhic status of *zivah*.

The Mishnah contains instructions for a woman who is unsure about the number of days that have elapsed and is thus uncertain whether or not the blood she sees is related to her menses (*m. Arakhin* 2:2). In addition to this relatively common case, however, the Mishnah does not waste the opportunity to address the borderline case wherein a woman saw blood during *bein ha-shemashot* at the end of the seventh day of menstruation or at the end of the eleventh day of the interval period. In both of these cases, her seeing blood produces a halakhic exception. What makes this discussion unique is that the Mishnah records a rare and sharp reaction against the very engagement with the borderline case of *bein ha-shemashot*:

> Regarding a woman who saw [a discharge of blood] on the eleventh day during *bein ha-shemashot*, at the beginning or end of the *niddah* period or at the beginning or end of the *zivah* period; or [if she saw blood] during *bein ha-shemashot* of the fortieth day [after the birth] of a male, or the eightieth day [after the birth] of a female—in all these cases, they are [assumed to be] in error. Rabbi Yehoshua said: Before you find remedies for the extraordinary women, find remedies for the ordinary women. (*m. Niddah* 6:14)

According to the first Tanna of this *mishnah*, seeing blood during *bein ha-shemashot* of the eleventh day is considered, due to uncertainty, as seeing both *niddah* blood and *zivah* blood, thus leading to an irregular halakhic result. Rabbi Yehoshua rejects the very discussion of this exceptional borderline case of *bein ha-shemashot*. According to him, such a discussion imposes an unnecessary burden in an area of halakhah that is already difficult.[11] Rabbi Yehoshua's dismissive and critical tone expresses discomfort with the attention to uncommon extreme cases, like seeing blood during *bein ha-shemashot* of a particular day.

---

11. The expression (*shotot*) in the Mishnah that refers to women who saw blood during *bein ha-shemashot*, is contrasted by Rabbi Yehoshua with *pikḥot*. Unlike its ordinary use *shotot* does not mean "lacking in intelligence" but rather "irregular." See the comment of Epstein, *Introduction to the Mishnaic Text*, 1:560. Ritva interpreted *shotot* to mean "irregular," as in an "irregular myrtle branch," referring to something that deviates from the norm. See Ritva to *Niddah* 54a, s.v. "*eima to'ot*."

In his *Commentary on the Mishnah,* Maimonides explains Rabbi Yehoshua's words at length and in depth:

> The meaning of the words of Rabbi Yehoshua, who says, "Instead of speaking about and discussing women who are extraordinary, let us discuss the status of those who are not extraordinary," is that he is intimating that this sort of discussion that we are in the midst of is very difficult; its laws are manifold, and we cannot completely explain all of the numerous differences whose possible existence is likely. So why should we make presumptions whose possible existence is unlikely, for instance, that she would see specifically at *bein ha-shemashot* of a particular day. This is unlikely to occur, but if we engage in discussion about what the law would be in this case, it will expand, and we will be too preoccupied to deal with things that are more necessary. (Maimonides, commentary to *Niddah* 6:14)

The imaginative engagement with these borderline cases does not contribute to the clarification of an area that is already difficult and complicated. As Maimonides put it, such exercises are liable to distract people from clarifying substantive issues.

Rabbi Yehoshua's critique of the attention given to the irregular borderline cases of *bein ha-shemashot* is itself an irregular moment in the Mishnah.[12] The development of complex halakhic results, born, inter alia, in the borderline states that the Mishnah invents, is an essential component of the Mishnah's character. One of the borderline states that the Mishnah invents is the transition from day to night as a place of uncertainty. Engagement with this state produces, as we have seen, a complex series of rulings.[13]

---

12. The rarity of Rabbi Yehoshua's criticism and its marginal place in the halakhic mainstream find expression, for example, in the fact that Maimonides, who developed and expanded upon Rabbi Yehoshua's words in his *Commentary on the Mishnah,* codifies this law in *Mishneh Torah* in accordance with the view in the *mishnah* that opposes Rabbi Yehoshua. See *Mishneh Torah,* Laws of Forbidden Sexual Unions 6:19.

13. There is another, highly instructive use of the concept of *bein ha-shemashot* in Tannaitic literature, namely, a list of items that were created at *bein ha-shemashot* on the eve of the first Sabbath of creation:

> Ten things were created on the eve of the [first] Shabbat at *bein ha-shemashot*: The mouth of the earth; the mouth of the well; the mouth of the donkey; the rainbow; the manna; the staff [of Moses]; the *shamir*-worm; the letters; the script; and the tablets. Some say: also the destructive spirits, and the burial place of Moses, and the ram of Abraham, our father. And some say, also the tongs with which [other] tongs are made. (*m. Avot* 5:6)

A similar list, with some changes, appears in *Sifre Devarim* 355 and *Avot De-Rabbi Natan,* version 2, chapter 37. Maimonides, in his commentary to *Avot,* associated the idea of creation during *bein ha-shemashot* with the notion that the future miracles done with these items were embedded in nature at the moment of creation. In answer to the question of why, of all miracles, only the items in this limited list are mentioned, Maimonides commented that all other

It is possible, therefore, to identify within Tannaitic literature three stages in the emergence of uncertain temporal intervals. The first stage is the invention of the concept of *bein ha-shemashot* as an uncertain time, the outgrowth of a challenge to the binary conception of the transition from day to night. This uncertain unit has no precedent in pre-rabbinic literature, and it appears in the rabbinical academy by the generation of Yavneh at the very latest.[14] The second stage is the broad development of the halakhic ramifications of the existence of this uncertain time and the setting of various rules for different halakhic contexts—circumcision, the Sabbath, sin and guilt offerings, and the laws of *niddah* and *zivah*. The third stage, which emerges from an inquiry into the time of *bein ha-shemashot* in various halakhic contexts, gave rise, in the generation after the sages of Yavneh, to a second-order disagreement about the nature of the uncertainty presented by *bein ha-shemashot*. At the heart of the debate is the question: Is *bein ha-shemashot* a temporal continuum of gradual change, about which there is uncertainty, or is there a single, abrupt but elusive moment of transition that is not discernible? Processes like these are typical of the emergence of halakhah in the Mishnah generally, but development of uncertainty in such borderline cases is surprising, as it is an outgrowth of the challenge to the binary distinctions that legal systems are generally interested in preserving. This trend appears in other halakhic contexts as well.

II

One of halakhah's central categorical distinctions is between man and woman. One's gender assignation has far-reaching consequences within Tannaitic halakhah: women are exempt from time-bound positive *mitzvot* in which men are obligated, and the patriarchal configuration of halakhah

---

miracles were embedded in creation on the day that the object of the miracle was created. It seems that this unique idea of the creation of additional objects at the last moment of creation on that first Friday is not connected to any resolution of the problem of miracles—that problem, as a metaphysical, theological problem, did not bother the sages. There is no trend, anywhere in Tannaitic literature, of transforming miracles into part of nature. Moreover, close scrutiny of the items on the list shows that not all of them are connected specifically to miracles—for instance, the burial place of Moses and the cave where Elijah stood, which is mentioned in *Sifre Devarim*. It seems that this addendum of things that were included in creation is an attempt to prefigure history with the creation story, which in Scripture addresses only nature in its original, fixed state. At the end of the process of creation, the greatest moments in all of history are prefigured. This teaches that the sacred history of the world, and especially of the Jewish people, is embedded within creation itself.

14. The dispute between Rabbi Eliezer and Rabbi Yehoshua in Sifra and in Mishnah *Kareitot* is aware of the unique character of *bein ha-shemashot*.

distinguishes between man and woman with respect to the laws of marriage and the laws of inheritance. There is not a single halakhic realm in all of Tannaitic literature from which gender distinction is absent: *mitzvot* and prohibition, testimony, the recitation of the Shema, prayer, blessings, purity and impurity, property, penalties, and family law with and all their ramifications.[15]

In Tannaitic literature, the distinction between man and woman is based on biological identifiers, which define man and woman by their sexual organs. A man is a person with male genitalia, and a woman is a person with female genitalia. However, the sages deal with borderline cases that challenge decisive gender definitions, and a whole world of uncertainty and the rules for dealing with uncertainty grow out of the comprehensive examination of such borderline cases.

The sages recognize two borderline cases that challenge the man/woman binary. The first is the *androginos*, a person who was born with both male and female genitalia. The second is the "*tumtum*," a person whose sexual organ is not apparent. As Charlotte Elisheva Fonrobert has shown, gender definitions are dictated by a sexual distinction based on the genitalia; therefore, Tannaitic literature, in contrast to Hellenistic literature, does not deal with feminine men or masculine women, definitions that are related to physical and other attributes like voice, body hair, gait, and musculature.[16] Likewise, in Tannaitic literature, gender is not a matter of consciousness but is, as mentioned, based on an evident biological difference; the borderline cases that challenge the man/woman binary, namely, *tumtum* and *androginos*, are themselves exceedingly rare biological phenomena.

Nevertheless, the rarity of these conditions did not have the slightest impact on the sages' comprehensive engagement with the status of the *tumtum* and the *androginos*. The gender borderline states of *tumtum* and

---

15. A systematic but noncomprehensive list of gender-based halakhic distinctions in Tannaitic literature can be found in *m. Sotah* 3:7–8 and *t. Sotah* 2:7–9.

16. See Charlotte Elishiva Fonrobert, "The Semiotics of the Sexed Body in Early Halakhic Discourse," in *Closed and Open: Readings of Rabbinic Texts*, ed. Matthew Kraus (Piscataway, NJ: Gorgias Press, 2005), 69–96. Joshua Levinson presents a different view in "Cultural Androgyny in Rabbinic Literature," in *From Athens to Jerusalem: Medicine in Helenized Jewish Lore and in Early Christian Literature; Papers of the Symposium in Jerusalem, 9–11 September 1996*, ed. Samuel Kottek et al., Pantaleon reeks 33 (Rotterdam: Erasmus, 2000), 119–40. Levinson links the sages' discussion of the *androginos* to Hellenistic literature that demonstrates fluidity in distinguishing gender. However, as will emerge from our analysis of halakhic material below, Fonrobert's view, that there is an essential difference between the halakhic literature of the sages and Hellenistic literature, seems correct. See further I. Rosen-Zvi, "Temple of the Body: The List of Priestly Blemishes in Mishnah Bekhorot and the Place of the Temple in Tannaitic Discourse" [Hebrew], *Mada'ei Ha-Yahadut* 43 (2005): 74–76. Regarding the discussion within Hellenistic literature, see Maud W. Gleason, *Making Men: Sophists and Self-Presentation in Ancient Rome* (Princeton: Princeton University Press, 1995), 389–415.

androginos are addressed dozens of times in Tannaitic literature, and an entire unit in the Tosefta of tractate *Bikurim* is devoted to the *androginos*. The sages linger among such borderline cases, which, as borderline cases, enable halakhic creativity that destabilizes accepted and familiar constructs. In this case, challenging the binary distinction between man and woman also allows the sages to map out the meaning of the distinction more clearly.

We begin the discussion of the *androginos*, and the uncertainty surrounding hir[17] in Tannaitic literature with an entirely incidental and exotic mention of the *androginos* in the Tosefta of tractate *Nazir*, dealing with conditional nazirism. This marginal invocation is unique in how it sets out the range of possibilities raised by the condition of the *androginos* vis-à-vis the erstwhile inflexible categories of man and woman:

> If one saw an *androginos* and said, "I am a nazirite if that is a man," and another says, "I am a nazirite if that's not a man." "I'm a nazirite if that's a woman," and another says, "I'm a nazirite if that's not a woman." "I am a nazirite if that is both man and woman," and another says, "I'm a nazirite if that is neither man nor woman."... They are all nazirites. (*t. Nezirot* 3:19)[18]

The Tosefta describes a tight series of conditional nazirism vows, wherein people see an *androginos* and condition six distinct and contradictory nazirism vows relating to the challenge of plotting hir along the gender spectrum.

In the first case, a person who sees hir declares that he will be a nazirite if ze is a man; in the second case, another person reverses the condition and declares that he will be a nazirite if ze is not a man; in the third case, a person makes his nazirism contingent on hir being a woman; in the fourth case, another person reverses the condition and makes his nazirism contingent on hir not being a woman; in the fifth case, a person conditions his vow of nazirism on hir being man and woman; in the sixth case, another person conditions his nazirism on hir being neither man nor woman. Each of these attempts at nazirism contradicts the preceding attempt, yet the Tosefta concludes that in each of these attempts, nazirism takes effect. One person who took these conditional vows one after another is obligated to fulfill six distinct vows of nazirism.

Conditional vows of nazirism are a relatively common phenomenon because the impulse to take a vow, of nazirism or otherwise, often gives expression to something that happened or is about to happen. However,

17. We have adopted the gender-neutral pronouns "ze" and "hir" to reinforce the uncertain status of the *androginos* in Tannaitic literature.

18. This passage is based on *m. Nazir* 5:7, which built the same series of nazirism vows around a different borderline case, namely, the *koi* (an animal whose status as wild or domesticated is ambiguous). See below, n. 43.

this Tosefta passage is certainly not intended to offer advance instruction about how to deal with situations of conditional nazirism that are likely to transpire. Life does not provide opportunities for people to condition the effectiveness of their nazirism vows on the gender status of an *androginos*, and people certainly do not make their nazirism vows contingent on a series of six contradictory conditions pertaining to hir status.

The engagement in hyperbolic and imaginary contingencies, such as this one, which focuses on the status of the *androginos*, is motivated by two factors that typify the halakhic creativity that is most fully expressed in cases of uncertainty. The first component is the virtuoso aspect of crafting a paradoxical halakhic result wherein a series of six nazirism vows, predicated on six different and contradictory conditions, all take effect. A halakhic result like this one is of the type of paradox that thrives in borderline cases; crafting such cases is typical of Tannaitic literature.

The second component, which is more significant for our purposes, is related to the challenge posed by the *androginos* to gender classification. The Tosefta is not primarily concerned with teaching the laws of nazirism. It is apparent, rather, that through this series of conditional vows, the Tosefta wishes to investigate the nature of the uncertainty presented by the *androginos*, and it teaches us that ze can be one of four possibilities simultaneously: man, woman, both man and woman, and neither man nor woman.[19]

The range of possibilities examined in *Nazir* serves as the organizing platform of an entire unit devoted to the *androginos* in the Tosefta of tractate *Bikurim*, which systematically classifies the laws of the *androginos* with respect to the gender-based features of halakhah. The subheadings of the unit appear in its opening passage: "An *androginos* is in some ways like men and in some ways like women; in some ways like men and women, and in some like neither men nor women" (*t. Bikurim* 2:3). This chapter of the Tosefta is in fact an attempt to collect the laws of the *androginos* that appear elsewhere in Tannaitic literature into a single unit. It also contains elements that are not discussed in other contexts.[20] The Tosefta organizes

19. The medieval Talmudists are divided over how to understand the effectiveness of these nazirism vows. The commentary attributed to Rashi (*b. Nazir* 34a, s.v. "*amar Rav Sheshet*," at the end), makes the claim that nazirism vows in borderline cases, like that of the *koi*, take effect uncertainly. Maimonides, in his *Commentary on the Mishnah*, maintains that these nazirism vows take effect with certainty, and see his formulation in the Laws of Nazirism 2:10. See also Saul Lieberman, *Tosefta Kifshutah: Nedarim–Nezirot* (New York: Jewish Theological Seminary, 1967), 542.

20. There are two versions of this chapter of Tosefta. The first is the version that appears in MSS Vienna and Erfurt of Tosefta, and the second is the version that was added to some editions of the Mishnah, which appears in Palestinian manuscripts of the Mishnah and in its first printed editions. As Lieberman shows, these variants do not stem from changes to a single ancient version. Rather, they represent two alternative traditions for the systematic

the details of these laws, as noted, in a way that emphasizes that the laws pertaining to an *androginos* are spread across a broad spectrum of four different possibilities across the continuum—and its ruptures—of the halakhic construction of gender. With respect to the *androginos*, there are laws linking to each of the four possibilities: man, woman, man and woman, neither man nor woman.

A close study of the various elements in the Tosefta of *Bikurim* and elsewhere in Tannaitic literature shows, first and foremost, the mainstream position, which establishes the status of an *androginos* as possibly a man and possibly a woman. As a result, the stringencies of both are imposed on hir. Thus, for example, with respect to purity and impurity:

> All are rendered impure through *zivah*: even converts, even slaves, whether they are manumitted or not manumitted, a deaf-mute, an imbecile, a minor, and a eunuch [whether castrated] by man or by nature. A *tumtum* and an *androginos* are imposed upon with the stringencies of the man and the stringencies of a woman; they are rendered impure with blood like a woman and with white [discharge] like a man, but their impurity is uncertain. (*m. Zavim* 2:1)

An *androginos* is thus rendered impure out of uncertainty, both by the impurity of a male who saw a white genital discharge, and by the impurity of a female who saw a red discharge.[21] The impurity of the *androginos* is an uncertain impurity, and therefore, if ze touched *terumah*, it is not incinerated, because *terumah* that is uncertainly impure is not incinerated. Likewise, a person who was rendered impure by contact with hir and then entered the Temple is not punished, due to this uncertainty.

In the *Bikurim* unit, this law from *Zavim* is broken down into three categories. Impurity due to a white discharge is a detail in which the status of an *androginos* is equivalent to that of a man: "[The *androginos*] is rendered impure through white discharge, like men" (*t. Bikurim* 2:4). Impurity due to a red discharge is a detail in which the status of an *androginos* is equivalent to that of a woman: "[The *androginos*] is rendered impure through red discharge, like women" (*t. Bikurim* 2:5). The fact that something rendered impure by an *androginos* is not incinerated, and that a person who was rendered impure by contact with hir and then entered the

---

and organized presentation of the laws of the androginos. Lieberman therefore printed both versions side by side in his edition of the Tosefta. Regarding the differences and the evolutions of the two variants, see Lieberman, *Tosefta Kifshutah: Shevi'it–Bikurim* (Jerusalem: Jewish Theological Seminary of America, 1993), 836–37. My citations and discussions are based on the Tosefta variant.

21. The same applies to the impurity of a woman who gives birth; out of uncertainty, the mother must observe the stringencies of giving birth to a male and a female: "A woman who delivers a stillborn *tumtum* or *androginos* must sit [i.e., observe impurity] for a male and for a female" (*m. Niddah* 3:5).

Temple is not punished, is unique to the impurity of an *androginos*, so this detail belongs to the category of laws pertaining to hir that are like the laws of neither men nor women: "We do not incinerate because of [the *androginos*'s] impurity ... unlike men and unlike women" (*t. Bikurim* 2:6).[22]

The fact of having a male component does not spare hir from halakhah's discrimination against women. Ze might be a woman and is therefore "disqualified from testimony like women. With respect to the laws of inheritance, ze is treated like a woman, who does not inherit if there are sons to inherit. The *midrash* that deals with those who are granted a homestead in the land of Israel includes the *androginos* with women, who are not privileged to inherit the land:

> "To these shall you apportion the land" (Num 26:53). This implies everyone; priests, Levites, Israelites, proselytes, women, slaves, *tumtum*, and *androginos* are implied. "And the Lord said to Aharon: You shall not inherit in their land" (Num 18:20)—this excludes priests. "They shall have no inheritance of homestead among the Israelites" (Num 18:24)—this excludes Levites. "They shall inherit according to the names of their fathers' tribes" (Num 26:55)—this excludes proselytes and slaves. "Each man according to his enrollment" (Num 26:54)—this excludes women, a *tumtum*, and an *androginos*" (*Sifre Bamidbar* §132).[23]

---

22. Tosefta *Zavim* 2:1 states:

> If a *tumtum* or an *androginos* saw [a discharge], whether white or red, we do not incinerate *terumah* on their account, and one is not liable on their account for making the Temple or its sacred object impure. If they saw both white and red discharges, we incinerate *terumah* on their account, but one is not liable on their account for making the Temple or its sacred object impure. One who touches the white and red discharges and enters the Temple is exempt. If [the *tumtum* or *androginos*] themselves touch the white and red discharges and enter the Temple, they are exempt.

It emerges from this Tosefta passage that an *androginos* who entered the Temple is exempt not only out of uncertainty, but even if the *androginos* is certainly impure. As Rabbi Naḥman says in the name of Rav in the Talmud:

> If a *tumtum* or an *androginos* saw ... both white and red discharges one is not liable on their account for making the Temple or its sacred object impure ... as [Scripture] states, "from male to female, send them away" (Num 5:3). A "male" for certain and a "female" for certain, but not a *tumtum* or an *androginos*. (*b. Niddah* 28a-b)

This explication of Num 5:3 is quoted by Rabbi Shimshon of Sens in his commentary on *m. Zavim* 2:1. And see *Sifre Bamidbar* on Num 5:3, which interprets the verse to mean that an *androginos* or *tumtum* is liable for entering the Temple: "'From male to female'—I only know about male and female. From where [do we derive] a *tumtum* and an *androginos*? It therefore teaches, 'send them away, outside the camp'" (Kahana edition, p. 6). See Kahana's note in his second volume, pp. 21–22.

23. In the unit in the Tosefta of *Bikurim*: "[An *androginos*] inherits all estates, like men and like women." The meaning here is that if there are no sons to inherit, just as the estate can then go to daughters, so can it go to an *androginos*. See also *Sifre Devarim* §215, which

The woman-like status with respect to the laws of inheritance and homesteads places the *androginos* in a group that is obligated to bring firstfruits to the Temple; yet ze is not among those who inherit the land as a homestead and therefore cannot recite the declaration over the firstfruits in the Temple, since the verses of the recitation by the bringer of the firstfruits express thanks for being given the land:

> A trustee, a slave, an agent, a woman, a *tumtum*, and an *androginos* bring [firstfruits] but do not recite [the declaration], for they cannot say, "That You, O Lord, have given me" (Deut 26:10). (*m. Bikurim* 1:5)[24]

In a world where an androgynous creature would be considered a full-fledged man and a full-fledged woman, being a woman as well would not withhold male privilege from this person. This is not the case in the Mishnah of the sages; the fact that an *androginos* is uncertainly a woman casts a shadow on the possibility of being a man with regard to such matters. Not only is ze not spared from the discrimination against women, but there are even circumstances when having the uncertain status of a man denies hir certain economic protections afforded to daughters: "[The *androginos*] is not given maintenance along with daughters, like men ... but does not take a share [of the inheritance] along with the sons, like women" (*t. Bikurim* 2:3–4).[25]

An *androginos*, who might be a man, is obligated in all time-bound positive commandments: "[The *androginos*] is obligated in all *mitzvot* stated in the Torah, like men." Yet, since this obligation is imposed out of uncertainty, ze cannot fulfill the obligation on behalf of men, only on behalf of others like hir:

> A *tumtum* and an *androginos* are obligated in the mitzvah of *shofar*, but they do not discharge the obligation of the masses. An *androginos* can discharge the obligation of a fellow *androginos*, unlike a *tumtum*.[26] Women

---

states that an *androginos* is not considered a son for the purposes of primogeniture: "'and the son'—not a *tumtum* or an *androginos*. 'The firstborn son'—not an uncertainty."

24. The status of the *androginos* has also been compared to that of a woman with respect to the priestly service. See *m. Parah* 10:11.

25. The negative impact stemming from hir borderline status as maybe-man-maybe-woman is established in *m. Bava Batra* 9:2:

> [If] he left behind sons and daughters and a *tumtum*, in the event that [the deceased's] assets are ample, the males push [the *tumtum*] toward the females. If the assets are sparse, the females push [the *tumtum*] toward the males.

The *mishnah* mentions only a *tumtum*, but this law, it stands to reason, was stated with respect to an *androginos* as well. Abaye and Rava disagree about whether the *androginos* indeed loses out from both sides; see *b. Bava Batra* 140a.

26. A *tumtum* cannot discharge the obligation of a fellow *tumtum* because one *tumtum* might be a man and the other might be a woman.

> are exempt and cannot discharge the obligation of the masses. (*t. Rosh Hashanah* 2:5)

An *androginos* is obligated, out of uncertainty, to observe all of the prohibitions that obligate only men: "[An *androginos* who is a priest] must not contract corpse impurity, like men, or violate 'do not round [the corners of your head]' and 'do not destroy [the corners of your beard]' (Lev 19:27), like men" (*t. Bikurim* 2:4).[27] Ze must be circumcised, but being a male only out of uncertainty, hir circumcision does not override the Sabbath: "We do not desecrate the Sabbath for an uncertainty [about the day of birth] or an *androginos*. Rabbi Yehudah permits in the case of an *androginos*" (*m. Shabbat* 19:3).[28] An *androginos* of priestly extraction may eat *terumah*, just as women of the priestly caste may. However, ze may not eat of sanctified foods given to (male) priests, because of uncertainty: "An *androginos* may eat *terumah* but not sanctified foods" (*t. Yevamot* 10:2). Due to the uncertain gender status, ze may not be in seclusion with men or women: "[An *androginos*] may not be secluded with women, like men ... and may not be secluded with men, like women" (*t. Bikurim* 2:4-5).

As mentioned, uncertainly being a man does not remove the *androginos*, who is also uncertainly a woman, from the inferior halakhic status of women. Nevertheless, an *androginos*, despite this abnormality, and despite being a borderline case that challenges the gendered order, does not inspire fear or disgust, which are liable to exclude hir from the protection of the law, as can happen in violent social contexts in which the appearance of such a figure can arouse cruel phobias. Like men and women, it is

27. A *mishnah* in Kiddushin lists these negative commandments as *mitzvot* that obligate men only:

> And [with regard to] every negative commandment, whether it is time-bound or it is not time-bound, both men and women are obligated, except for "You shall not destroy [the corners of your beard]," "You shall not round off [the corners of your head]" (Lev 19:27) and "You shall not contract corpse impurity" (Lev 21:1). (*m. Kiddushin* 1:7)

The parallel version of the Tosefta list that appears in some versions of the Mishnah states: "[An *androginos*] does not violate 'do not round,' 'do not destroy,' or 'do not contract corpse impurity,' like women" (*m. Bikurim* 2:3). It seems that this version does not disagree with the Tosefta version; the Mishnah version deals with penalties, from which the *androginos* is exempt due to uncertainty. See Lieberman, *Tosefta Kifshutah: Shivi'it-Bikurim* (Jerusalem: Jewish Theological Seminary of America, 1993), 841.

28. It stands to reason that Rabbi Yehudah maintains that an *androginos* is obligated in the *mitzvah* of circumcision, despite not being a male for certain, because the *mitzvah* is to remove the foreskin and thus applies to anyone who has a foreskin, whether a male or an *androginos*. It is also possible that Rabbi Yehudah maintains that an *androginos* is a full-fledged male; see below, and see *Sifra, Sheratzim*, 11:2: "'His foreskin'—if certain, it overrides the Sabbath, but an uncertainty does not override the Sabbath. An *androginos* does not override the Sabbath, for Rabbi Yehudah says, 'We override the Sabbath on behalf of an *androginos*, and we are liable for excision [for failure to circumcise an *androginos*].'"

forbidden to harm or injure an *androginos*, and one who does so is punished accordingly: "The ways in which [the *androginos*] is similar to men and women: both men and women are liable for damages [against hir]. One who murders [an *androginos*] on purpose, is put to death; by accident, is exiled to a city of refuge" (*t. Bikurim* 2:6). Ze thus has the same protections of criminal and tort law afforded to men and women alike.[29] Due to this uncertainty, the *androginos* has the obligations of both men and

29. In addition to these criminal and tortious protections, the midrash derives that the obligation to honor and revere one's father and mother applies to hir as well:

> "Honor your father" (Exod 20:12). Since it says, "Every man, if he curses his father and mother" (Lev 20:9), I have learned only of a man. Whence do I derive [the same for] a woman? Whence do I derive a *tumtum* or an *androginos*? It therefore teaches, "Honor your father and your mother"—in any case. Just as regarding honor there is no distinction between man and woman, *tumtum* and *androginos*, so too, regarding reverence, do not distinguish between man and woman, *tumtum* and *androginos*. These are the words of Rabbi Yishmael. Rabbi Yehudah ben Beteira says: It is written: "A man, shall revere his mother and his father and keep My Sabbaths" (Lev 19:3). Just as with regard to the Sabbath there is no distinction between a man and a woman, so, with honor (of parents), there is no distinction between man and woman, *tumtum* and *androginos*, so too, with regard to reverence, do not distinguish between man and woman, *tumtum* and *androginos*. (*Mekhilta De-Rabbi Yishmael, Ba-ḥodesh*, 20:12)

Ze is likewise obligated to bring a guilt offering just like a man or woman: "Why does it say, 'And that person becomes aware of their guilt' (Num 5:6)? Because it says 'a man or woman,' so I only know of a man or a woman. From where do we know [that this applies to] a *tumtum* or *androginos*? It therefore teaches, 'And that person becomes aware of their guilt'" (*Sifre Bamidbar* §2, Kahana edition, p. 11). The protections of criminal and tort law are also expounded in *Mekhilta De-Rabbi Yishmael*: "'Or if it gore a son, or if it gore a daughter' (Exod 21:31). This tells me only a full son or daughter. Whence are a *tumtum* and an *androginos* derived? It therefore teaches, 'Or if it gore a son, or if it gore a daughter'" (*Nezikin* 11). Perhaps a certain unique variation of the sort of uncertainty posed by the *androginos* can be inferred from the language of Sifre and Mekhilta. As noted, one way to understand the uncertainty is that ze is one or the other, either fully a man or fully a woman. At first glance, according to this view, there would be no need to make these derivations; the verses say "a man or woman" and "if it gore a son, or if it gore a daughter," and ze is, in all cases, one of the two. It is possible that these derivations are based on Rabbi Yose's view, to be discussed below, that an *androginos* is not an uncertain man or an uncertain woman but a being unto hirself. Another possibility that can be raised, and is even implied by the formulation of *Mekhilta*, is that ze is not "fully" a son or "fully" a daughter. The uncertainty stems from hir being both man and woman, but not fully either one. This position arose among the medieval commentators. For instance, this is the view of Raavad (Rabbi Avraham ben David). According to Raavad, an *androginos* can discharge an obligation on behalf of those like hir only according to the view that ze is a being unto hirself (see below regarding this view): "But [according to] one who maintains that [an *androginos*] is half male, [an *androginos*] cannot discharge the obligation on behalf of that type [i.e., another *androginos*] or someone of a different type, like one who is half-slave and half-free" (Raavad, gloss to *Mishneh Torah,* Laws of Shofar 2:2). The most interesting expression in Raavad's comment is "half male"; according to Raavad, the uncertainty of the *androginos* is that of a half-man, half-woman, not of someone who is either man or woman.

women and is afforded the basic protections that the law grants to the two genders.[30] Being an uncertain male does not protect hir from the legal discrimination against women. Thus, ze has the obligations of a man and the inferior status of a woman at the same time.[31] By incorporating all gender categories in a single legal personality, the *androginos* becomes a subject who signifies the law's gender divisions within a single figure.

One way in which gender distinctions are preserved is the prohibition for a man to dress in a woman's clothing and for a woman to dress in a man's clothing. A regime based on inequality and domination will tend to create the means of identification and separation that will prevent the dilution of a distinction that is central to the very construction of society and law. "A woman must not put on man's apparel, nor shall a man wear woman's clothing; for whoever does these things is abhorrent to the Lord

30. On the question of the humanity of the *androginos*, the legal protections afforded by the Tosefta of *Bikurim*, and an analysis of the significance of this unit in general, see the in-depth discussion in Max Strassfeld, "Categorizing the Human, The *Androginos* in Tosefta *Bikurim*," www.academia.edu/9625276/Categorizing_the_Human_The_androginos_in_Tosefta_Bikurim.

31. The only context in which it is possible that the *androginos*, as a mixed creature, is established as being inferior to both men and women is in the laws of valuations (*arakhin*). The biblical treatment of valuations determines a sum that a person must give to the Temple in the event that he pledged his own value or the value of another. The biblical passage establishes different sums, depending on age, for males and females: "the valuation shall be: For a male from twenty to sixty years of age, the valuation shall be fifty shekels of silver by the holy shekel; if it is a female, the valuation is thirty shekels" (Lev 27:3–4. With regard to the laws of valuations, the Mishnah establishes the following principle:

> All are fit to pledge value and to have their value pledged, to vow [another's worth] and to have their worth vowed: priests, Levites, Israelites, women, and slaves. A *tumtum* and an *androginos* are fit to vow [on another's worth], to have their worth vowed, and to pledge value, but they are not fit to have their value pledged, as only a definite male or definite female can have their value pledged. (*m. Arakhin* 1:1)

This law is based on the expounding of the verses in Leviticus: "'A male'—not a *tumtum* or *androginos*. One might think that they are excluded from the category of 'man' but included in the category of 'woman.' It therefore states, 'if it is a female.' A definite male and definite female" (*Sifra Beḥukotai* 3:1). This law establishes that if a person pledged the value of an *androginos* to the Temple coffers, he is not obligated to pay a set sum, because the sums specified by Scripture are for a definite male or female. This law is recorded in the systematic chapter in *Bikurim*, among the laws wherein an *androginos* is neither man nor woman: "[The *androginos*] is not valued, not like men and not like women" (*t. Bikurim* 2:7). The question is, Does this law express an inferior status of *tumtum* and *androginos*, as being valueless with respect to the sacred? Or does this discussion simply emerge from the precise language of Scripture—"male" and "female"—from which nothing can be discerned about the status of the *androginos*, especially since, as we have seen, the *androginos* is not discriminated against when it comes to the equal protections of tort and criminal law? A similar reading of the precise language of Scripture is found in another law, where the *androginos* is considered neither man nor woman, and is linked to the fact that ze is not liable for entering the Temple. See *t. Zavim* 2:1, and above n. 22.

your God" (Deut 22:5). This construction of prohibition, which is anchored by enlisting the language of "abhorrence" (*to'eivah*), blocks the possibility of imposing the stringencies of both women and men on hir.[32] It is possible, in principle and in an exceptional case, to rule, as the Tosefta indeed rules, that an *androginos* is obligated in all time-bound commandments like a man, yet disqualified from testifying like a woman. It is impossible, however, to rule that an *androginos* must wear hir hair like a man and like a woman. Here, the unique halakhic case of the *androginos*, wherein one person bears the legal status of both genders, reaches its limit. When it comes to clothing, the *androginos* cannot conform to both the obligations incumbent on a man and the obligations incumbent on a woman simultaneously; ze must be identified with one side of the gender divide, and, however ze is identified, ze is likely to violate the prohibition out of uncertainty. If ze wears a man's clothes, ze may be in violation of "nor shall a man wear woman's clothing," and vice versa.

On this issue, the Tosefta rules that an *androginos* may not wear the clothing of a woman: "[The *androginos*] may not be wrapped or get a haircut, like men."[33] The ruling that an *androginos* dresses like men and not women teaches that the concern about a man becoming a woman is greater than that about a woman becoming a man. The "feminization" of a man terrifies the sages more than the transformation of a woman into a man. It is better that someone who might be a woman becomes a man than that someone who might be a man becomes a woman. We find a similar ruling, but far more complex and important, in the laws of marriage and homosexuality. These demand separate treatment.

A *mishnah* in *Yevamot* establishes the status of the *androginos* vis-à-vis marriage as follows:

> Rabbi Yose and Rabbi Shimon said: A priest who is an *androginos* who married the daughter of an Israelite grants her the right to eat *terumah*. Rabbi Yehudah said: [If] a *tumtum* ruptured and was found to be male, he may not perform *ḥalitzah*, because he is like a eunuch. An *androginos* may marry [a woman] but may not be married [to a man]. Rabbi Elazar[34] said: [If one has relations with] an *androginos*, he is liable to be stoned [to death], like [a man who has relations with] a male. (*m. Yevamot* 8:6)

---

32. The Talmudic tradition recognizes articles of clothing that are not specific to either sex. See, in this regard, *b. Nedarim* 49b, on the cloak that Rabbi Yehudah and his wife would alternate using.

33. See the comments of Saul Lieberman in his brief elucidation: "That is, [the *androginos*] may not be wrapped as a woman wraps, nor get a woman's haircut, but behaves like men" (*Tosefta Kifshutah: Zera'im*, 290 n. 14).

34. Thus MS Parma. It is likely that the correct text is "Rabbi Eliezer"; see Epstein, *Introduction to the Mishnaic Text*, 2:1163–64; and Lieberman, *Tosefta Kifshutah*, 94, until line 18.

An *androginos* may marry a woman but may not marry a man. Thus, with respect to marriage, hir status is like that of a man, not a woman.[35] One could argue that this is simply a guideline for cases of uncertainty; since halakhah is more lenient about homosexual relations between women than between men, an *androginos* can marry a woman but not a man. However, according to the straightforward meaning of the *mishnah*, the marriage of an *androginos* to a man is forbidden and not deemed an "uncertain marriage" that would require a writ of divorce, lest the *androginos* is really a woman. Likewise, the marriage of an *androginos* to a woman is valid and effective not merely out of uncertainty, as is evident from the fact that if the *androginos* is a priest who marries an Israelite woman, hir wife may partake of *terumah*, like any Israelite woman who married a priest. Had this marriage been merely uncertain, the wife of an *androginos* priest would not be permitted to eat *terumah*.[36]

---

35. With regard to the laws of levirate marriage, see also *t. Yevamot* 11:2:

> A natural eunuch, an *androginos*, a maternal half-brother, a proselyte, and a manumitted slave perform neither levirate divorce nor levirate marriage. How so? If they died and left wives, and they have brothers, and the brothers came and [one] made a verbal declaration [*ma'amar*] [of intent to perform levirate marriage], gave a writ of divorce, or performed levirate divorce, they have accomplished nothing. If [one of the brothers] engaged in relations with her, they disqualify her from marrying into the priesthood and are liable to bring an offering. If the brothers died and left wives, and there are other brothers, and [one of these disqualified individuals] made a verbal declaration [of intent to perform levirate marriage], gave a writ of divorce, or performed levirate divorce, they have accomplished nothing. If [one of them] engaged in relations with her, they disqualify her from marrying into the priesthood and are liable to bring an offering.

It emerges from this Tosefta passage that the wife of an *androginos* undergoes neither levirate marriage nor levirate divorce, and the *androginos* performs neither levirate marriage nor levirate divorce for the widow of hir deceased brother. This law stems not from the notion that the marriage of an *androginos* is not considered marriage, but from the fact that an *androginos* cannot sire children, like a eunuch. Therefore, ze is not subject to the rules of levirate marriage, whose purpose is to perpetuate the seed of the deceased brother.

This Tosefta passage maintains that hir marriage is a bona fide marriage, for since ze is not subject to the rules of levirate marriage, hir widow is prohibited to hir brothers by dint of the prohibition against marrying a brother's wife. As the Tosefta puts it, if they marry hir widow, they disqualify her from marrying a priest and incur liability to bring a sacrificial offering. See also *t. Yevamot* 2:5–6.

36. In the Bavli on this *mishnah* in *Yevamot*, the question of whether the marriage of an *androginos* is considered a definite marriage or an uncertain marriage is explained as a matter of dispute between Amoraim: "Resh Lakish said, 'He grants her the right to eat *terumah* but does not grant her the right to eat from the breast and thigh [i.e., the parts of a peace offering that are given to the priests].' Rabbi Yoḥanan says, 'He even grants her the right to eat from the breast and thigh.'" The Talmud then limits the words of Resh Lakish to *terumah* that is given "nowadays," which is of rabbinic provenance, and therefore can be eaten in cases of doubt (see *b. Yevamot* 81a). Later in the same discussion, the Talmud asserts that an *androginos*

The end of the *mishnah* that establishes that an *androginos* is considered a male with respect to marriage records Rabbi Elazar's view that a man who has sexual intercourse with an *androginos* is liable for death by stoning, as the Torah requires death by stoning for sexual intercourse between males.[37] Like the *mishnah,* Rabbi Elazar considers the *androginos* to be male, and this law, too, is not a rule governing an uncertainty, for in rabbinic halakhah, a person who uncertainly committed a transgression is not punished by the court and certainly not put to death. It seems that the fact that ze has a male sexual organ is what determines an *androginos* to be a man with respect to marriage and homosexuality, in the view of these Tannaim.[38]

The question is whether the sages who appear in the *mishnah* in *Yevamot,* who maintain that an *androginos* is male vis-à-vis marriage and homosexuality, also consider hir to have the status of a man with respect to other areas of halakhah. That is, do they disagree with the laws that equate an *androginos* with a woman? Do they consider hir to be a valid witness and heir? Or is their view limited to the issue of marriage and homosexuality, because with regard to these issues in particular, the male genitalia are what establish the *androginos*'s male identity, whereas in other areas, ze has the status of both man and woman out of uncertainty?[39] The Tosefta

---

may marry a woman only ex post facto, not ab initio. In the Yerushalmi, the positions of Rabbi Yoḥanan and Resh Lakish are reversed; Rabbi Yoḥanan maintains that the marriage of an *androginos* is an uncertain marriage. See *y. Yevamot* 8:6, col. 872, lines 342–43. On the difference between the discussions in the Bavli and Yerushalmi, see Lieberman, *Tosefta Kifshutah: Yevamot – Ketuvot,* 94–96. In any event, the Amoraic position—whether that of Resh Lakish according to the Bavli or that of Rabbi Yoḥanan according to the Yerushalmi—that the marriage of an *androginos* is uncertain runs counter to the straightforward meaning of the *mishnah.*

37. Tosefta *Yevamot* 10:2 states:

> Rabbi Elazar said: I heard that one is liable for death by stoning on account of intercourse with an *androginos,* as with a male. When does this apply? When one penetrates [the *androginos*] by way of [hir] masculinity [i.e., anally], but if he did not penetrate [hir] by way of [hir] masculinity, he is exempt.

See the discussion in *b. Yevamot* 83b, which cites a view that the category of homosexual intercourse with an *androginos* includes even intercourse that is not "by way of [hir] masculinity."

38. The status of an *androginos* as a male with respect to marriage, and the significance of this ruling for all that pertains to hir gender identity, was discussed by Charlotte Elisheva Fonrobert in an article that provides an in-depth analysis of the status of the *androginos* while discussing the Tosefta of *Bikurim* ("Regulating the Human Body: Rabbinic Legal Discourse and the Making of Jewish Gender,"in *The Cambridge Companion to the Talmud and Rabbinic Literature,* ed. Charlotte Elisheva Fonrobert and Martin S. Jaffee (Cambridge: Cambridge University Press, 2007), 287–90.

39. The question as to whether Rabbi Elazar thinks that an *androginos* is a man in every respect just as ze is a man with respect to homosexuality seems to be a matter of dispute between the Talmudim. The Bavli records the following view: "Rabbi Shezvi said in the

of tractate *Bikurim*, which sets out the laws of the *androginos*, maintains that there is a difference between the status of the *androginos* vis-à-vis marriage and hir status with respect to other matters. On one hand, it states, "[The *androginos*] marries [a woman] but is not married [to a man], like men" (2:4). On the other hand, it equates the *androginos* with women, disqualifies hir from testifying, and excludes hir from inheritance: "[The *androginos*] is disqualified from all testimony from the Torah, like women" (2:5). The Tosefta (which does not mention the law regarding homosexual penetration) thus maintains that these issues are distinct; the *androginos* is considered a definite man with respect to marriage; ze may marry a woman; and hir marriage is considered valid out of certainty, not uncertainty.[40] Yet ze is still considered a woman with respect to matters of testimony and inheritance. Moreover, the uniqueness of the ruling in the Tosefta—considering the *androginos* to be a man with respect to marriage, placing hir unambiguously on the male side of the gender divide—is sharpened by the fact that, with respect to illicit sexual unions, the *androginos* is considered a woman as well: "If [ze] has prohibited sexual relationships, [ze] is disqualified from the priesthood, like women" (2:5). A woman who had a prohibited incestuous sexual relationship is considered a *ḥalalah* and may neither marry a priest nor eat *terumah*. Likewise, an *androginos* who is a priest is barred from eating *terumah* if ze had prohibited sexual relationships—a rule that does not apply to male priests (i.e., if a male priest has prohibited sexual relationships, he is not disqualified thereby from eating *terumah)*. Thus, in every respect, even when it comes to forbidden sexual unions, the *androginos* is on both sides of the gender divide—except when it comes to marriage.

---

name of Rabbi Ḥisda: It was not in regard to everything that Rabbi Eliezer said that an *androginos* is a bona fide male…" (*b. Yevamot* 83b). In the Yerushalmi, this is raised as a question: "What else should he have revealed? [Whether ze may] inherit, testify, [whether hir] meal-offering can be brought at all, and whether [ze] can be included in a *zimmun*, like a male" (*y. Yevamot* 8:6, col. 872, lines 41–42). See the commentary of Penei Moshe *y. Yevamot* 8:6, which states that Rabbi Eliezer maintains that an *androginos* is considered male with respect to testimony, inheritance, and other laws.

40. A comparison to the laws of marriage of a *tumtum* clearly shows that the laws of an *androginos* vis-à-vis marriage are not rules for uncertain situations. With regard to the *tumtum*, the following rule is established: "If a *tumtum* betrothed [a woman], hir betrothal is a valid betrothal. If ze was betrothed, hir betrothal is a valid betrothal" (*t. Yevamot* 11:1). Since it is unknown whether the *tumtum* is a man or woman, the halakhah is to be stringent about hir betrothal in either direction. As Saul Lieberman wrote in his commentary (on *t. Yevamot* 11:1, n. 1): "It is uncertain whether [the *tumtum*] is man or woman, and therefore [ze] both betroths and is betrothed, out of uncertainty, and as a stringency." In contrast to the *tumtum*, the law regarding an *androginos* is that ze may marry a woman but not a man. As the Tosefta states, citing the Mishnah's formulation: "The *androginos* marries [a woman] but is not married [to a man]." Had this law of the *androginos* been based on uncertainty, there would have had to be symmetry, as in the case of the *tumtum*, and the *androginos* would have been capable of marrying [a woman] or being married [to a man] out of uncertainty.

Despite the rare incidence of the biological phenomenon of hermaphroditism or androgyny, the figure of the *androginos* draws a great deal of attention and intensive halakhic study in Tannaitic literature.[41] The picture that emerges from Tannaitic literature and the way that the legal status of the *androginos* is organized in the Tosefta of tractate *Bikurim* demonstrates how the sages developed the *androginos* as a legal personality who signifies, on hir body, the gender map of halakhah more generally. The *androginos*, as a subject of the halakhah, simultaneously bears the laws of men and the laws of women. Out of uncertainty, ze causes impurity like a man and like a woman; ze may not be secluded with men or with women; hir status as a man—out of uncertainty—obligates hir in time-bound positive commandments, yet does not release hir from the inferior status of women with regard to the laws of testimony and inheritance. In this sense, halakhah creates a legal subject that has what the medieval halakhists called a "man aspect" and a "woman aspect."

It emerges, however, from the unit in the Tosefta of tractate *Bikurim* and from the views of sages throughout the Tannaitic corpus that, when it

---

41. Another context in which the male/female categorization has halakhic significance is the laws of sacrificial offerings and sanctified objects. Here, too, there is systematic engagement in the question of the *androginos*, which sheds light on how the uncertainty presented by the *androginos* is understood. Some offerings must come from male animals. For instance, the Paschal offering must be of a male sheep, and a burnt offering must be of male sheep or cattle. An *androginos* animal is excluded from both of these offerings; see *Mekhilta De-Rabbi Yishmael, Mesekhta De-Pasḥa* 4; and, with regard to the burnt offering, *Sifra, Nedava* 4:1. The sin offering must come from a female animal, and here, too, an *androginos* is disqualified (*Sifra,* Ḥova 10:5). There are offerings, like the peace offering, that can come from either male or female animals; however, here, too, the *androginos* is disqualified: "'Male or female'—a definite male, a definite female, but not a *tumtum* or *androginos*" (*Sifra, Nedavah* 16:2). This exegesis seems to consider the *androginos* as a mixed being, half male and half female. See also *m. Temurah* 2:3. When it comes to burnt offerings of fowl, where the Torah mentions no gender, the following is expounded:

> Rabbi Eliezer says: Wherever it says "male and female," a *tumtum* and an *androginos* are disqualified therefrom. With respect to fowl, regarding which male and female are not mentioned, a *tumtum* and an *androginos* are not disqualified. (*Sifra, Nedavah* 7:1)

And see *t. Bekhorot* 5:16, where the sages disagree about an *androginos* firstborn animal:

> Rabbi Ilai says in the name of Rabbi Yishmael: An *androginos* is a firstborn, and it is blemished. It may be slaughtered on that basis. But the sages say: Sanctity does not devolve upon it; rather, it may depart and pasture with the flock. Rabbi Shimon says: It says, "All firstborns that are born among your sheep and cattle, you shall sanctify the males to the Lord your God" (Deut 15:19). Wherever it says "male," it excludes a *tumtum* and an *androginos* from the group. See also the dispute between the sages and Rabbi Yishmael in *m. Bekhorot* 6:12. We may ask whether this Tosefta passage preserves a Tannaitic tradition that an *androginos* is a male with a blemish, as Rabbi Yishmael states. Alternatively, Rabbi Yishmael maintains that the *androginos* is an uncertain case, whereas the sages maintain that ze is not an uncertain case but a category of hir own. See the statement of Naḥmanides in chapter 6 of his Laws of Firstborns.

comes to marriage, the construction of the *androginos* as simultaneously man and woman is foreclosed; Tannaitic halakhah deems it necessary to establish hir as being unambiguously on one side of the gender divide. The marital relationship does not tolerate the sort of vagueness in which a single subject simultaneously constitutes, out of uncertainty, a man and a woman; therefore, the penis is what determines whether one is man or woman in this carnal relationship. An *androginos* who marries a woman is considered a *bona fide* man, even as ze retains the status of maybe-man-maybe-woman with regard to other areas of law. Ze thus demarcates, as a subject, the boundaries of an uncompromising differentiation of gender and of the application of conflicting gender categories on a single subject. At the same time, ze demarcates the limits of what is possible within the sort of vagueness that applies to cases of gender differentiation.

At the end of the list of halakhot in the Tosefta of *Bikurim* is a Tannaitic opinion that disputes the conception that characterized the entire unit and fundamentally challenges viewing the *androginos* as a double legal subject who is either a man or a woman, though we are uncertain which:

> Rabbi Yose says: An *angroginos* is a being unto [hirself], and the sages could not decide whether [ze] is a man or a woman. However, this is not so with respect to a *tumtum*, who is either a man out of uncertainty or a woman out of uncertainty. (*t. Bikurim* 2:7)

According to Rabbi Yose, a *tumtum* is indeed a man out of uncertainty and a woman out of uncertainty, for ze is presumed to have a sexual organ that remains unknown, but which may become revealed in the future. An *androginos*, however, is not uncertainly a man and uncertainly a woman, but a separate class of being. The greatest of the medieval halakhists disagreed about the extent to which Rabbi Yose undermines the conception that guided the halakhah of the *androginos* as a case of uncertainty. According to Naḥmanides, whose reading of the text seems correct, Rabbi Yose disputes the construction of the laws of *androginos* as developed in Tannaitic literature and organized in the Tosefta. This construction is premised on the *androginos* being a maybe-man-maybe-woman, and many of the laws pertaining to hir are derived from this conception. Rabbi Yose disagrees with the notion that an *androginos* is maybe-man-maybe-woman, and therefore, in his opinion, the laws of men and women are not applied to hir out of uncertainty. Thus, for example, as Naḥmanides says, Rabbi Yose maintains that an *androginos* does not render others impure out of uncertainty; if ze experienced a white discharge or a red discharge, ze is not impure out of uncertainty. Rather, the category of *zav* impurity applies to men and women, and an *androginos* is neither of those, not even out of uncertainty.[42]

---

42. See *Ḥiddushei Ha-Ramban* to *Yevamot* 83a, s.v. *"ha de-amar Rabbi Yose"* (concluding

According to Rabbi Yose, the phenomenon of the *androginos* teaches that the human species cannot be sorted into men and women. There are human phenomena that defy this division, which does not cover the more variegated spectrum of humanity. The construction of gender, therefore, is not exhaustive of human variety.

Contra Rabbi Yose, the earlier Tannaitic tradition maintained that the division of gender is complete and applies to all humans. The *androginos* does not stand outside the gender division but exposes the fuzzy margins of the distinction and the fact that there are cases in which a subject of the law cannot be placed clearly and fully on one side of the divide. Since, according to this view, the *androginos* is both man and woman, ze signifies the entire halakhic gender map within one persona, and, at the same time, also signifies the limits of this sort of vagueness when it comes to marriage.[43]

---

essay). Ritva attests that his teacher, Rabbi Aaron ha-Levi, followed Naḥmanidies; see *Ḥiddushei Ha-Ritva* to *Niddah* 28b, s.v. "*zakhar vadai nekeivah vada'it.*" The leading Tosafists disagreed with this view and held that Rabbi Yose also maintains that an *androginos* is still uncertainly man and uncertainly a woman. In this regard, see the view of Rabbi Isaac of Dampiere ("Ri ha-Zaken") cited in Tosafot to *Yevamot* 83a, s.v. "*beriyah.*" And see the view of Rabbi Samson of Sens in his commentary to *m. Bikurim*, where he writes that in Rabbi Yose's view, an *androginos* is uncertainly a man, uncertainly a woman, and uncertainly a being unto hirself. The contrast between the *tumtum* and the *androginos* in the Tosefta seems to clearly favor Naḥmanides's view; Rabbi Yose thought that an *androginos* is a separate class of being because the sages found no clear signs of hir being a man or woman.

43. A similar pattern of investigation of borderline cases is applied in Tannaitic literature to a different categorical halakhic distinction: the distinction between a *behemah* and a *ḥayah*. In rabbinic literature, quadrupedal mammals are divided into the categories of *behemah* and *ḥayah*. A *behemah* lives within civilization and is domesticated, whereas a *ḥayah* lives outside of civilization and is wild. Because it is untamed, bringing it under human control requires an act of trapping or hunting. The division of kosher animals into the categories of *behemah* and *ḥayah* has halakhic implications in various contexts. The blood of a slaughtered fowl or *ḥayah* must be covered, whereas the blood of a *behemah* need not be covered. It is permitted to eat the *ḥelev* (certain fats around the kidneys) of a *ḥayah*, but the *ḥelev* of a *behemah* is forbidden. According to the sages' tradition, the biblical prohibition against eating milk and meat applies only to the milk and meat of a *behemah*, not of a *ḥayah*. The gifts that must be given to the priests and Levites apply to the meat of a *behemah*, not that of a *ḥayah*. Therefore, the obligation to tithe the flocks—"*ma'aser behemah*"—does not apply to *ḥayot*; there is no obligation to give the foreleg, jowl, and stomach of a slaughtered *ḥayah* to a priest; and a firstborn *ḥayah* does not belong to the priest. Likewise, the prohibition against slaughtering a *behemah* and its offspring on the same day does not apply to a *ḥayah*.

With regard to this categorical distinction between *behemah* and *ḥayah*, the sages created an animal called a *koi* as a borderline case in which it is uncertain whether the animal is a *ḥayah* or a *behemah*. Its status is thoroughly investigated in various contexts within Tannaitic literature. The identity of the *koi* is unclear, and it may well be an imaginary creature whose entire manifestation is designed to produce the uncertainty of borderline situations, by means of which it is possible both to examine and to challenge halakhic categorical distinctions.

There are parallels between the *koi* and the *androginos* with respect to the way their laws are organized and formulated. Accordingly, the four uncertain possibilities that organize the

The commonality between the borderline cases of *bein ha-shemashot* and the *androginos* is that additional information will not resolve the uncertainty pertaining to them. In this sense, these realms of uncertainty are not similar to uncertainties in the realms of forbidden foods, purity, or

---

laws of the *androginos* correspond to the four uncertain possibilities organizing the laws of the *koi*: *behemah*, *ḥayah*, both *behemah* and *ḥayah*, and neither *behemah* nor *ḥayah*. The *mishnah* in *Bikurim* that organizes the laws of the *koi* is formulated thus: "A *koi* is in some ways like a *ḥayah* and in some ways like a *behemah*; in some ways like a *ḥayah* and a *behemah*, and in some ways like neither *ḥayah* nor *behemah*" (*m. Bikurim* 2:8). As in the case of the *androginos*, these possibilities are raised and tested by means of a thought experiment involving conditional nazirism:

> If one saw a *koi* and said, "I am a nazirite if that is a *ḥayah*," and another says, "I am a nazirite if that's not a *ḥayah*." "I'm a nazirite if that's a *behemah*," and another says, "I'm a nazirite if that's not a *behemah*." "I am a nazirite if that is both *ḥayah* and *behemah*," and another says, "I'm a nazirite if that is neither *ḥayah* nor *behemah*." "I am a nazirite if one of you is a nazirite." "I am a nazirite of none of you are nazirites." "I am a nazirite if you are both nazirites." "I am a nazirite if you are all nazirites." They are all nazirites. (*m. Nazir* 5:7)

As in the case of the *androginos*, the stringencies of both *ḥayah* and *behemah* are applied to the *koi* out of uncertainty:

> How is it similar to a *ḥayah*? Its blood must be covered, as the blood of a *ḥayah*. It may not be slaughtered on a festival, but if slaughtered, its blood should not be covered. Its *ḥelev* cause impurity like the carcass of a *ḥayah*, but its impurity is uncertain. The firstborn donkey cannot be redeemed through it.
>
> How is it similar to a *behemah*? Its *ḥelev* is prohibited like that of a *behemah*, though eating it is not punishable by excision. It may not be purchased with tithe money to be eaten in Jerusalem. Its foreleg, jowl, and stomach are due [to the priest]; Rabbi Eliezer exempts this, because one who seeks to expropriate from his fellow—[the burden of] proof is upon him.
>
> How is it like neither a *ḥayah* nor a *behemah*? It is forbidden as *kilayim* [and may not be yoked or crossbred] with a *ḥayah* and with a *behemah*. If one writes that his *ḥayah* or *behemah* shall pass to his child, he did not write over the *koi*. If one said, "I am hereby a nazirite if this is a *ḥayah* and a *behemah*," he is a nazirite. In all other ways, it is like both a *ḥayah* and a *behemah*. It requires ritual slaughter like both, imparts carcass impurity, and [one may not eat] the limb of the living [*koi*], like both of them. (*m. Bikurim* 2:9–11)

With respect to the *koi*, as with the *androginos*, there is a Tannaitic view that maintains that this borderline condition should be categorized in a completely different way: "Rabbi Yosah bar Rabbi Yehudah says: A *koi* is a being unto itself, and the sages could not decide whether it is a *ḥayah* or a *behemah*" (*t. Bikurim* 2:1). This structural similarity is what caused the joining of these two lists—the *koi* list and the *androginos* list—into a single literary unit in the Mishnah and Tosefta of tractate *Bikurim*.

The *koi*, however, unlike the *androginos*, can bear being a combination of both *ḥayah* and *behemah* without difficulty. It adapts completely to the structure proposed at the beginning of the unity. In contrast, in the case of the *androginos*, because gender categories pose a far more difficult and weighty challenge when it comes to the laws of marriage, as we saw, the organizing structure of the uncertainty is undermined. The structural parallel between these two borderline cases thus demonstrates the way of thinking about the organization of uncertainty in Tannaitic literature, but close study of the halakhic details also indicates that the *androginos* defies the ostensibly pure logic of conceptualization of borderline cases.

pedigree, which are treated extensively in Tannaitic literature. In principle, if we have all the facts, it is possible to resolve all the uncertainties created when a baby is found in a mixed city, or when one purchases fruit in the market and it is unknown whether it had been tithed properly. This is not the case with respect to *bein ha-shemashot* and the *androginos*; in these cases, the uncertainty arises not from lack of knowledge of the facts but from the limitations of the categorical halakhic distinctions between day and night, man and woman—and of their ability to crisply and binarily organize the reality to which they are applied.

The establishment of these borderline cases and the comprehensive formation and investigation of their character in various halakhic contexts within Tannaitic literature, which we have addressed in this chapter, allow us to raise two common elements. The first element is the very establishment of these phenomena as uncertain possibilities that are defined and accepted as borderline cases. One can imagine an alternative in which, due to the special importance of preserving the binary character of legal categories, such borderline cases would have been decided one way or another, even arbitrarily, if only because the ambiguous borderline case is both unwanted and unseemly. We can imagine an opinion that resolves the question of *bein ha-shemashot* in one direction or the other and does not establish it as a time of uncertainty, with respect to which the halakhic regime is complicated and convoluted. The very enshrinement of a time that is uncertainly the Sabbath, which is accepted as an uncertain situation to which special laws are applied, is truly a halakhic scandal, as it asserts that there is a time interval at the onset of the Sabbath and at the end of Sabbath about which we are uncertain whether it is the Sabbath or weekday. It is no wonder that the category of *bein ha-shemashot*, which is uncertainly the Sabbath, was unknown to pre-rabbinic halakhah; its emergence is one of the characteristics of Tannaitic literature.

This is no less true of the case of the *androginos*. We can imagine a world in which the gender of the *androginos* is decided one way or the other, perhaps even arbitrarily. The existence of the *androginos* as a legal subject to whom opposing gender categories simultaneously apply is itself a unique and astonishing situation. It seems that the sages themselves attempted to reach an unequivocal decision about the gender identity when it comes to marriage.

We see that, by establishing these realms of uncertainty at the borders of categorical distinctions, the sages did not hesitate to challenge the binarity of legal categories; instead of deciding, even arbitrarily, they develop and approve of these uncertain situations, which, from that point forward, will require the application of special instructions.

The second component common to the development of these borderline situations is apparent from the way that Tannaitic literature is not content to establish them as realms of uncertainty but goes on to develop second-order disputes about the nature of the uncertainty that these borderline cases raise. By investigating different cases to which the vagueness of legal categories applies, different positions about the nature and meaning of this vagueness emerge. The rare halakhic situations that are created and discussed in this context enable the isolation of the element that defines the nature of the vague phenomenon. This gives rise to different potential understandings of the transition from day to night—as a gradual continuum or as an unidentifiable discrete moment. Similarly, in discussing the question of gender, a problem arises as to whether the limitations of gender categories and distinctions stem from the fact that they do not cover the range of humanity, or whether the range of humanity presents these distinctions with phenomena that cannot clearly be placed on any one side of the gender divide. Vagueness such as this is not the sort of murkiness that the sages are quick to dispel; rather, they tarry in it, develop it, and attempt to characterize its hazy essence. They thus create additional realms of uncertainty that, through the course of the history of halakhah, enjoyed their own spectacular development.

Conclusion

Tractate *Kinnim*, the last tractate in the Mishnaic Order of *Kodashim*, is mostly devoted to uncertainty, and it presents the most extreme and bewildering treatment of doubts in all of the Tanaitic literature. Its subject matter, as part of the order dedicated to sacrifices, is the obligatory and voluntary offerings of fowl. In several of the sacrificial laws in the book of Leviticus, the sacrifice of two turtledoves or two pigeons is required, one of which is sacrificed as a sin offering and the other as a burnt offering.[1] The laws of the burnt offering and the sin offering are different, as are the way they are sacrificed. Therefore, according to the halakhah established in the Mishnah, a turtledove or pigeon that was designated as a burnt offering and brought as a sin offering is disqualified, and vice versa (*m. Kinnim* 1:1). The vast majority of the three-chapter tractate *Kinnim* introduces cases of uncertainty regarding fowl offerings that became mixed up with one another and develops a complex and dizzying set of rules relating to these cases of uncertainty. Thus, for example, the first *mishnah* to deal with these cases of uncertainty discusses a case in which a turtledove or pigeon designated as a sin offering or burnt offering gets mixed up with a pair of turtledoves or pigeons—a "nest" (*ken*; pl. *kinnim*)—designated as an obligatory sacrifice, such that it is impossible to identify which of the birds are from the original nest, and which one later joined.

The Mishnah then goes on to discuss increasingly exotic cases in which a pair or multiple pairs of obligatory sacrifices get mixed up with other pairs of obligatory sacrifices, both of the same species and of the other species. The second chapter of the tractate deals with the case of a pigeon or turtledove that flew from one nest (containing a pair of obligatory sacrificial birds) to another, and then more complicated cases of multiple pigeons or turtledoves that flew to other nests. Generations of students have struggled to follow the baffling combinatorics of the rules governing uncertainty that tractate *Kinnim* established for the cases of uncertainty that it invented. This tractate therefore drew the attention of

1. See Lev 5:7; 12:8; 15:14, 30; Num 6:10.

some of the greatest medieval and modern commentators, who devoted works to decoding its meaning.[2]

Tractate *Kinnim* is perhaps the starkest example in all of Tannaitic literature of developing cases of uncertainty that have nothing to do with any attempt to guide human behavior in the event that someone encounters such uncertainty in real life.[3] Other cases of uncertainty discussed in the Mishnah pertain to legal circumstances that will never happen in real life, and the three compact chapters of *Kinnim* are the clearest demonstration of the development and broadening of "imaginary halakhah" in Tannaitic literature. This development was motivated by the sages' fondness for legal paradoxes and unusual halakhic results for which these states of uncertainty are a gold mine, and whose formulation is a sort of test of a sage's virtuosity. In addition, the postulation of these imaginary cases is of great service for conceptual clarification and for the examination of a variety of underlying principles that inform different fields of law. In the various boundary cases of uncertainties that were discussed in each chapter of this book, this function of the imaginary cases was manifested, such as in the laws of uncertainties and mixtures of forbidden foods addressed in tractate *Orlah*, or in the case of the switched babies and their impact on the laws of the priesthood and levirate marriage, or in the gradation of uncertainties regarding a firstborn among other offspring vis-à-vis priestly gifts and the burden-of-proof rule, or in the case discussed by the sages regard-

2. Inter alia, the Mishnah of tractate *Kinnim* has running commentaries by Raavad, Rabbi Zeraḥiah ha-Levy, and Rabbi Asher ben Yeḥiel. On the medieval commentaries on *Kinnim*, including the text of a commentary that appears to have been written by Rabbi Shimshon of Sens, see Pinchas Roth, "A Commentary on Tractate *Kinnim* by One of the Tosafists (Rabbi Shimshon of Sens?)" [Hebrew], *Netu'im* 7 (2000): 9–45. Moshe Koppel, a mathematician, devoted a work specifically to this tractate, in which he formulates the exceedingly complex rules of the Mishnah using abstract mathematical notations (*Seder Kinnim: A New Mathematical Commentary to Tractate Kinnim* [Jerusalem: Alumah, 1995]). These two commentaries, along with *Motar Kinnim*, a commentary by Rabbi Yitzḥak (Aizik) Yehudah Yeḥiel Safrin of Komarno, were recently published together in a booklet. See *Al Gozalav Yeraḥef*, ed. Elli Fischer (Modiin: NP, 2017). The booklet is available for download at http://bit.ly/AlGozalav.

3. The exceptional aspect of tractate *Kinnim* is that it distinguishes the rules of uncertainty it formulates to deal with cases where a priest asked the sages what to do in such cases of uncertainty that arise from the rules it formulates for cases where the priest acted without clarifying the law for the case of uncertainty. The first *mishnah* of chapter 3 of *Kinnim*, which begins with the statement, "About what is this said? About a priest who consults. However, a priest who does not consult…," divides the tractate in two. The first part, which includes chapters 1 and 2, issues instructions to a priest who asks what to do in cases of uncertainty that have arisen. The third chapter deals with cases wherein the priest acted without asking for instruction. The *mishnayot* in the third chapter determine which of the offerings that the priest brought are valid and which are disqualified. The surprising thing about this distinction is that it is primarily a distinction within an "imaginary" world where there is a difference between a priest who asked and a priest who did not ask.

ing one who performs *melakhah* during *bein ha-shemashot* between Yom Kippur and the Sabbath, and in the discussion of the nazirite who conditions six contradictory nazirism vows that hinge on the gender status of the *androginos*.

One of the reasons for the birth of uncertainty in Tannaitic literature is thus linked to the broader and more significant innovation of this literature vis-à-vis Second Temple literature. The Mishnah, the Tosefta, and the Tannaitic *midrashim* reflect a worldview that was unfamiliar prior to the emergence of halakhah in Tannaitic literature—a worldview that sees halakhah and its development not only as a set of instructions that purports to guide human behavior but also as a system that constructs a world alongside the real world. The thick, complex web of rules that this literature produces, itself an object of constant contemplation and expansion, conceives of an alternate universe wherein dwell those who spend their lives within the tent of Torah. The expansion and engagement of this alternate universe of situations and directives itself became a matter worthy of its own study and solutions, treated with the same seriousness and devotion as halakhic questions that would be relevant in the future and that, by their very nature, demand response.

The development of borderline questions introduced by the world of uncertainties is part of the emergence of this new conception of halakhah and of the meaning of Torah study, and the twilight zone of doubt and uncertainty proved to be fertile soil for the construction of a world alongside the real world. Tractate *Kinnim*, which was edited relatively early and is ascribed to Rabbi Yehoshua, demonstrates that this conception of halakhah and its reinforcement through cases of uncertainty emerges already at the beginning of the Yavneh period.[4] In the entire Second Temple legal corpus, we find no cases that correspond to the borderline cases of the halakhah's creative imagination, because this corpus presumes as self-evident that its rules should guide human action in one way or another. Since Second Temple legal compositions contain no borderline cases, they are also devoid of the further development of uncertainties and the rules that emphasize the law's imaginary borderline contexts. One who considers the enormous project of halakhah's emergence in Tannaitic literature will thus identify an ambiguity running through it. Sometimes it seems that the purpose of halakhah is to create a world alongside this world, yet,

4. On the attribution of *m. Kinnim* to the editing of Rabbi Yehoshua, see J. N. Epstein, *Introduction to Tannaitic Literature* [Hebrew] (Jerusalem: Magnes, 1957), 62–63. See also *b. Zevaḥim* 67b–68a, which attributes the tractate to Rabbi Yehoshua, and Rashi to *b. Zevaḥim* 67b, s.v. "*ḥatat le-zo ve-olah le-zo*." Moshe Weiss even claims that the first chapters were edited before Rabbi Yehoshua's time ("The Order of the Mishnah in Tractate *Kinnim*: The Question of Toseftan Mishnah Chapters" [Hebrew], *Sidra* 13 (1997): 78; Moshe Koppel, "*Kinnim*'s Composition: A Philological-Mathematical Analysis," *Netu'im* 13 (2005): 9–25.

at the same time, the objective of halakhah is directed toward the real world; its goal is to improve and sanctify it by means of a set of rules that indicate proper action and encompass every facet of human life.

However, in addition to the broader context of the birth of uncertainty as part of the new halakhic discourse of Tannaitic literature more broadly, the center of gravity of the rules and cases of uncertainty developed in Tannaitic literature reside in the encounter with the uncertainties that are essential to the living reality of halakhah. In these contexts, which touch on a key element of a human existence plagued by uncertainty about what happened in the past, what the future holds, and what is happening in the present, Tannaitic literature develops a new and startling system of rules. In examining this unprecedented emergence of regulating uncertainty *three* main guiding principles and sensibilities can be discerned. The *first* guiding principle pertains to the relationship between the threshold of certainty and the price of error. Tannaitic literature does not present one principle for states of uncertainty in every realm of the law; rather, it produces a variety of rules—from imposing a higher threshold for incrimination in capital cases, to imposing a low threshold of probability to warrant the violation of prohibitions in order to save lives, to a dispute about the warrant of self-defense in cases of uncertainty. This broad spectrum of rules for cases of uncertainty stems from the relationship between the required level of certainty and the cost of error; conversely, the gravity of error produces different probabilistic requirements and different attitudes toward uncertainty. The study of the rules governing uncertainty is thus a key to understanding the varying weight that halakhah assigns to different potential errors, and such study is a way to understand Tannaitic halakhah's hierarchy of considerations and value judgments.

Close study of monetary uncertainties, like uncertainty about forbidden foods, reveals a basic sensibility of the Tannaitic halakhic system. With regard to monetary uncertainty, minimizing the potential cost of error by instructing the parties to divide the disputed asset in cases of uncertainty is in tension with the tendency to preserve the status quo in uncertain situations. This tension exposes two simultanous contradictory trends that undergird law and halakhah: the law's attempt to bridge the gap between the ideal and the real, and the law's goal of maintaining a stable, predictable, and enduring existence in a world of uncertainty.

The existence of cases like *agunah* cases, which required a high degree of certainty in order to rule permissively for marriage in given cases of uncertainty, serve to magnify the great innovation of the laws governing uncertainty about forbidden foods. In this area of law as we saw, a bare statistical majority renders the uncertainty permitted. In examining the diverse rules concerning forbidden foods and impurities in relation to the concern with the price of error, the *second* main guiding principle emerged. The variety of rules based on statistical majority, *ḥazakah,* and annulment by majority were made possible by liberating the realms of forbidden foods and impurty from realist assumptions, thereby allowing us to view the prohibited or impure item not as a toxic spiritual entity but as a prohibition or impurity that is solely constituted by the law. Due to the nominalist assumption, the nature of the prohibition and its scope can be shaped and directed in relation to different policies and interests that constitute the ways in which uncertainty is encounter. Without such nominalism, most of the uncertainty rules that were created in early rabbinic literature would not have been possible.

But, while such princples based on a nominalistic approach to the nature of the prohibited or impure object stood as a shared basis of the formation of rules in cases of forbidden foods and impurties, attempts to come to grips with uncertainties about lineage were attended by deep disputes that tore Tannaitic halakhah apart from within. Unlike forbidden foods, attitudes toward the doubtful *mamzerut* were highly charged, because this issue pertains to a sin punishable by excision, and, even more importantly, because the transmission of the stain of *mamzerut* to all future generations ad infinitum invites an essentialist conception of profound revulsion. However, this strict attitude toward the *mamzer* as a contagious and infectious subject of prohibition is itself the reason for far-reaching and unprecedented leniency when it comes to lineage, because stringency in the case of a *mamzer* is self-defeating. Those who attempt to isolate pure-blooded aristocratic families from within a sea of uncertainty are also liable to be "carriers" of this spreading epidemic of *mamzerut*. The heavy shadow of uncertain lineage, which stems from the definition of *mamzerut*, is the source of messianic longing to purify *mamzerim* and the impetus for complex halakhic processes that address uncertain pedigrees in an attempt to overcome the explosive sectarian potential inherent in them.

As was shown in earlier chapters, each different realm in which the sages developed their doctrine of uncertainty posed unique questions, which induced answers that followed the logic internal to each realm. Nevertheless, in the realms of sumptuary prohibition, impurity, and lineage, the emergence of uncertainty is bonded to a shared concern and to a similar response to the problem of uncertainty. In this shared concern, the *third* and most central guiding principle driving the rules of uncertainty was manifested. This guiding principle pertains to the rejection of the default sectarian alternative. In the realm of forbidden foods, Tannaitic literature produced rules for states of uncertainty based on following the majority (even a bare majority), on *ḥazakah*, and on nullification by majority. The impetus for these rulings is not the dread of uncertainty; rather, they are an attempt to enable continued existence even in the heart of uncertainty. A mixed city of Jews and gentiles, and especially the marketplace, are spaces that invite halakhic uncertainty, and the ways in which this uncertainty is decided make it possible to tolerate such complicated friction with heavily trafficked (and thus uncertainty-riven) spaces.

Likewise, the primary distinction in the laws of uncertain impurity, namely, that an uncertainty in the public domain is deemed pure, while uncertainty in the private domain is deemed impure, reflects the same policy considerations as the laws governing uncertain forbidden foods. The public domain is filled with uncertainty, and without the sages' ruling on this uncertainty, it would be closed off to those who are meticulous about purity. By distinguishing between the public and private domains in their rulings on uncertainty, the sages made room for meticulousness without incurring the cost of separatism.

Following a bare statistical majority in the marketplace to permit forbidden foods, like the rule that uncertain impurity—and even probable impurity—in the public domain is deemed pure, are rulings that comprise a rejection of the sectarian alternative. Within such an alternative, it is forbidden to consume any food unless one knows its provenance for certain, and it is forbidden to walk or linger in a space where there is a high likelihood of coming into contact with impurity. The implication of a separate, sectarian existence is the creation of a closed world that is as self-contained as possible—a world that avoids brushing up against uncertainty. In such a world, one eats only from the communal table and refrains, to the degree possible, from any contact with an environment that is not meticulous about purity and impurity, and certainly from the public domain, which is riven with such obstacles. It is therefore likely that the absence of rules governing uncertainty from Second Temple legal material stems from the basic sectarian conception of uncertainty, which contains only one all-encompassing rule: "Where there is uncertainty, it has to be avoided and prohibited." The ramified development of states of uncertainty and rules governing them within Tannaitic literature stems from the rejection of the basic premise of sectarianism, so when a person loyal to halakhah finds himself in spaces that are always susceptible to uncertainty, the Mishnah and Tosefta provide him with rulings that allow him to chart his course through an uncertainty-laced world.

In the history of halakhah and Talmudic learning, the realms of uncertainty have undergone massive and systematic development since the eighteenth century. The great classic compilations of innovative legal and conceptual virtuosi—*Takfo Kohen* by Rabbi Shabbetai Kohen ("the *Shakh*"); *Kuntres Ha-sfeikot* by Rabbi Yehudah Kahana Heller; *Shev Shemateta* by his brother, Rabbi Aryeh Leib Kahana; and *Sha'arei Yosher* by Rabbi Shimon Shkop—are devoted to developing a comprehensive conceptual investigation into the laws of uncertainty, *ḥazakah,* nullification by majority, and other rules governing various forms of uncertainty. To these works, we can add dozens and hundreds of short monographs and transcribed oral lessons devoted to clarifying these questions, for in the world of the *yeshivot* and beyond, the realm of uncertainty has become the primary arena of Talmudic education, through which the Talmud scholar proves his intellectual and conceptual abilities. Of all the different realms of halakhah, it is arguably the rules of uncertainty that are the densest and most tumultuous. A return to the earliest stages of the halakhah, as it is solidified in the Mishnah, allows for a clear and penetrating look into the processes by which the basic templates of the rules governing uncertainty were formed, before they became self-evident, and before they became the foundation for an ever-growing internal discourse. The close study of these Tannaitic sources invites us to ask anew and attempt to answer some of the big questions: Why were such rules for cases of uncertainty established? What alternatives did these rules reject and replace? And what broader assumptions enabled the birth of the realm of uncertainty and the expansive rules that grew up in its wake?

Bibliography

Primary Sources

The translations are those of the author and the translator. The translator was aided in many cases by the translations available at Sefaria.org, especially Mishnah translations, translations of the Bavli, and, to a lesser extent, of the halakhic midrashim. The translations of Yerushalmi and Tosefta passages are by the translator. Mishneh Torah passages are from the Yale Judaica translation, with minor adjustments as needed. Biblical citations are generally from the 1985 JPS translation, though again with adjustments as needed.

As a rule, the form of citation of Yerushalmi is based on the Bomberg edition (Venice, 1524). This is a standard mode of reference.

Aderet Eliyahu [1530]. Odessa, 1870.

The Apocrypha and Pseudepigrapha of the Old Testament in English: With Introductions and Critical and Explanatory Notes to the Several Books. Edited by R. H. Charles. Oxford: Clarendon, 1913.

The Dead Sea Scriptures. Edited by Theodor H. Gaster. Revised and enlarged edition. Garden City, NY: Doubleday Anchor, 1964.

The Dead Sea Scrolls: The Hebrew Writings [Hebrew]. Edited by Elisha Qimron. Jerusalem: Yad Ben Zvi, 2010–2013

The Dead Sea Scrolls Reader. Edited by Donald W. Parry and Emanuel Tov. 6 vols. Leiden: Brill, 2004–2005.

The Dead Sea Scrolls Study Edition. Edited by Florentino García Martínez and Eibert J. C. Tigchelaar. 2 vols. Leiden: Brill, 1997–1998.

Hadasi, Rabbi Yehuda. *Eshkol ha-Kofer.*

Maimonides. *The Code of Maimonides, Book Five: The Book of Holiness*. Translated by L. Rabinowitz and P. Grossman. New Haven: Yale University Press, 1965.

———. *The Code of Maimonides, Book Thirteen: The Book of Civil Laws.* Translated by J. J. Rabinowitz. New Haven: Yale University Press, 1949.

———. *Commentary on the Mishnah.*

———. *Laws of Other Sources of Impurity.*

Mekhilta de-Rabbi Shimeon Ben Yohai on the Nezikin Portion: Text, Terms, Sources and Editing. Edited by Liora Elias Bar-Levav. Jerusalem: Magnes, 2014.

Qimron, Elisha, and John Strugnell. *Qumran Cave 4.V: Miqsat Ma'ase ha-Torah.* Discoveries in the Judaean Desert 10. Oxford: Clarendon, 1994.

Shkop, Shimon. *Sha'arei Yosher.* 2 volumes. Warsaw: Pospiech, 1925.

Secondary Sources

Albeck, Hanoch. *Shisha Sidrei Mishnah Meforashim Bidei Hanoch Albeck Seder Kodashim.* Tel Aviv: Dvir, 1959.

Albeck, Shalom. *Evidence in Talmudic Law* [Hebrew]. Ramat Gan: Bar-Ilan University Press, 1987.

Alexander, Larry. "Scalar Properties, Binary Judgments." *Journal of Applied Philosophy* 25.2 (2008): 85–104.

Alon, Gedaliah. "The Bounds of the Laws of Levitical Cleanliness." Pages 190–234 in *Jews, Judaism, and the Classical World: Studies in Jewish History in the Times of the Second Temple and Talmud.* Translated by Israel Abrahams. Jerusalem: Magnes, 1977.

Alster, Ruth. "Mashma'ut Ha-munaḥ 'Demai' Be-sifrut Ha-Tanna'it" (The Meaning of the Term "Demai" in Tannaitic Literature), *Sidra* 29 (2014): 5–38.

———. "Religious and Social Aspects of the Laws of Demai in Talmudic Literature" [Hebrew]. PhD dissertation. Bar-Ilan University, 2010.

Baker, Cynthia. *Rebuilding the House of Israel: Architectures of Gender in Jewish Antiquity.* Divinations. Stanford, CA: Stanford University Press, 2002.

Balberg, Mira. *Purity, Body, and Self in Early Rabbinic Literature.* Berkeley: University of California Press, 2014.

Bar-Asher, Elitzur, and Yair Furstenberg. "A Reexamination of the Talmudical Discussion 'teqafo kohen'" [Hebrew]. *Sinai* 125 (2000): 48–80.

Bar-Ilan, Meir. "The Attitude toward *Mamzerim* in Jewish Society in Late Antiquity." *Jewish History* 14 (2000): 125–70.

Bar-On, Shraga. *Lot-Casting, God and Man in Jewish Literature, from the Second Temple Period to the Renaissance* [Hebrew]. Ramat Gan: Bar-Ilan University Press, 2020.

Blankovsky, Yuval. "Essay on Talmudic Interpretation" [Hebrew]. At http://www.daat.ac.il/daat/vl/belan-talmud/belan-talmud01.pdf.

Bodsien, Susanne. "Chrysipppus and the Epistemic Theory of Vagueness." *Proceedings of the Aristotelian Society* 102 (2002): 217–38.

Boswell, John. *The Kindness of Strangers: The Abandoment of Children in Western Europe from Late Antiquity to the Renaissance.* 1988. Reprint, Chicago: University of Chicago Press, 1998.

Brandes, Yehuda. "Agunot: Chained Women and Meta-Halakhic Principles" [Hebrew]. *Akdamut* 18 (2007): 55–72.

———. "Living and Learning in a World of Doubt: Thoughts on Shev Shmateta." *Akdamut* 19 (2007): 143–64.

Buchak, Lara. *Risk and Rationality*. Oxford: Oxford University Press, 2013.

Büchler, Adolf. *The Galilean Am Ha-Aretz* [Hebrew]. Translated by I. Eldad from the German. Jerusalem: Mossad Harav Kook, 1964.

Carmichael, Calum M. *The Laws of Deuteronomy*. Ithaca, NY: Cornell University Press, 1974.

Cohen, Shaye J. D. "The Origins of the Matrimonial Principle in Rabbinic Law." *AJS Review* 10 (1985): 19–53.

———. "Some thoughts on 'The Attitude toward *Mamzerim* in Jewish Society in Late Antiquity.'" *Jewish History* 14 (2000): 171–74.

Epstein, J. N. *Introduction to Tannaitic Literature* [Hebrew]. Jerusalem: Magnes, 1957.

———. *Introduction to the Mishnaic Text* [Hebrew]. 2 vols. Jerusalem: Magnes, 2001.

Fisch, Yael. "Bones in the Temple." Pages 485–92 in *Between Josephus and the Rabbis*. Edited by Tal Ilan and Vered Noam. Jerusalem: Yad Ben Zvi, 2017.

Fischer, Elli, ed. *Al Gozalav Yeraḥef*. Modiin: NP, 2017. Available at http://bit.ly/AlGozalav.

Fonrobert, Charlotte Elisheva. "Regulating the Human Body: Rabbinic Legal Discourse and the Making of Jewish Gender." Pages 270–94 in *The Cambridge Companion to the Talmud and Rabbinic Literature*. Edited by Charlotte Elisheva Fonrobert and Martin S. Jaffee. Cambridge: Cambridge University Press, 2007.

———. "The Semiotics of the Sexed Body in Early Halakhic Discourse." Pages 69–96 in *Closed and Open: Readings of Rabbinic Texts*. Edited by Matthew Kraus. Piscataway, NJ: Gorgias, 2005.

Furstenberg, Yair. "Eating in a State of Purity in the Tannaitic Period: Tractate *Tohorot* and Its Historical and Cultural Contexts." PhD dissertation, Hebrew University, 2010.

———. *Purity and Community in Antiquity: Traditions of the Law from Second Temple Judaism to the Mishnah* [Hebrew]. Jerusalem: Magnes, 2016.

Gafni, Isaiah. "Expressions and Types of 'Local Patriotism' among the Jews of Sasanian Babylonia." Pages 63–71 in *Irano-Judaica* II: *Studies Relating to Jewish Contacts with Persian Culture throughout the Ages*. Edited by Shaul Shaked and Amnon Netzer. Jerusalem: Ben-Zvi Institute, 1990.

Gleason, Maud W. *Making Men: Sophists and Self-Presentation in Ancient Rome*. Princeton: Princeton University Press, 1995.

Gulak, Asher. *The Foundations of Jewish Law* [Hebrew]. 4 vols. Tel Aviv: Dvir, 1922.

Halberstam, Chaya. *Law and Truth in Biblical and Rabbinic Literature.* Bloomington: Indiana University Press, 2010.

Haque, Adil Ahmad. "Killing in the Fog of War." *Southern California Law Review* 86 (2012): 63–116.

Hayes, Christine. "Intermarriage and Impurity in Ancient Jewish Sources." *Harvard Theological Review* 92 (1999): 25–35.

———. "Legal Realism and the Fashioning of Sectarians in Jewish Antiquity." Pages 119–46 in *Sects and Sectarianism in Jewish History.* Edited by Sacha Stern. IJS Studies in Judaica 12. Leiden: Brill, 2011.

Hidary, Richard. *Dispute for the Sake of Heaven: Legal Pluralism in the Talmud.* Brown Judaic Studies 353. Providence, RI: Brown Judaic Studies, 2010.

Jackson, Frank, and Michael Smith. "Absolutists Moral Theories and Uncertainty." *Journal of Philosophy* 103 (2006): 267–83.

Katz, Leo. *Why Is Law So Perverse?* Chicago: University of Chicago Press, 2011.

Kehat, Baruch. "'The Burden of Proof Lies with the Claimant' in Rabbinic Literature" [Hebrew]. PhD dissertation. Bar-Ilan University, 2010.

———. "'The Burden of Proof Lies with the Claimant' in Tannaitic Sources and Their Interpretation in the Talmuds" [Hebrew]. Master's thesis. Bar-Ilan University, 2006.

Kister, Menahem. "Concerning the History of the Essenes: A Study of the Animal Apocalypse, the Book of Jubilees and the Damascus Document" [Hebrew], *Tarbiz* 56 (1987): 1–18.

———. "Romans 5:12–21 against the Background of Torah Theology and the Hebrew Usage." *Harvard Theological Review* 100 (2007): 391–424.

———. "Studies in 4QMiqṣat Ma'aśe Ha-Torah and Related Texts: Law, Theology, Language and Calendar" [Hebrew]. *Tarbiz* 68 (1990): 317–71.

Kolber, Adam J. "Smoothing Vague Laws." Pages 275–98 in *Vagueness and Law: Philosophical and Legal Perspectives.* Edited by Geert Keil and Ralf Poscher. Oxford: Oxford University Press, 2016.

Koppel, Moshe. "Kinnim's Composition: A Philological-Mathematical Analysis." *Netu'im* 13 (2005): 9–25.

———. *Seder Kinnim: A New Mathematical Commentary to Tractate Kinnim.* Jerusalem: Alumah, 1995.

Koren, Yedida. "'Look through Your Books and Make Me a Perfect Match': Talking about Geneology in Amoraic Palestine and Babylonia." *Journal for the Study of Judaism* 49 (2018): 417–48.

Laskar, Daniel. "Karaism and the Study of Judaism" [Hebrew]. *Mehkarei ha-Katedra Al Shem Yosef ve-Sil Maiser* (2000): 26–27.

Lazar, Seth. "In Dubious Battle: Uncertainty and the Ethics of Killing." *Philosophical Studies* 175 (2018): 858–83. (i4)

Levinson, Joshua. "Cultural Androgyny in Rabbinic Literature." Pages 119–40 in *From Athens to Jerusalem: Medicine in Hellenized Jewish Lore and in Early Christian Literature; Papers of the Symposium in Jerusalem, 9–11 September 1996*. Edited by Samuel Kottek et al. Pantaleon reeks 33. Rotterdam: Erasmus, 2000.

Lieberman, Saul. *Meḥkarim Be-Torat Eretz Yisrael*. Edited by David Rosenthal. Jerusalem: Magnes, 1991.

———. *Tosefta Kifshutah: Bava Kamma–Bava Metzi'a*. New York: Jewish Theological Seminary of America, 1988.

———. *Tosefta Kifshutah: Beitzah–Ḥagigah*. New York: Jewish Theological Seminary of America, 1962.

———. *Tosefta Kifshutah: Berakhot–Terumot*. Jerusalem: Jewish Theological Seminary of America, 1993.

———. *Tosefta Kifshutah: Nedarim–Nezirot*. New York: Jewish Theological Seminary of America, 1967.

———. *Tosefta Kifshutah: Shevi'it–Bikurim*. Jerusalem: Jewish Theological Seminary of America, 1993.

———. *Tosefta Kifshutah: Sotah-Kiddushin*. New York: Jewish Theological Seminary of America, 1973.

———. *Tosefta Kifshutah: Yevamot–Ketubot*. New York: Jewish Theological Seminary of America, 1967.

———. *Tosefta Kifshutah: Zera'im*. Jerusalem: Jewish Theological Seminary of America, 1992.

Lockhart, Ted. *Moral Uncertainty and Its Consequences*. Oxford: Oxford University Press, 2000.

Lorberbaum, Yair. "Halakhic Realism." *Dine Israel* 30 (2015): 9–77.

Menirav, Joseph. *Prakmatia: The Marketing System on the Jewish Community in Palestine during the Mishna and Talmud Era* [Hebrew]. Ramat Gan: Bar-Ilan University Press, 2009.

Milgrom, Jacob. *Leviticus 1–16: A New Translation with Introduction and Commentary*. Anchor Bible 3. New York: Doubleday, 1991.

Mishnah and Tosefta Ketubbot: Text, Exegesis, and Redaction [Hebrew]. Edited by Robert Brody. Jerusalem: Magnes, 2015.

Moscovitz, Leib. "Le-ḥeker Dinei Ta'arovet 'Yavesh Be-yavesh' Be-sifrut Ḥazal" [A Study of the Laws of "Dry with Dry" Mixtures in Rabbinic Literature]. *Asufot–Yearbook of Jewish Studies* 11 (1998): 309–58.

Noam, Vered. "The Bounds of Non-Priestly Purity: A Reassessment" [Hebrew]. *Zion* 72 (2007): 127–60.

———. "Essentialism, Freedom of Choice and the Calendar: Contradictory Trends in Rabbinic Halakhah." *Dine Israel* 30 (2015): 121–37.

———. *From Qumran to the Rabbinic Revolution: Conceptions of Impurity* [Hebrew]. Jerusalem: Yad Izhak Ben Zvi, 2010.

———. "Is It True That 'A Corpse Does Not Defile'? On Ritual Contamination in Tannaitic Literature" [Hebrew]. *Tarbiz* 78 (2009): 157–88.

Novick, Tzvi. "'They Come against Them with the Power of the Torah': Rabbinic Reflections on Legal Fiction and Legal Agency." *Studies in Law, Politics and Society* 50, edited by Austin Sarat (2009): 1–18.

———. *What Is Good and What God Demands: Normative Structures in Tannaitic Literature.* Journal for the Study of Judaism Supplements 144. Leiden: Brill, 2010.

Rosen-Zvi, Ishay. "Introduction to the Mishnah." In *Rabbinic Literature: Introductions and Studies* [Hebrew]. Edited by D. Rosenthal et al. Jerusalem: Yad Ben Zvi, 2018.

———. *The Rite That Was Not: Temple, Midrash, and Gender in Tractate Sotah* [Hebrew]. Jerusalem: Magnes, 2008.

———. "Temple of the Body: The List of Priestly Blemishes in Mishnah Bekhorot and the Place of the Temple in Tannaitic Discourse" [Hebrew]. *Mada'ei Ha-Yahadut* 43 (2005): 49–87.

Rotenberg, Michael. "Ha-ḥayim Be-tzel Ha-maḥloket: Darkhei Ha-kiyum Ha-meshutaf Be-matzavei Maḥloket She-lo Hukhre'ah Be-mishnat Ḥazal" [In the Shadow of Dispute: Modes of Coexistence in Conditions of Unresolved Dispute in the Teaching of the Sages]. PhD dissertation. Hebrew University of Jerusalem, 2012.

Roth, Pinchas. "A Commentary on Tractate *Kinnim* by One of the Tosafists (Rabbi Shimshon of Sens?)" [Hebrew]. *Netu'im* 7 (2000): 9–45.

Rubenstein, Jeffrey. *The Culture of the Babylonian Talmud.* Baltimore: Johns Hopkins University Press, 2003.

———. "Nominalism and Realism Again." *Dine Israel* 30 (2015): 79–120.

Safrai, Ze'ev. *Mishnat Eretz Yisrael, Demai* [Ramat Gan: Bar-Ilan University Press, 2012).

Samet, Noam. "'Ketsot Ha-choshen': The Beginning of 'Lamdanut'—Features and Tendencies" [Hebrew]. PhD dissertation. Ben-Gurion University, 2016).

Satlow, Michael. *Jewish Marriage in Antiquity.* Princeton: Princeton University Press, 2001.

Schremer, Adiel. *Male and Female He Created Them: Jewish Marriage in Late Second Temple Mishnah and Talmud Periods* [Hebrew]. Jerusalem: Schazar Center, 2003.

———. "Seclusion and Exclusion: The Rhetoric of Separation in Qumran and Tannaitic Literature." Pages 127–45 in *Rabbinic Perspectives: Rabbinic Literature and the Dead Sea Scrolls; Proceedings of the Eighth International Symposium of the Orion Center for the Study of the Dead Sea Scrolls and Associated Literature, 7–9 January, 2003.* Edited by Steven D. Fraade, Aharon Shemesh, and Ruth A. Clements. STDJ 62. Leiden: Brill, 2006.

Schlesinger, Haggai. "Din Ha-ba Ba-maḥteret Be-mishnatam shel Tanna'im: Bein Haganah Atzmit Le-anishah" ("The Law of the Tunneler in Tannaitic Teachings: Between Self-defense and Punishment"). *Shnaton Ha-mishpat Ha-Ivri* 29 (2017–2018): 181–234.

Schwartz, Daniel. "Law and Truth: On Qumran, Sadducean, and Rabbinic Views of Law." Pages 229–40 in *Dead Sea Scrolls: Forty Years of Research.* Edited by Devorah Dimant and Uri Rappaport. Studies on the Texts of the Desert of Judah 10. Leiden: Brill, 1992.

———. "On Two Aspects of a Priestly View of Descent at Qumran." Pages 158–66 in *Archaeology and History in the Dead Sea Scrolls: The New York University Conference in Memory of Yigael Yadin.* Edited by Lawrence H. Schiffman. Journal for the Study of Pseudepigrapha Supplement Series 8. Sheffield: JSOT Press, 1990.

Segal, Moshe H. *Sefer Ben-Sira ha-Shalem.* 2nd ed. Jerusalem: Bialik, 1958.

Shemesh, Aharon. *Halakhah in the Making: The Development of Jewish Law from Qumran to the Rabbis.* Taubman Lectures in Jewish Studies. Berkeley: University of California Press, 2009.

———. "The History of the Halakhic Concept '*Piku'aḥ Nefesh Doḥe Shabbat*'" [Hebrew]. *Tarbiz* 80.4 (2012): 481–506.

———. "Incest Prohibitions in Judean Desert Scrolls and their Importance to the History of Halakhah," *Sidra* 24–25 (2010): 441–57.

Shiffman, Pinchas. "Al Yakir ve-al Yastir: Emet Uvdatit ve-Emet Mishpatit be-Ḥashash le-Mamzerut" [Don't Ask, Don't Tell: Factual Truth and Legal Truth in Suspicion of *Mamzerut*]. Pages 201–22 in *Studies in Law and Halakhah: Menachem Elon Memorial Volume.* Edited by A. Edrei et al. Jerusalem: Nevo, 2018.

———. "On the Concept of Doubt ('Safek') in Halakha and Law." *Shenaton ha-Mishpat ha-Ivri* 1 (1974): 328–52.

Silman, Yochanan. "Halakhic Determinations of a Nominalistic and Realistic Nature: Legal and Philosophical Considerations" [Hebrew]. *Dine Israel* 12 (1984): 249–66.

Sinai, Yuval. "Burden of Persuasion in Civil Cases—A New Model" [Hebrew]. *Bar-Ilan Law Studies* 24 (2008); 213–16.

Strassfeld, Max. "Categorizing the Human, The Androginow in Tosefta Bikurim." www.academia.edu/9625276/Categorizing_the_Human_The_androginos_in_Tosefta_Bikurim.

Ta-Shma, Israel. "A *Mamzer* Is Not Alive?" [Hebrew], *Beit Mikra* 34 (1968): 33–36.

Tikochinsky, Michal. "'*Kuntres HaSfekot*' (Studies in Uncertainty): Methodology, Objectives, and Meaning" [Hebrew]. *Shenaton ha-Mishpat ha-Ivri* 25 (2008): 1–44.

Urbach, E. E. "'Whoever Preserves a Single Life …': The Evolution of a Textual Variant, the Vagaries of Censorship, and the Printing Business," *Tarbiz* 40 (1971): 268–84.

Weiss, Moshe. "The Order of the Mishnah in Tractate Kinnim: The Question of Toseftan Mishnah Chapters" [Hebrew], *Sidra* 13 (1997): 61–91.

Williamson, Timothy. *Vagueness.* Problems of Philosophy. London: Routledge, 1994.

Wozner, Shai. *Legal Thinking in the Lithuanian Yeshivoth: The Heritage and Works of Rabbi Shimon Shkop*. Jerusalem: Magnes, 2016.

Yankelevitz, Raphael. "Mishkalo shel Ha-yiḥus Ha-mishpaḥti Ba-ḥevrah Ha-Yehudit Be-Eretz Yisrael Be-tekufat Ha-Mishnah Ve-haTalmud" [The Significance of Family Pedigree in Palestinian Jewish Society in the Era of the Mishnah and Talmud]. Pages 151–62 in volume 1 of *Uma Ve-toldoteha*. Edited by Menahem Stern. Jerusalem: Zalman Shazar Center, 1983.

Zimmerman, Michael J. *Ignorance and Moral Obligation*. Oxford: Oxford University Press, 2014.

———. *Living with Uncertainty: The Moral Significance of Ignorance*. Cambridge: Cambridge University Press, 2000.

Index of Ancient Sources

Tosefta

Halakhic Midrashim

Jerusalem Talmud

Babylonian Talmud

General Index

CPSIA information can be obtained
at www.ICGtesting.com
Printed in the USA
BVHW030325021121
620500BV00002B/43

9 781951 498757